Navigating Ethical Dilemmas in Social Work Practice

Navigating Ethical Dilemmas in Social Work Practice

Mark Doel and Paula Beesley

BLOOMSBURY ACADEMIC
LONDON • NEW YORK • OXFORD • NEW DELHI • SYDNEY

BLOOMSBURY ACADEMIC
Bloomsbury Publishing Plc, 50 Bedford Square, London, WC1B 3DP, UK
Bloomsbury Publishing Inc, 1359 Broadway, New York, NY 10018, USA
Bloomsbury Publishing Ireland, 29 Earlsfort Terrace, Dublin 2, D02 AY28, Ireland

BLOOMSBURY, BLOOMSBURY ACADEMIC and the Diana logo are trademarks of
Bloomsbury Publishing Plc

First published in Great Britain 2026

Copyright © Mark Doel and Paula Beesley, 2026

Mark Doel and Paula Beesley have asserted their right under the Copyright, Designs and Patents Act, 1988, to be identified as Authors of this work.

Cover design: Terry Woodley
Cover image © ink drop/Adobe Stock

All rights reserved. No part of this publication may be: i) reproduced or transmitted in any form, electronic or mechanical, including photocopying, recording or by means of any information storage or retrieval system without prior permission in writing from the publishers; or ii) used or reproduced in any way for the training, development or operation of artificial intelligence (AI) technologies, including generative AI technologies. The rights holders expressly reserve this publication from the text and data mining exception as per Article 4(3) of the Digital Single Market Directive (EU) 2019/790.

Bloomsbury Publishing Plc does not have any control over, or responsibility for, any third-party websites referred to or in this book. All internet addresses given in this book were correct at the time of going to press. The author and publisher regret any inconvenience caused if addresses have changed or sites have ceased to exist, but can accept no responsibility for any such changes.

A catalogue record for this book is available from the British Library.

A catalog record for this book is available from the Library of Congress.

ISBN: HB: 978-1-3505-0888-0
PB: 978-1-3505-0887-3
ePDF: 978-1-3505-0889-7
eBook: 978-1-3505-0890-3

Typeset by Newgen KnowledgeWorks Pvt. Ltd., Chennai, India
Printed and bound in Great Britain

For product safety-related questions contact productsafety@bloomsbury.com.

To find out more about our authors and books visit www.bloomsbury.com and sign up for our newsletters.

Contents

	List of Figures	x
	Acknowledgements	xi
1	**Introduction**	1
	Ethical dilemmas in twelve objects	2
	Starting with questions	4
	Ethical dilemma 1: Co-habitation and soft-boiled eggs	5
	Definitions	8
	Ethical codes and guidance	11
	Ethical reference group	12
	Organization of the book	14
	Think further about …	17
	The big picture	18
	Ethical dilemmas with twelve people	18
	Further reading	20
2	**Rights and wrongs**	21
	Introduction	21
	Ethical dilemmas in twelve objects	21
	Think about …	23
	Finding your inner moral philosopher	23
	Different approaches to ethics	24
	Critical thinking	31
	Ethical dilemma 2: Discretion at the coffee shop	33
	Guidance from codes, standards and principles	36
	Global Statement of Ethical Principles (IFSW 2018)	37
	Conclusion	37
	Think further about …	38
	Ethical dilemmas with twelve people	39
	Further reading	39

3	**Value conflicts and choices**	41
	Introduction	41
	Ethical dilemmas in twelve objects	41
	Think about …	43
	Origins of value conflicts: Personal, professional and structural	43
	The big picture	50
	Four responses to value conflicts	50
	Ethical dilemma 3: Two 'lives' – the story of Charlotte and Daniella	51
	Alternative paradigms	60
	Guidance from codes, standards and principles	61
	Conclusion	62
	Think further about …	63
	Ethical dilemmas with twelve people	63
	Further reading	64
4	**Power**	65
	Introduction	65
	Ethical dilemmas in twelve objects	65
	Think about …	66
	Power	66
	The big picture	69
	Oppression, equality and social identity	72
	Empowering practice	74
	Self-determination	75
	Ethical dilemma 4: The medication	76
	Guidance from codes, standards and principles	79
	Conclusion	80
	Think further about …	81
	Ethical dilemmas with twelve people	81
	Further reading	82
5	**Professionalism**	83
	Introduction	83
	Ethical dilemmas in twelve objects	83
	Think about …	84
	Professionalism	85
	Personal and professional ethics	86

	The big picture	87
	Professional standards	89
	Personal and professional identity	90
	Professional integrity	92
	Ethical dilemma 5: The gift	93
	Guidance from codes, standards and principles	99
	Conclusion	101
	Think further about …	102
	Ethical dilemmas with twelve people	102
	Further reading	103
6	**Working relationships**	**105**
	Introduction	105
	Ethical dilemmas in twelve objects	105
	Think about …	106
	Working relationships	106
	Another picture	107
	Relationships with service users	108
	Relationships with professionals	110
	Boundaries	111
	Ethical dilemma 6: The adoption	114
	Guidance from codes, standards and principles	120
	Conclusion	122
	Think further about …	122
	Ethical dilemmas with twelve people	122
	Further reading	123
7	**Decision making**	**125**
	Introduction	125
	Ethical dilemmas in twelve objects	125
	Think about …	126
	Risk in decision making	126
	The big picture	127
	Ethical decision making	130
	Ethical dilemma 7: The Friday afternoon enigma	136
	Guidance from codes, standards and principles	146
	Conclusion	147

	Think further about …	148
	Ethical dilemmas with twelve people	148
	Further reading	149
8	**Rules, disobedience and whistleblowing**	151
	Introduction	151
	Ethical dilemmas in twelve objects	151
	Think about …	152
	Duty to obey; duty to rebel	152
	The big picture	155
	Moral luck	158
	Whistleblowing	161
	Ethical dilemma 8: Stan and the files	164
	Guidance from codes, standards and principles	174
	Conclusion	175
	Think further about …	175
	Ethical dilemmas with twelve people	176
	Further reading	177
9	**Use of technology in social work practice**	179
	Introduction	179
	Ethical dilemmas in twelve objects	179
	Think about …	179
	Technology etiquette	180
	Remote communication	181
	Social media	182
	The big picture	183
	Artificial intelligence (AI)	190
	Ethical dilemma 9: The petition	191
	Guidance from codes, standards and principles	195
	Conclusion	196
	Think further about …	196
	Ethical dilemmas with twelve people	197
	Further reading	197
10	**Conclusion**	199
	Objects	199
	The importance of questions	200

Singularities	201
Complexity	201
Power	202
Different ethical positions	203
Procedures, guidance and the wise professionals	204
Bigger pictures	206
Navigating the future: Thinking further about …	208
Further reading	208
Glossary	209
References	213
Index	225

Figures

3.1	Social work's reason for being	44
3.2	Social work and social systems	45
3.3	Pros and cons (1)	58
3.4	Pros and cons (2)	59
4.1	Words associated with power	67
8.1	Moral compass	160

Acknowledgements

All stories are true and some actually happened.

Many people want to know *did that happen*? – or are convinced *that can't be true*. So, whether it matters or not, we would like to state that all the illustrations in this book are based on actual happenings. They are all true.

Specifically, we are indebted to Pete Nelson, Carol Cohen, Marianne Chierchio, Lesley Best, the late Nasa Begum, Judith Livesey, Leo Selleck, Anne Hollows, Caroline Goy, Paul Stapleton and Liz Allam for their various roles in bringing stories to light.

Our thanks, too, to the team at Bloomsbury.

I (Mark) am indebted to all my colleagues, my students, my tutors and mentors, and the many people I have worked with as a social worker for the ethical challenges and insights they have shared. It has been a delight to share the learning from these experiences in this book.

I (Paula) would like to thank everyone who contributed formally and informally to the development of this book, in particular ethical discussions with Ade, Lily and Alice and friends that enabled my external reflector to develop ideas.

1

Introduction

Welcome to the start of a journey to explore ethical dilemmas in social work. In this book we will be approaching the theory and practice of ethical dilemmas in a variety of ways. Our principal tools are detailed examples drawn from social work practice, designed to illuminate the theories, concepts and guidance that support an understanding of ethical dilemmas in professional practice.

Each chapter will be introduced via an Object, building in total to a set of twelve objects and their stories. *Object-stories* give us an opportunity to approach the theme of the chapter in a rather different way from conventional text. Object-stories can express the meaning of social work in strikingly direct ways when contrasted with theoretical discourse and practice examples (Doel 2019). Two websites, socialworkin40objects.com (English language) and 40objetos.ulagos.cl/galeria (Spanish language) have collected over two hundred object-stories from around the globe, which together display the broad canvass of social work and give meaning to the idea of social work as a *contested* profession; in other words, there are many different perspectives on what social work is.

We will use some of these object-stories to introduce and illuminate the themes of each chapter. As the authors, we begin with our own chosen objects, to open a door to ethical dilemmas in social work and ways of navigating them. Our objects have a common theme, of journeys taken. However, one of our objects is a personal artefact and the other serves a symbolic, metaphorical purpose. These different purposes – personal and symbolic – are reflected in the other objects that introduce the chapters in this book.

Ethical dilemmas in twelve objects

City of Sheffield Official Street Guide (map book)

On the morning that I started my first job as a qualified social worker I was given a map book of the city where I would be practising my profession. The book was already well-used and had clearly passed through many hands, so I was reminded straight away that I was part of an ongoing history, and that I would be passing it on, too – the map book and the story of my own social work journeys. *(As it happened, I worked for the city for seventeen years, and was allowed to keep the map book on my departure!)*.

The map book was a practical aid to finding my way around a new city in the days well before GPS and satnav. I soon learned the streets in my 'patch' of the city, but when I visited various children's homes, old people's homes, foster homes, day centres, hospitals, schools and the like all over the city, the map book was indispensible. It is a creature of its times: it's not produced by a commercial company but by the City Council itself, with a brief history of the city, contact details for general civic information, and a map of the political wards.

The map book reminds me that social work, perhaps more than any other profession, is about *context*. Certainly, 'clients' as we called the people we worked with, were individuals, but they lived in households in connected streets that made up communities; the map book reflected my own vision of a social work that was community-based. A significant part of my practice as a social worker was groupwork and community development. The social workers in our patch were known – for instance, I would be in someone's home when there would be a knock at the outside door and one of the neighbours would ask if I could visit them afterwards!

My own street, the one where I lived, was in this map book too. It was near to but not in my patch. I was minded that we all shared this city together, but that there was often a social distance as well as the literal one.

The map book helped me find my way around the physical city, but I soon realized that I needed something more to chart an ethical course through my travels in this city – the kind of professional *compass* described in the next chapter.

The Path Walked

Unlike Mark's map book above, this is more of a concept than an object. The object is a footpath, which reflects my love of countryside that enables a mindfulness that clears my head and allows me to think clearly and critically. However, there is often more than one path where the object becomes the *path walked*, where the landowner tarmacs a path, but everyone cuts the corner off as it is quicker, resulting in a designated path and a desire path. Here we can see that the planners have decreed that walkers will take the tarmacked route whilst walkers have assessed the situation and taken the shorter route. In making this decision, they have likely weighed up civil responsibility (what they are being asked to do) against their own wishes and feelings – as well as taking into account the distance they will need to walk versus risk of dirty shoes.

This parallels with decision making in ethical dilemmas. You will frequently be given a variety of options that you need to consider in order to make a decision about what you will do and how you will respond. You may be required to consider competing person-centred needs, agency philosophical and procedural requirements, legal expectations, social work values and your practice-wisdom and evidence base. Social work does not give us simple and neat solutions particularly often and social workers are often required to critically think about the situation they find themselves in to determine a course of action.

Alternatively, you may be told to undertake a task in a certain way and you may see that there are different routes to consider that aren't set out for you. If you consider this scenario without a muddy path, would you consider walking the shorter way anyway or would you accept the tarmac path without question? In social work practice, will you do as you are told to unthinkingly or will you critically think about the why, to ensure that it is the best solution for the given situation, even if that is the originally presented solution?

This book enables you to consider the *path that you will walk* by providing discussion about different ethical perspectives that will enable you to weigh up complex situations.

Starting with questions

How do you know what is right? Then, if and when you know what is right, how do you *do* what is right? Is doing right *as a social worker* different? And, as a social worker, once you know what is right how do you *do* what is right? Ought we to cultivate social workers who are like the general populace, or do we want social workers who have special qualities and, if so, what are these special qualities? How ought you to decide what to do in those situations where doing right for one person conflicts with doing right for another – is there an overriding 'rightness'? Is it more important to do good or to avoid harm? And how do all these questions connect to values, ethics and morals?

This book is based on the premise that good social work springs from a better understanding of rights and wrongs. Social work is not at all unique in this respect (think of the complexity of medical and legal ethics) but social workers are particularly entwined with notions of rights and wrongs, with the relationship between the individual and society, and with the struggles of power and marginality. Social work's holistic perspective on individuals in their families in their communities in their society makes the social worker's moral landscape especially broad and challenging; and the powers that social workers can exercise give them a particular responsibility to be accountable, morally accountable, for their actions. This duty is the keener because the individuals and communities with whom social workers engage are often poor and marginalised, though not without their own resilience and strengths.

A fundamental tenet of this book is that an understanding of rights and wrongs is crucially important to social work, and that this understanding is best cultivated by asking questions – then asking the further questions that arise from these first questions, and so on. That is not to say that we can avoid considering responses to questions, but that these responses are seldom definitive answers. Questioning a fact – *what colour is that wall?* – can have an answer: *it is yellow*; but an ethical question – *ought that wall be yellow?* – does not have an answer, merely an endless set of further questions (*what other colours could it be?*), observations (*being yellow helps to keep the room looking light*), or reflections (*why do you ask that?*). This book is designed to help this process of asking questions and to ask increasingly *better* questions, if not necessarily the 'right' ones; and to help in formulating further questions, observations and reflections. It is based on the belief that through this process we approach a better awareness of rights and wrongs in social work.

Ethical dilemma 1: Co-habitation and soft-boiled eggs

In the following ethical dilemma, questions are posed not necessarily to elicit your opinion, but to facilitate your acquisition of information, to further your understanding of the issues at stake and to interrogate the ethical dimension to these issues.

Oaklands is a privately run residential care home for older people with facilities for people who need supported living. Helen is a student social worker on placement at Oaklands. Marie is Helen's work-based supervisor, and Rajitha is her off-site practice educator. Helen is key worker for some of the residents, including Mr Porter (Gordon) and Mrs Loxley (Joyce) who are both in their late seventies. They are experiencing various degrees of dementia; Gordon is in earlier stages than Joyce. Both are widowed and have known each other since they came, separately, to live in Oaklands two years ago.

Helen has come to know Gordon and Joyce well over the five weeks she has been on placement so far, and she appreciates the bond of affection and connection between the two. Gordon is more cogent than Joyce and does most of the talking for them. His uninhibited conversation often includes sexual matters.

A double room has come vacant and Gordon says they want to move in together. Joyce agrees, but it is uncertain what kind of consent she is giving as she is frequently unclear. However, Helen has caught Joyce at lucid times and believes it to be Joyce's wish also.

Gordon's family are in regular contact, visiting him at Oaklands twice-weekly and having him to stay with them regularly. They are supportive of the proposal, especially his son, Ashley, who comes every Sunday. Joyce's family see her only occasionally, and they are implacably opposed to her moving in with Gordon. One of Joyce's daughters, Bella, says it would be wrong because her mother and Gordon aren't married. She also claims that her mother is in no state of mind to make that kind of choice and so it would amount to sexual exploitation.

Helen has spoken further with Gordon and Joyce and supports the move. Her work-based supervisor, Marie, indicates support when in Helen's company, but soon backs down in the face of scepticism from Sharon, the manager of the home.

1 Ought Gordon and Joyce to be supported to move in together?

Gordon and Joyce are adults and are entitled to enjoy all the pleasures of adulthood. Ought the question, then, be how best to elucidate Joyce's 'true' feelings. However, these feelings might be ambivalent at the best of times, even if Joyce were able to give full and articulate expression to them. Is Gordon's motivation, then, central to the moral equation? Ought we to aim to find out whether he has Joyce's best interests at heart? Or ought Joyce and Gordon be allowed to make their own mistake, if that is what this move and intimacy proves to be? Making mistakes is easier when you have the support of your family, so ought the lack of this support in Joyce's case have a bearing on the decision?

Write down your responses to the questions posed in the preceding paragraph. What other information would you like to know? What questions are needed to elicit this information, and whom will you ask? Again, write your questions down.

A week has passed and Joyce and Gordon have not moved into the empty double room. The owners of Oaklands press for the room to be filled (they are not bothered who occupies it), as discussions continue about whether this is 'suitable'. Helen notes in her sessions with Rajitha, her off-site practice educator, that 'suitable' and 'appropriate' seem to be the terms that are used instead of 'right' – terms that are, in fact, about values but seek to obscure the fact. Rajitha uses the term 'sub-ethical' for this kind of language – value-laden, but only implicitly so.

What values do you think lie beneath the various opinions that people in this situation – to cohabit or not to cohabit – are expressing?

New information can alter the way we might perceive the situation and, at the same time, change the decisions we make, or limit them. Introduce some 'What Ifs' to experiment with how they might change this situation. For instance, what if Bella had Power of Attorney over Joyce and decided to use it to prevent her from moving in together with Gordon?

Here is another 'What If' for you to factor into your considerations: Conversations with Joyce are elusive because of her moderate dementia, but

Helen gathers from one of these conversations that there is every probability that she and Gordon have, in fact, already been intimate.

2 What ought Helen to do with this new knowledge?

Before responding to this question, consider who has the power, and who *ought* to have the power, to make the choice about what ought to be done with this information. In other words, dig behind the question rather than offering an immediate opinion.

Meanwhile ... a separate and seemingly minor incident has arisen over the weekend, concerning eggs. Ashley visited on Sunday and was told by his father, Gordon, that he was no longer allowed soft-boiled eggs or – even worse – his favourite poached eggs, at breakfast. Sharon had decided that the risk of salmonella from soft yolks is too great for a 'vulnerable population' such as the residents at Oaklands and that she doesn't want to be responsible for any 'unnecessary deaths' just for the sake of 'not eating a hard-boiled egg'. She has returned from a training course in which these dangers have been highlighted and a rumour is also going around that the owners of Oaklands are concerned about the risk of litigation should one of the residents fall sick. Ashley has worked himself up and is claiming a violation of his father's human rights. Gordon is meanwhile claiming that Joyce, too, likes soft-boiled eggs, and wants to be allowed to eat them.

3 Who ought to determine the eggs policy? And who ought to take responsibility if it goes wrong?

Consider the eggs policy from these different perspectives (below). What interests do the various players have in this policy? Where do you think the major differences and similarities might lie?

Joyce *(resident and egg-eater)*
Gordon *(resident and egg-eater)*
Bella *(Joyce's daughter)*
Ashley *(Gordon's son)*
Helen *(student social worker)*
Marie *(Helen's on-site supervisor)*
Rajitha *(Helen's off-site practice educator)*
Sharon *(Oaklands manager)*
Rajiv *(Oaklands head cook and egg-maker)*

Owners of Oaklands
Oaklands **management committee**
The local **Health and Safety officer**
The **local press**
The **Regulator** for Care Homes

Consider whose voices are the most powerful and the least powerful. What role does professional social work have in these issues?

You might consider the question of a possible cohabitation for two people where notions of consent and agency are blurred to be of far greater ethical import than whether somebody is denied their favourite soft-boiled egg. And, of course, at one level you would be correct. However, what interests us as ethical social workers is the fact that the tools available to us – the lines of questioning – are parallel in both cases. Just as the rules of mathematics apply whether you are multiplying 2 x 2 or 16,746 x 183,982, so the ethical considerations that apply to decisions large or small are guided by similar ethical principles. We will consider these in greater detail in the next chapter.

In the ethical dilemma above, we have focused on the people and the institutions involved, and we have begun to interrogate how their perspectives might coincide or differ; we have encouraged you to consider how social work might work with the gaps between these perspectives. In the next chapter, a range of ethical theories will be presented that help you to consider how the actors in the Oaklands scenario are motivated by different ethical worldviews. Frequently, there is a gap between the worldview and an awareness of this worldview. It is our belief that one of the social worker's principal roles is to make this gap explicit and to help people to bridge it. Needless to say, you can't help others to bridge this gap until you are aware of it yourself. This book is designed to help you mind the gap and to know what to do with it.

Definitions

Values, ethics, morals

The terms *values*, *ethics* and *morals* are often used interchangeably, but Joseph and Fernandes (2006: 25) think it careless to mix them indiscriminately and they make these distinctions:

Values: Moral principles and standards
Ethics: The study or the science of morals, or *principles* of behaviour
Morals: A sense of right and wrong, or a *standard* of behaviour.

Ethics are 'concerned with what people consider "right" while values are concerned with what people consider "good"' (Dubois and Miley 1996: 122). Terms from moral philosophy are highlighted in the text (*utilitarianism*) and are explained in the Glossary on pages 209–12.

Social work values are a range of beliefs about what is worthy and valued in a social work context and include general beliefs about the nature of a good life and a good society and how to achieve this through social work practice. Banks and Nøhr's (2012) research into fifteen different countries' ethical codes revealed a consensus of four guiding ethical principles: 'respect for persons, service user self-determination, social justice (equality) and professional integrity'.

These are very broad principles about which it would be difficult to find disagreement, but which might find themselves open to quite disparate interpretation when put into practice (Doel et al. 2010). Hence the use of singularities, moments of decision making, in the dilemmas in this book to pin down these and other values.

Dilemmas, issues, problems, challenges

A dilemma is:

> A situation that often involves an apparent conflict between moral imperatives, in which to obey one would result in transgressing another.
>
> (Zerbe 2008: 115)

> When two or more ethical imperatives are equally important but require opposite behaviours.
>
> (Hardcastle 2011: 4)

> … a purposefully disorienting experience from which transformative learning can be gained.
>
> (Mann 2016)

Is there a difference between a difficult decision and a dilemma? Between a practice dilemma and an ethical one? Ethical problems involve difficult choices, but it is clear what is the right action to take; the difficult choices in ethical dilemmas are compounded because it is not clear what is the right course of action. Banks (2020) describes an ethical dilemma as 'a choice between two equally unwelcome alternatives' and draws a distinction between ethical issues, problems and dilemmas. In this book, we will be using 'dilemma' more broadly, largely because we think the choices can be various and not necessarily undesirable. It is a moral responsibility to choose the best course of action even when both or many are considered desirable. A fine distinction between a practice problem and an ethical dilemma usually proves difficult in reality, as most of social work practice (indeed, most of life) rubs against ethical issues, sometimes recognized as posing a dilemma, other times not. Let's take this simple example:

> There is a rainstorm and I have an umbrella. No dilemma of any kind here – I take out my umbrella and use it to keep off the wet. But in this next rainstorm I have an umbrella and I am with a group of four friends, none of whom has an umbrella. Now there is a dilemma and the choices are many, not just two; some may be desirable, others not. That is part of my dilemma, because I am ignorant as yet of what I *ought* to do. What are the ethical issues? I have yet to think about them. At first sight, it is a practical dilemma, whether to use the umbrella alone or to share it, and if sharing it in what manner, as it will not cover the five of us. However, this practical dilemma is shot through with ethical ones – early on in my decision making I will be asking 'What *ought* I to do?' and reaching to moral philosophy for an answer, whether I know it or not. And, of course, decision making is usually time-limited: if I don't put up the umbrella while I am weighing up the problem, we all get wet!

Parting ethical issues from practice problems seems as difficult and unnecessary as separating the red and the blue in the colour purple. This is not to say that it isn't helpful sometimes to consider what are ethical issues and what are practice problems within a dilemma, but it is unnecessary to struggle to define the dilemma as *either* ethical *or* practical.

Banks (2020) usefully reminds us that it is important to see the whole of social work as comprising ethical dimensions and to focus on the ethical issues in practice as much as the ethical problems and dilemmas. To get you started, each chapter in this book contains a 'Think about …' introductory dilemma which has both practice and ethical dimensions which lead into the more complex dilemmas explored in each chapter. The chapters conclude with a 'Think further about ...' section to help you reflect on your learning.

Ethical codes and guidance

Other guidance about the nature of social work values comes from a *Statement of Principles* jointly agreed by the International Federation of Social Workers and the International Association of Schools of Social Work (IFSW/IASSW 2018). The Statement focuses on two primary values: human rights and human dignity (a *duty-based, deontological* ethical approach); and social justice (a *consequentialist, teleological* approach). We will explore these ethical approaches in more detail in Chapter 2. The Statement is explicit about social workers' ethical responsibilities:

- Social workers should foster and engage in ethical debate with their colleagues and employers and take responsibility for making ethically informed decisions.
- Social workers should be prepared to state the reasons for their decisions based on ethical considerations, and be accountable for their choices and actions (IFSW/IASSW, 2018).

The IFSW/IASSW statement is one of principles and core values, not a code; it is expected that each national social work association derives its own code of ethics. In the UK, social workers in the public sector (the majority) are expected to subscribe to a public service ethos which includes service to others and putting the needs of others first (Nolan 1995). However, the ethics of the very notion of a statement of values and a code of ethics are controversial, seen by some as an example of one philosophical mindset (Western) imposing its way of thinking on other less powerful mindsets.

Our own position on codes is one of healthy scepticism and a possible concern that their existence might induce ethical torpor rather than rigour – a sense that 'some-one else has done the thinking, so we don't have to.' What little research knowledge we have about reference to codes of ethics in daily practice suggests that it is minimal (Doel et al. 2010), perhaps because codes are conceived at such a level of generality that social workers struggle to apply them to the singularities of practice. This same research seems to indicate that social workers are more likely to take a *case-based* approach to ethics than on one based on principles.

Comparing Italian and British codes of ethics for social workers, Cavaliere (2014: 66) noted interesting differences in 'authorial attitude' – in the Italian code, 'we find a bare, detached definition of the code and an introduction to rules to be complied with', whilst the British code 'relies on terms which come within the "affective" sphere' to convey the social workers' emotional and empathic commitment towards service users. Whereas the British (BASW) code chooses the word 'should', the Italian uses the prescriptive modal, *deve* (must). Cavaliere's study was restricted to the British and Italian codes, but an exploration of the grammar of the Indian code (a 'Declaration of Ethics') reveals the style of a personal commitment in the words, 'I pledge to … ' (BATSW 2002). These textual differences ('cultural grammars') between codes convey subtle cultural meanings that are not immediately evident.

Illustrative sections from ethical codes and statements are included towards the end of each of the themed chapters.

Ethical reference group

'There are value judgements on which reasonable people might differ.'
(Ian McEwan's *The Children Act* 2014: 13)

Earlier we professed a degree of scepticism for codes and formulae, at best ensuring things are done *correctly* but not necessarily *rightly*, at worst excusing active engagement with ethical issues. So, is the alternative that social workers just do what they think is right? Clearly, this is not a satisfactory alternative. So, what might prevent social workers from becoming ethically passive?

What is most likely to sustain the kind of ethical enquiry we are advocating in this book is the commitment that comes from group loyalty and obligation, such as knowing you are needed to make up the number for a team event. This *ethical reference group* could be your own professional work colleagues, in which case it is important to build in ways to combat the risk of groupthink, where a lack of divergent reasoning becomes the norm. A reference group should be ethically sharp, regularly tussling with moral issues in professional practice – a group of amateur ethicists whose questions go to the heart of social work's meaning and purpose.

Your reference group can be 'virtual', not necessarily in an on-screen way, but an imagined group that we might refer to as the 'wise professionals'. There are different ways to ponder these wise professionals. They could be real people whom we hold in high regard because we admire their personal and professional qualities and seek to emulate them. They might be imagined professionals, idealized versions of ourselves perhaps, the practitioner we seek to become. Perhaps the wise professional is the inner dialogue in our own head, if we only take the time to listen. The wise professionals are the embodiment of reflection and mindfulness, the 'Voice of Experience' (Thompson 2016) that challenges received wisdom and reframes it; they perfect the improvised performance of the 'wise person' (Payne 2007, 2009). They engage in *phronesis*; that is, they are virtuous people who are able to use practical reasoning born from experience. In summary, the wise professionals are an ethical reference group helping you to exercise *philosophic scepticism* and to engage in *Socratic dialogue* (Yassour-Borochowitz 2004).

Early in your social work studies it might, admittedly, be challenging to conjure the idea of the 'wise professionals', as you might be at the beginning of the journey to discover what it is to be 'professional'. Don't worry, just keep this idea in the back of your mind and come to it when you are ready. In particular, seek out and observe people whose professional practices look like those you aspire to in your own future practice.

The wise professionals are plural because they embody diverse value judgements, and it is these differences that are illuminating, so we listen to them all, respect them and understand each to have its own value. Much moral philosophy takes the individual as its basis, so the *group* of wise professionals is a reminder that any dialogue is better when we invite many voices to join.

The wise professionals' understanding of morality is that it cannot be based solely on one's own interests and should be based on a belief in others' interests too. This is a good fit for the principles of public service (Nolan 1995) and it is consistent with the social work role, first to understand a situation from everybody's position and then to find ways to help these others to do similarly – to bridge the gaps in communication and understanding. These wise professionals do see a place for reason and argument in morality rather than a purely intuitive, non-rational commitment. If morality is not open to reason, then we are doomed at best to live in isolation from one another and, at worst, to throw things at one another from our respective corners of the world. However, it is wrong to deny the force of emotions and intuitions in moral life. Above all, the wise professionals guide us to the significance of interpersonal ethics, the relationships between ourselves and, indeed, between humans and the ecological environment, too.

Trust and care

There are two central qualities for ethical practice. The first is trust. Trust is a key component in professional integrity (BASW 2021: 10) and central to the development of relationships, which are crucial for social work practice (Ruch et al. 2018). We should place trust in our wise professionals, too; and we should trust the journey they take us on. As the French saying goes, *le chemin se fait en marchant* – 'the path is made by walking it.' We should, therefore, be wary of following well-worn tracks, precisely because they are well worn.

The second quality is care. Care emphasizes the interpersonal and relational aspects of social work and its empathic qualities. In the next chapter, we will see how an *ethics of care* has developed to address the inadequacies of classical ethics theories – one more suited to the values of social work.

Organization of the book

There exists a considerable literature on values, ethics and dilemmas in social work, which includes Akhtar 2012; Banks 2004, 2010, 2014, 2020; Barsky 2019; Barnard et al. 2008; Bauman 1993; Beckett et al. 2017; Bell and Hafford-Letchfield 2015; Green and Carey 2013; Clark 2000; Dickens 2012; Dolgoff et al. 2009; Gray and Webb 2010; Hardwick and Worsley 2011; Held 2006; Horne 1999; Hugman 2013a, 2013b; Hugman and Smith 1995; Joseph and Fernandes 2006; Lonne et al. 2015; Parrott 2014; Parsons, 2001; Porter 1999; Pullen-Sansfaçon and Cowden 2012; Reamer 2023a; and, more generally, Warnock 1998. There are whole books written on topics merely touched upon in the chapters that follow, so we approach this task modestly. Our hope is that another book is justified by the particular organization of the material and the treatment of the issues in the chapters that follow.

We have centred the seven themed chapters (Chapters 3–9) around a core set of dilemmas. Each of these chapters cluster around a theme that is central to the everyday experiences of social workers. Of course, in any single sequence of events, a social worker might encounter ethical issues and practice problems that relate to all seven of these themes; but frequently there is a core category, for example, *power* (Chapter 4). Indeed, in gathering sixty-six different dilemmas from social workers at a conference workshop, it was found that each dilemma sat comfortably in one or more of the seven themes. However, the organization of themes into discrete chapters is not intended to obscure the messy reality of practice, with its smudgy overlaps between these categories; the boundaries between the chapters are very porous. To use a navigational metaphor, each chapter maps the same island, but from different points of the compass.

Singularities – significant moments in time

There are variations in the way we each learn best, but the power of example seems to be universally effective in triggering deep learning. The introduction of a concrete, specific situation onto the page is designed to pin down the questioning process. This method is well established in adult pedagogy (Freire 1968/2018) and reflected in research methods such as critical incident analysis (Butterfield et al. 2005) and narrative inquiry (Clandinin and Huber 2010; Gardner and Poole 2009), where no hypothesis is to be proved and there is no single truth. However, this method is more easily supported in live workshops where interaction is possible; on the page, the challenge is to have a conversation with the reader that avoids bulleted lists of trite trigger questions, whilst not overloading the page with the authors' own beliefs. We hope that balance is achieved in the chapters that follow.

The style of the theme-based chapters draws from *narrative* and *case-based ethics* – in which stories and case-based reasoning are used to reveal ethical issues (Banks and Nøhr 2012). In particular, we use the notion of a singularity to help with this questioning process. There are various meanings attached to the word 'singularity', but we are taking it to signify a moment in time when a very particular action or question has a significant impact on what happens next, and a different action or question would entail an alternative future. The film *Sliding Doors* (1998) is an entertaining example, in which entering (or not entering) a carriage on the London Underground is the difference between the lead character meeting the love of her life, or not meeting him. Being a film, she gets the chance to replay this singularity. *Groundhog Day* (1993) is another fictional example; indeed, so common is this device in cinematography that we can surmise that the idea has a strong hold on the collective imagination, and it is something we draw learning from.

The singularities presented in the dilemmas in each chapter are points when the social worker is caught in a significant moment in time, presented with a choice which sometimes might not even be seen as a choice, so it is not necessarily recognized as a road travelled or not. The occasion might or might not be experienced as a dilemma and the social worker might or might not be aware of ethical issues. The value of the singularity is that it pauses time in a way that is not possible *off-page* in the 'real' world, so it allows a rehearsal of the range of issues associated with any action or question. In the actual world, these issues are too often unexposed, either by the forgetfulness of routine or the push of other events pressing on available time.

Some readers might wonder whether the scenarios you will encounter are 'true'. As it happens, the vast majority of situations have been taken from fact, though the alternative futures suggest different trajectories for the stories. Flanagan (2015) makes the observation that 'the difference between stories perceived as factual and those viewed as fiction is not as distinct as it may appear.' The artist Lucien Freud (1922–2011) noted: 'There is a distinction between fact and truth. Truth has an element of revelation about it' (cited at a 2015 exhibition at Christchurch Mansion, Ipswich).

There are big events in social work, such as whether to take someone's liberty because they are judged to be a threat to themselves or others; or to remove a child from the care of its parents. These big events are rarely *moments*; usually they are the accumulation of many preceding singularities, everyday moments, some of which came and went without any recognition of their significance. Yet it is the singularities that add up to the big event; by the time the big event arrives, in all likelihood it is inevitable. As we will explore in more detail in the next chapter, the ethics to suit singularities – the *everyday ethics* (Banks 2016) – is not as available as the *epic ethics* of much classical theorizing. Our hope is that the example dilemmas, with their moments in time, will contribute to our understanding of an *everyday ethics* and its relationship to the big events; also, that these dilemmas will help your deliberations about not getting it wrong, as well as those about getting it right. Being wrong (or the fear of it) can provoke practice that is risk averse and feels oppressive to practitioners. So, thinking about 'not getting it wrong' is just as significant as getting it right.

Some chapters incorporate a 'balance sheet' method, with a list of pros and cons. This approach can be helpful in steering towards a decision or a moral conclusion, but it is rarely a clincher. The length of one side of the balance sheet does not reveal the relative importance of each 'fact'. Balance sheets indicate the value of marshalling facts, but also expose the ultimate limitation: that knowing *what is* does not point in a clear direction to *what ought to be*.

The singularities are contextualized alongside these kinds of broader ethical issues. The 'big picture' sections frame the everyday ethical issues faced by social workers with contemporary news stories, in which *epic ethics* parallels the *everyday ethics* of social work encounters.

Think further about …

… the idea of a singularity and how to begin to recognise it in practise. Make a start by considering a recent dilemma in your personal life, something rather more *everyday* than *epic,* and a decision you made in relation to this dilemma.

- What choices were open to you in relation to the dilemma?
- What questions would you ask someone else facing this dilemma to help them make a decision about what action to take? *(They might make a different decision to yours.)*
- Was there a singular moment when 'the die was cast' – that decided you take the course of action you did? Why was this 'the moment'?
- Is there an ethical dimension to the dilemma? What is it? *If at this stage you don't see any ethical dimension, return to this after you have read Chapter 2.*

> ## The big picture
>
> It is important to place the daily ethical issues faced by social workers into the larger frame (see Wolff 2011, for a philosophical enquiry into ethics and various aspects of public policy). For instance, is it possible to pursue ethical social work practices in an agency organized around profit? Is it inevitable that the imperative for profit will conflict with the imperative for professional practice and, when this happens, is it also inevitable that the profit motive will be paramount? Or is there no difference between the need to balance the books in a publicly funded or not-for-profit agency and the need to balance those same books in a private agency?
>
> The big picture is also the connection between individual professionals' ethical decisions and the broader ideologies that underpin (or undermine) them. As the Swedish ethical code for social work professionals notes:
>
>> Ethical dilemmas in social work may be related to overall ideological issues: To what degree is the public society responsible for the individual citizen? How much of the responsibility for a person's situation and future is entirely his own? Which ethical values and norms are essential for judging the balance between the responsibility of the public society and that of the individual?
>>
>> (SSR 2006: 6)

Ethical dilemmas with twelve people

At the end of each chapter, we introduce the person who donated the object that began the chapter. As a group, the biographies of these donors reflect the diversity of social work and the many reasons why people come to the profession.

Mark Doel (Map book)

> In professional terms, I am a child of the Seebohm era – that is, I qualified just as the Seebohm Report recommendations were being put into practice in the mid-1970s. This brought all the various social work services into one unitary Social Services Department. It led to a specialism that is very different from the kind we are familiar with now – to a geographical specialism (hence

the map book) rather than ones based on children, adults, mental health, etc. Rather like General (medical) Practitioners, we were General (social) Practitioners and our specialism was the small neighbourhood ('patch') in which we worked. It led to a notion of radical social work with its focus on community as well as family and individuals. We worked with everyone in our geographical patch 'from cradle to grave'. My other specialism was, and continues to be, groupwork. My PhD was groupwork-based and I have been an active member of the International Association for Social Work with Groups (IASWG) for many years.

I have occupied many spaces. As well as knocking on doors, I've supervised students on placements, taught and learned with them in class, been an academic manager as Head of a School of Social Work, and directed research projects large and small. In addition to my writing, some of my most fulfilling work is leading training workshops with practitioners. I've been fortunate that my work has taken me to many countries, living and working for two separate years in the US, and directing research and development projects – in Eastern Europe especially. I have an Honorary Doctorate from Tbilisi State University in Georgia.

My undergraduate studies were in philosophy and politics. In the half-century since those times, I continually find this to have been an excellent grounding for my professional social work. I would like to see moral philosophy as core to social work qualifying education.

Paula Beesley (The Path Walked)

I am a qualified social worker, practice educator, social worker and researcher. My first time of walking my own path was when I was on the conveyor belt of education, where I was expected to move from school to university and study a career that followed in one of my parents' footsteps. Whilst my dad was a boring accountant, my mum had worked on one of the country's first computers, a history of which I am proud. Yet neither appealed to me, and worse I was not ready to go to university.

Instead, I became a social care worker with adults with learning disabilities, which led me to become a social worker and travel the world. I love the concept of a singularity, where one decision changes your life course. I have had an amazing and fulfilling career, which I value, and thank my younger self for making that brave decision. Yet, it was not easy. I had to weigh up so many different factors and I applied critical thinking to the situation which led me to go against the established norms. Ultimately, I am now working at Leeds Beckett University (an irony my parents still point out to me) supporting the next generation of social workers to determine their path *walked*.

Further reading

It may be helpful to familiarize yourself with ethics as you begin to approach this book. Generic guides are available such as:

Blackburn, S. (2021), *Ethics: A Very Short Introduction*, Oxford: Oxford University Press.

Hugman, R. (2014), *A–Z of Professional Ethics*, Houndmills, Basingstoke: Macmillan.

Salmon, P. (2024), *The Little Book of Ethics: An Introduction to the Key Principles and Theories You Need to Know*, Chichester: Summersdale Publishers.

Or you may chose to access the works of Socrates, Plato, Aristotle, Kant, Sartre, Rawls and Fletcher.

2

Rights and wrongs

Introduction

This chapter will help you reflect on your engagement with ethical and moral issues. How deep is it? We will introduce you to ethical perspectives and formal ethical theory and help you to navigate these long-established ethical discourses alongside the everyday judgements that social workers must make during the course of their work. We will consider virtue ethics, duty ethics, situational ethics, existentialism, consequentialism and the new ethics in providing a brief introduction to a range of perspectives that can be applied to the same ethical dilemma. An example of an ethical dilemma in a non-social work setting will be presented to illustrate in a light-hearted way the impact of applying different ethical perspectives.

Ethical dilemmas in twelve objects

Scales

> For his object, Asian British social worker Omar chose a pair of *Scales*, as social work as a profession is always balancing out themes, concepts and dilemmas. He believes that Scales provide a direct link to the ethics and values around promoting social justice, equity, human rights and fairness, as Scales are often represented in the justice and legal systems. Social workers are often dealing with unbalanced Scales, in the sense that there is an overwhelming amount of social injustice that takes place in societies, and social workers are contributing to the movement of the Scales either

through promoting empowerment and social justice, or by engaging in oppressive practices. This can sometimes be deliberate but is often found in the structures, systems and processes that social workers work within, such as social workers wanting to promote anti-racism in their practice, although the systems we work within were imbued with institutional and systemic racism. This is a key ethical dilemma that social workers often face and battle with, although the expectation of all social workers is that our values and ethics are strong, and that they should guide us when it comes to ethical dilemmas.

Compass

> Russian social work educator Boris chose a *Compass* as his object, as social work needs to determine the right direction towards social and personal well-being. He believes that a *professional compass* is needed to determine this 'right direction', one that provides security for society in the widest sense of this notion.

A set of Scales and a Compass are material objects that are, nonetheless, used metaphorically to express ideas of social work that are complementary, yet also indicate difference. In Scales, we are being invited to consider which of two choices (left pan or right pan) has the greater weight – perhaps we are gathering evidence to see which side is the most convincing and this determines our decision or recommendation. In proposing Scales, Omar is also suggesting that a sense of balance, of proportion, fairness and even-handedness, is needed in social work practice; and, additionally, we might consider balance to be important in the work/life judgements of social workers in order to avoid burn-out.

The idea of the Compass is not as either/or as Scales. A Compass helps us to get our bearings, but we need to know what the ethical equivalent of 'magnetic north' is before we can begin to understand whether we are going in the right direction. Moreover, although magnetic north might be the desired direction, we might find it necessary to plot detours in order to return to the right direction. How, in making pragmatic detours, do we ensure that we keep our bearings?

Think about …

On a home visit, you observe a dog that looks gaunt. Your remit is child or adult protection. Does that give you the right to enquire about a dog's welfare?

Is there a dilemma? If so, what is the nature of your dilemma? And what do you do?

What might make a difference to the nature of your dilemma? Consider if you have the right (duty?) to challenge any pet owner or whether it would be wrong to raise this: 'it's not my responsibility' or 'it will undermine my relationship.'

Finding your inner moral philosopher

The ethical and moral issues at the heart of this book have been the subject of serious thought for many millennia. As a starting point, it can be helpful to reflect on what we are calling your *inner moral philosopher* (see the discussion about the 'wise professional' in Chapter 1).

Let's start by considering how interesting you find these following questions:

1. Is it better to remain true to yourself or compromise yourself for fame and financial gain?
2. Can someone be too virtuous for their own good?
3. Can you really be cruel to be kind? Is an extreme action worth taking for the greater good?
4. Is there such a thing as moral weakness and moral ignorance? If so, what are they and how might they show themselves?
5. Do you think that each individual human person has an 'infinite worth'? What is a human life worth?
6. Is it right to practise self-denial? Is it right to follow the path of pleasure whatever?
7. Are good intentions good enough?
8. What ought to happen when your own moral compass no longer aligns with social norms?

The eight questions above are abstract ones – there are no illustrative examples to pin them down. Perhaps you are a concrete thinker and prefer your moral philosophy shaped into real, if hypothetical, situations:

9. Is a fatally ill young person better off knowing the unhappy truth that they are nearing the end of their life, or believing a reassuring lie that they are in recovery?
10. Would it be right for a person balancing on a small but stable raft in a flood to ignore cries for help from others in the water?

In responding to these questions, you might take a step back and ponder how these responses are being framed. What guides your thinking? Are they well-worn thinking tracks or are you finding yourself in new territory? One of this book's aims is to help you connect with your 'inner moral philosopher' – in other words, how you connect with 'rights' and 'wrongs' in your life in general, not just your professional life. The first step is to become self-aware about how exercised in this area you are already. To stretch the metaphor – do you take brisk 'moral walks' regularly, or are you out of condition? This is the time to be honest with yourself.

Different approaches to ethics

Ethics is a branch of philosophy that comes from the Greek word *ethos*, meaning moral character. Ethics are a socially constructed and agreed set of beliefs and values that inform behaviour, the rights and wrongs of individual behaviour and collective society. In social work, ethics are seen as a set of guiding principles, often codified into practices to promote professionalism and integrity, and boundaries that should not be crossed: the rights and wrongs of social work. However, different philosophies offer different approaches to ethics. What follows are explorations of Western ethical developments; we will consider alternative paradigms in Chapter 3.

Virtue ethics

When we ask people about their positive experiences of social work, we find that they are more likely to be concerned with the virtues of their particular social worker – their honesty, warmth, trustworthiness and intelligence – rather than whether they comply with an abstract ethical code or a set of moral standards.

(Doel and Best 2008: xi)

Virtue ethics places individual practitioners firmly centre stage, in terms of their character and their ability to live 'a good life' rather than live up to their role (Clark 2006; Marquis and Jackson 2000; Saarnio 2000). These ideas arise from the works of Socrates, Plato and Aristotle in which these ancient Greek philosophers developed ideas through reflective discussion. Plato, developing Socrates' ideas, argued that people should pursue virtue and excellent moral habits rather than material wealth or physical pleasures because it was rational to do so. He argued that there are four virtues: wisdom, courage, temperance and justice. Social work's core ethical basis of social justice and professional integrity can be argued to be virtue-based, though Plato's assertions of moral absolutism (there is one moral right and one alone) is less in keeping with social work's relativism (discussed later).

Aristotle's more nuanced approach, for example, in his *Nicomachean Ethics*, argued that ethics should consider the individual situation. This aligns more with social work's reflective and reflexive approach. Aristotle argued that developing a virtuous character enables virtuous acts, particularly when faced with an ethical dilemma. However, there are difficulties with virtue theory, most notably the difficulty of agreeing what these virtues are and whether they reflect, or ought to reflect, different societies.

Principlism

The use of principles to guide ethical practice was exemplified in social work by Biestek's (1961) seven principles for 'the casework relationship':

- Individualization
- Purposeful expression of feelings
- Controlled emotional involvement
- Acceptance
- Non-judgemental attitude
- Client self-determination

- Confidentiality.

Biestek's principles have been adapted by Doel (2023: 11) for a contemporary practice beyond social work just as casework. Hardwick and Worsely (2011) reflect on the use of general principles as 'illuminators' but not 'directors' in the context of social work research ethics and Banks (1995: 37) identified four 'first-order' principles in social work:

- Respect for and promotion of individuals' rights to self-determination
- Promotion of welfare or well-being
- Equality
- Distributive justice.

A reliance on principles aligns most closely with the idea of the moral compass that introduced this chapter – that there is a steady 'ethical north' that is unchanging and must always guide us.

Duty-based ethics

Duty-based ethical theories (also known as deontological theories) assert that acting morally means doing your duty regardless of consequence. An example is Judaeo-Christian ethics, beginning with the catalogue of absolute duties and restrictions listed in the Ten Commandments and, for Christians, incorporating the teachings of Christ, such as 'love thy neighbour.' Duty-based moral philosophies, faith-based or otherwise, are generally based on dos and don'ts.

Kantian ethics are duty-based but do not rely on a belief in a god, and they concern themselves more with motivation and *will* (intent). Kant describes some duties as 'categorical'; they are unconditional and must always be followed, such as the duty never to kill anyone. Other duties are hypothetical, for instance, if you want to be trusted then you ought to tell the truth. These moral precepts can be made universal, such as 'do to others as you would have them do to you', where it is possible and desirable for everyone to act on this. However, what to do when there are conflicts in duties? We will explore this in more detail in later chapters.

Human rights are part of the duty-based family of ethics. Inalienable rights are those that are categorical, non-negotiable and not dependent on consequence, time, or place – they are universal. The best-known expression of this is the United Nations' Declaration of Human Rights in 1948:

> Human rights are rights inherent to all human beings, whatever our nationality, place of residence, sex, national or ethnic origin, colour, religion, language, or any other status. We are all equally entitled to our human rights without discrimination. These rights are all interrelated, interdependent and indivisible.
> (The United Nations Office of the High Commissioner for Human Rights [OHCHR] http://www.ohchr.org)

Human rights are mentioned in 75 per cent of national social work codes of ethics (Keeney et al. 2014) and underpin social work's philosophy of social justice.

It is worth noting that different cultures put varying emphases on duties and rights. For instance, Muslim communities have a strong sense of duty towards family and community, not dissimilar to white working-class communities before neoliberalism diminished these duties in favour of individualism. Where does your sense of duty lie most strongly – with community, family, or yourself?

From a duty-based point of view, it is not, therefore, a *moral* choice to become a social worker if that choice is made because of the need of an income, or even because of compassion for oppressed persons; these are all pragmatic or emotive motivations, rather than springing from a sense of duty. A moral choice to become a social worker may stem from a sense that it is right and good to do so, for example, a belief in the need to fight social injustice at ground level. Kant discounted the moral emotions, yet many people feel intuitively that emotions are inherent in ethics. Does it matter whether social work is founded on an altruistic desire to alleviate the sufferings of those who are wronged, or on a collective guilty conscience that relative wealth and fortune comes on the backs of the poor and the dispossessed? Advocating that a child is placed with a same-race adoptive placement to promote identity despite a short delay can be perceived to be a moral choice by a social worker, even if the social worker is motivated in their work because they have to pay their bills.

Kant (1784/1998) argued that moral choices are not dependent on outcome. For instance, even if a social worker fails to prevent elder abuse, their actions can be considered *moral* when acting from a sense of duty to take steps to both protect and honour the person's right to make an informed decision.

Situation ethics (casuism)

In situation ethics, each instance is decided not by prescriptions or universal law, but case by case, with attention to the person in their specific context. This enables flexible, responsive decision making and actions to be taken that allow the individual to assess multiple courses of action dependent on the circumstances they find themselves in. In situation ethics, the dominant moral principles of society, and in the case of social work practice, the professional Code of Ethics, provide a foundation to work from but are not absolutes and can be reflected upon and adapted, or even dismissed, to meet the needs of the situation.

In Fletcher's (1967) *Moral Responsibility: Situation Ethics at Work*, love (thy neighbour) is the central motivation that governs the morality of decisions, and concern for people is the core principle. He argued that moral judgements are decisions made at the time for the *well-being* of the people involved, meaning that moral judgements should be subject to review and can change as the situation changes. It can be argued that situational ethics takes its core principles from other ethical philosophies, allowing flexibility. Fletcher felt that everyone has a duty to put people first and, like duty ethics, he concluded that actions rather than results indicate morality. To some extent, he aligned with *utilitarianism* (the greater good) in that he promoted human welfare and happiness as the key to morality and as such, he argued that situational ethics promoted social justice.

The principle of love and concern for people indicates an alignment with human rights, but love is dependent on subjective interpretation: when considering the criminalization of the burqa in France, or female genital mutilation in some African communities, both sides of these moral choices would likely argue that they come from a position of 'love'. If a practice is accepted as the norm in one society, do other societies have the right to impose their definition of acceptable behaviour?

To what extent, then, can and ought the social worker's judgement of right and wrong sit with a service user's alternative visions of good and bad? Can an expression of love by instilling discipline through physical chastisement be considered a moral choice by a social worker practising in a country where it is deemed morally and legally acceptable? It is here that boundaries and agreed norms play their part in supporting moral choices.

Discretion – the ability to make ethical judgements based on the particular circumstances – is seen as part of what it is to be professional, and yet service users should be able to rely on something *common* to all social workers, too. It this *essence* that is so difficult to define and yet it is what ultimately makes a social worker a social worker. Each social worker applying their own values to each separate situation they meet does not seem satisfactory; and yet a social worker as a rule-driven, standardized clone is equally unattractive.

Existentialism

Existentialism is a philosophy that seeks to describe the world as it is (i.e., ontologically) rather than as it ought to be. However, Sartre (1946) argued in *Existentialism and Humanism* that there is an obligation to value your own freedom and therefore a moral value in the freedom of others. Existentialists believe we cannot escape making choices (we all have this inalienable freedom), and we arrive at our value judgements without any reliable external guidance.

As a social worker, an existentialist would make decisions based on how they feel and see the world, whilst also respecting the right of people with lived experience to make their own choices. In many ways, the right to make an unwise decision, enshrined in mental health legislation, reflects this philosophy, yet social work is often faced with the ethical dilemma of the right to make an unwise decision impacting on the safeguarding of family members or public safety.

Consequentialism

Kant's dismissal of consequence as irrelevant seems intuitively wrong; surely what happens as a result of our actions must be weighed on the ethical scales (sometimes referred to as teleology). *Utilitarianism* is one such ethical theory, one that aligns most closely with the idea of the Scales that introduced this chapter. It is based on the pursuit of pleasure and a belief that the right course of action is the one that is likely to bring the greatest sum of happiness for everyone who will experience the consequences (Mill 1863) or, conversely, the least amount of unhappiness. Mill's 'greatest happiness' principle, often referred to as the 'greater good', relies on making a moral choice based on what benefits the most people. However, this can prove difficult to weigh up.

Mill believed 'higher' pleasures (largely intellectual) to be more deserving than 'lower' pleasures (largely physical), a sense of hierarchy that seems to presage Maslow's (1943) hierarchy of needs. Calculating consequences is complicated and, like duty-based ethical theories, there are some aspects that seem intuitively wrong. For instance, even if the hanging of a man brings more overall happiness to the people (by way of a deterrent to violent crime) than the unhappiness of that one guilty man, does this make hanging 'right'? Consequence might be an important facet of our moral world, but it fails to wholly complete it.

Interestingly, Gawronski (2022) found that those who followed a duty-based, deontological, ethical philosophy and conformed with moral norms were perceived to have a greater morality than those following a consequence-based utilitarian ethical base.

New ethics

The moral theories propounded so far have autonomous, independent, rational beings at their core, but this is an idealized picture. The ethics of care (Held 2006; Meagher and Parton 2004; Parton 2003) and relationship ethics (Banks 2020) focus on interpersonal relationships, rather than the individual's rights or virtues, or calculations of utility. One premise of these new ethical frameworks is that a significant experience for human beings is their dependency on the care of others, especially, but not exclusively, through childhood. Though relationship ethics are not anti-reason, they do embrace (some) emotions rather than rejecting them. Another premise is that people need to feel sufficiently connected to one another to *care* about values and rights (Hugman 2013b).

The ethics of forgiveness and a belief in the possibility of change through redemption has traditionally been central to social work and probation practice. Probation officers were called on to 'advise, assist and befriend' the offenders with whom they worked, in the hope and belief that this kind of relationship could bring about change sufficient to move their clients away from criminal behaviour. This form of *redemptive ethics* also included positive action in the employment of ex-offenders in these services. A greater emphasis on risk and the assessment of risk, and a less forgiving climate, has put redemptive ethics in the shade, but stories of forgiveness might change this (Cantacuzino 2015).

Moral relativism

Moral relativism reminds us that ethics and morals are socially constructed, in contrast with moral realism, which sees ethics as more objective, with an absolute right existing.

In this book, we argue that inevitably all ethics are socially constructed. For example, Aristotle's assertion that women were lesser humans surely reflected the patriarchal society of his time. Nearer to our own times, we can reflect on considerable changes to acceptable behaviours. What might future generations see as unacceptable in our current practices?

Kant reflected that irrespective of taking a rational or an empirical view, knowledge is subjective and will change and develop as our worldview changes. This emphasizes the importance of continuous professional development and critical thinking to ensure that we do not become complacent and unthinking in our social work knowledge, skills, behaviours and values.

Philosophers are those who have made it their main work to investigate how *what is really important* can be understood or explained. Ultimately, moral discourse is about finding out what it is that is really important for us, what we value, as individuals, as communities and as a common humanity. How do we live well together? And what do we do when others want to do wrong? This book takes an approach that moral issues cannot be resolved in a prescriptive manner, but rather by the application of philosophic scepticism, a process that helps to arrive not at a definitive conclusion but at a point where action can be taken.

Critical thinking

Effective critical thinking involves the ability to evaluate sources of knowledge, such as law, policy, research and theories, to draw and articulate reasonable and verifiable conclusions.

Most social work education and training implicitly relies on a belief that if you reflect long and hard enough, the outcome will be *better* practice. Indeed, there is an explicit reliance on experiential learning to develop knowledge, skills and behaviours (Beesley 2024) and to promote the *reflective practitioner*. However, reflection needs to be undertaken critically, where the first response is interrogation of other perspectives: 'Decisions should always be informed by empirical evidence; practice wisdom; and ethical, legal, and cultural considerations. Social workers must be prepared to be transparent about the reasons for their decisions' (IFSW 2018).

Critical thinking has its roots in Socratic questioning. Socrates' students were asked open and challenging questions to stimulate thought and development. Socrates likened himself to a gadfly (horsefly), stinging his students by playing devil's advocate to encourage them to consider a situation from a wide range of perspectives, to develop understanding. It is this approach that social workers are encouraged to take. The social worker should never accept the first explanation of a situation, but should delve deeper and wider to analyse and assess the situation to ensure that an informed decision can be taken. Indeed, his statement that 'an unexamined life is not worth living' illustrates the value Socrates attributed to critical thinking.

Terminology

In this chapter, we have been using various terms as shorthand for a number of different ethical approaches. Every profession has its own terms, and one of the most controversial in social work is 'service user': someone who was previously referred to as 'client' and is now more often expressed as 'a person with lived experience'. The words social workers use in their practice reflect, often implicitly, their ethical stance. 'Person with lived experience' might be a lengthy descriptor, but it more accurately indicates the importance of listening to an individual's experiences to facilitate a person-centred response, one that is more likely to meet the needs of the person as expressed by themselves. Social workers cannot assume how a person with lived experience feels nor understand how they have experienced their life. Instead, a non-judgemental and open assessment of the situation is required to understand their individual, social, cultural and educational experiences. The terms we use reflect our ethical understanding.

Epic ethics and everyday ethics

The literature on moral philosophy tends to use examples from extreme situations, what we might describe as 'epic ethics'. For instance, the tram dilemma (Foot 1967; Jarvis Thomson 1976) is an ethical dilemma in which a tram is heading towards five people stuck on the track, with the choice to transfer to another track where there is only one person. The greater good would be to kill one person rather than five, but the problem is that by consciously changing tracks the situation is transformed from an unavoidable accident to an informed choice, leaving the tram driver feeling responsible for the death of a person. The focus of the tram dilemma can be altered by adding a personal element: what if the one person is your child? Or what if one of the five was Hitler? Other epic ethics are generated by big questions such as euthanasia, abortion, wartime killings, nuclear weaponry, (de) criminalization of sex work and the like. However, most moral dilemmas are more humdrum and it is these everyday ethical dilemmas that social workers face most regularly.

We need to understand how moral philosophy helps us with the routine dilemmas and not just the life-changing ones. We will be visiting dilemmas arising from professional life in the chapters ahead, so let us indulge first in an example that seems on the surface to have nothing to do with social work.

Ethical dilemma 2: Discretion at the coffee shop

Throughout the following ethical dilemma you will be asked questions designed to stimulate critical thinking to develop your understanding of the ethics involved in an everyday situation that you might not recognize as having an ethical dimension.

A coffee chain aims to 'alleviate poverty, hunger and help break the cycle of homelessness by donating unsold food … and giving opportunities to those in need of a second chance'. Is this an altruistic, charitable mission that enriches society from the profits of a large organization? Certainly, it echoes the historical philanthropic work of Lever and Rowntree, where wealthy men believed that it was their duty to give something back to society.

The coffee chain decided to allow counter staff the discretion to give free drinks to customers as part of the 'random acts of kindness' policy which has been designed to align with the company's charitable aims. However, receiving free coffee became a different act when it caught media attention as a means to an end, where it was argued that the seemingly altruistic act of kindness was portrayed as a manipulative act to increase the morale of the member of staff giving the drink and, ultimately, adding to the profits of the owners. The backlash illustrated the complexity of motivation and the strong sense of revulsion that people feel to being used as a means rather than being treated as an end.

The company undoubtedly saw the act of giving as an uncomplicated one, but how might we understand this situation from different ethical theoretical perspectives? How do counter staff make a *good* decision about who ought to be the beneficiary of their gift? What is the *right* way to make this decision? First, and most importantly, contact with ideas of moral philosophy has made us aware that the gifting is, in fact, a *moral* event. Without this, the gifting might just have seemed to be a pragmatic choice, for example, giving it to the first customer you serve after noon, or some example of *convenience ethics*.

Might you wait for a friend or family member to walk in? Certainly, the notion of *moral relativism* helps us understand that in a coffee shop located in a very traditional community there would be no question that the counter server should reserve their free coffees for their close family and friends and that to do otherwise would be disloyal, possibly bringing shame by breaching their society's strongest code. Other customers from this same traditional community would understand this as the right thing to do and not call it out as favouritism or nepotism, as would likely be the case in a so-called 'meritocratic' society.

Would it be unethical for the counter staff to take the free cup for themselves? This would likely be seen as selfishness, possibly even corrupt. However, is this viewpoint changed if the staff are subsisting on minimum wage with intolerable expenditures and unable to afford to eat properly? Does that alter the moral balance? An *existential* view would consider a person to be free to make this decision anyway, whatever the context.

Is the counter server inclined to gift the person who is friendly, as a reward or positive reinforcement or, conversely, the person who looks in need of cheering up? Perhaps they ought to make their judgement on the basis of who they think is most deserving, such as a harassed parent with screaming toddlers, or a homeless person outside on the street? Or should kindness only go to kind people as *virtue ethics* would suggest and, if so, how to make that judgement? Can appearances really indicate whether a person is kind or not? Might a uniform indicate public service, for instance, a nurse, or the often-maligned traffic warden, who bravely takes a lot of stick in order to keep the pavements clear of illegally parked cars so wheelchair users are not endangered? These judgement calls on customer virtue are very likely to be heavily influenced by the societal, educational, cultural and familial past experiences, all of which inevitably have an impact on the server's ethical decision making. Would an understanding of ethical theories, as outlined earlier in this chapter, influence the way in which the server went about making their decision, and would this make for *better* decision making?

Another approach is to base the gifting of free drinks on *fairness*, perhaps expressed as proportional fairness or representativeness. This would mean that over the course of a month, the gifted coffees would go equally to women and men, to represent their distribution in the population as a whole. How far does the duty of fair distribution extend: ethnic balance, age range, etc. and how is this tracked and monitored? If something is difficult or cumbersome to put into effect, does this influence whether it *ought* to be put into effect?

A *consequentialist* approach would consider the likely consequences of the different choices and, if specifically *utilitarian*, aim to achieve the greatest happiness. However, might one consequence of giving a free coffee actually increase the unhappy beneficiary's displeasure, as they interpret the gesture as pitying or patronizing? What are the consequences for the happiness of others in the queue who are not chosen? Might the sum of the unhappiness of six overhearing customers substantially outweigh the happiness of the chosen one? So, should the beneficiary be chosen on the basis that they are the only person in the queue? However, if that person later tells their friends, will they not feel even more displeasure that this gifting activity has been going on 'behind their backs'? It becomes quickly clear that weighing consequences is complex. Even so, as we will see in later chapters, consequentialism is commonly employed, if usually implicitly, in decision making.

Much moral philosophy takes the individual as the starting point, but ought we come to a *collective* position? How are colleagues arriving at their choices and how ought theirs influence ours? For the coffee company who ostensibly wished to give flexibility and choice to their employees to promote kindness, the consequence might be a complex ethical weight placed on their staff. One response might be to impose a rigid policy which not all staff would want but alleviates them of the moral responsibility to make a choice. Does the moral responsibility, therefore, lie with the company to provide clearer but flexible guidance, or perhaps within the more complex corporate relationships between owners, managers, staff and customers?

Finally, what about the coffee itself, no matter who or how it is given? Does the company have a moral responsibility to the coffee-bean growers and buyers to pay ethical prices and use Fair Trade products? Do they have a moral responsibility to ensure quality-assured and fair-priced goods to their customers? They have a responsibility to their shareholders to make a profit – is this an *ethical* duty? If one of these responsibilities conflicts with another, which 'wins'?

Do you think that counter servers who have studied moral philosophy will make *better* decisions or just *slower* ones? Keep your response to this question in mind as you read the book, because it influences how you think about the very question of ethical issues and practice dilemmas, well before you consider what you ought to do about them.

Guidance from codes, standards and principles

All values might appear equal on the pages of the codes of ethics, but some are perhaps more equal than others, and some require long-term advocacy in order to be realized (Beresford and Croft 2001; Beresford and Holden 2000; Warren 2007). The value in which service users are held, the respect for the individual and for the right to self-determination, remain central to social work and these are embedded in professional ethical codes. Nevertheless, ethical codes should be open to debate and regularly reviewed. Individual social workers have a professional and moral duty to participate in each fresh consideration of these codes.

It is reasonable to query whether there can 'be an effective, overarching code of professional ethics if all our values are grounded in different cultures and personal beliefs' (Hugman 2013b: 385). The adoption of a single ethical code could be an example of a powerful elite imposing its own ethical hierarchy. So, instead of an international professional code of ethics, social work has agreed a *Global Statement of Ethical Principles* which aims to provide a 'moral tent' under which all social workers can shelter, wherever they practice (IFSW 2018), supplemented with numerous national Codes of Ethics. Even so, the difficulties when principles conflict will inevitably result in varying interpretations of ethical practice; it is this that lies at the heart of the dilemmas that illustrate the subsequent chapters.

Global Statement of Ethical Principles (IFSW 2018)

1. Recognition of the Inherent Dignity of Humanity.
2. Promoting Human Rights.
3. Promoting Social Justice.
4. Promoting the Right to Self-Determination.
5. Promoting the Right to Participation.
6. Respect for Confidentiality and Privacy.
7. Treating People as Whole Persons.
8. Ethical Use of Technology and Social Media.
9. Professional Integrity.

https://www.ifsw.org/global-social-work-statement-of-ethical-principles/

Throughout the book, the IFSW (2018) *Global Statement of Ethical Principles* and the Codes of Ethics from different nations will be referred to in relation to the chapter topic.

Conclusion

This chapter has introduced the notion of critical thinking in social work practice, outlined different approaches to ethics, and reflected on how these can be applied to a non-social work example from the everyday world, in this case in a coffee shop chain. As you continue through the book, we hope you will reflect on how an ethical dilemma is one that can be subjected to multiple approaches and ethical perspectives, and have varied potential outcomes. An ethical dilemma should be considered from a wide range of perspectives, that take account of social work knowledge, values, practice wisdom and skills. The social worker needs to consider the perspectives of all involved in order to facilitate good decision making. There is never, or certainly very seldom, just one singular, right response, and the social worker's job is to help determine the best decision available.

The ways in which ethical codes are interpreted varies surprisingly within the same profession (Doel et al. 2010), with quite contrary actions springing from commonly held values and principles. This can often best be explained by different practitioners' responses to *conflicting* principles and values (Joseph and Fernandes 2006). Value conflicts will be a recurring theme in the book. Good practice requires social workers to have access to regular supervision and reflective discussion to support critical thinking and rounded deliberation of ethical dilemmas.

The importance of 'morally exceptional figures' should not be underestimated. Gawronski (2022) found that decision making in ethical dilemmas is often modelled by these individuals, thereby illustrating the importance of strong social work educators, both in university and in practice placements, to support the development of social work students' ethical and moral codes. Finding a role model and mentor can be an effective skill development strategy in navigating the rights and wrongs of social work practice.

Think further about …

… a time this week when you had a choice to make, one that had an ethical dimension, but not one connected with social work or professional practice:

- What was the ethical nature of this choice and did it present a dilemma for you?
- Did the choice result in a specific decision and, if so, why did you come to the decision you made?
- What alternative decisions were available to you?
- Can you relate your thinking to any of the ethical approaches that you have read about in this chapter?

- Has the discussion of ethical approaches in this chapter had any impact on the way you would now make your decision?

Ethical dilemmas with twelve people

Omar Mohamed (Scales)

I am a 24-year-old, Asian British male, born and raised in London, with family and ancestral roots from East Africa, India and Persia. I am a lived experience activist and sibling kinship carer and use my role as a social worker as a platform to help make changes in the world that link to promoting social justice, equity and human rights. I sit on a variety of committees and leadership groups, provide training and consultancy, and regularly contribute to the next generation of social workers through international work and education. I regularly publish contributions to knowledge related to anti-racism and decolonization, with a drive to continually promote diasporic, embodied and indigenous knowledge.

Boris Shapiro (Compass)

In the early 1990s, social work as a helping profession started to develop strongly in Russia and I was involved in creation of curricula and courses for social workers at an international level. Then I have been for many years Dean of Faculty of Social Administration and Social Work at the Moscow School of Social and Economic Sciences (Russian-British postgraduate university). I have a PhD in psychology and I became Pro-Rector for Teaching and Learning at the Moscow School.

Further reading

Banks, S. (2020), *Ethics and Values in Social Work*, 5th edn, London: Bloomsbury.
Jarvis Thomson, J. (1976), 'Killing, Letting Die, and the Trolley Problem', *The Monist*, 59: 204–17.

3

Value conflicts and choices

Introduction

This chapter consider the kinds of value conflict that social workers experience and the complex intertwining of personal, professional and structural values. We consider a variety of different value conflicts and introduce a framework to help make choices in the light of these conflicts. A conflicted situation in social work is presented in some detail to help you to grapple with the complexities involved and the 'wise professionals' (see Chapter 1) are consulted towards the conclusion of the chapter.

To begin this chapter, we borrow two objects from the socialworkin40objects. com collection to help lead us in beginning to navigate the significant issues that will be presented and discussed in the rest of the chapter. Both objects serve a symbolic purpose: the first object is no longer in existence whilst, in contrast, the second object is found in every home.

Ethical dilemmas in twelve objects

Jane Addams' coat

> [Count] Tolstoy, standing by clad in his peasant garb, listened gravely but, glancing distrustfully at the sleeves of my traveling gown which unfortunately at that season were monstrous in size, he took hold of an edge and pulling out one sleeve to an interminable breadth, said quite simply that 'there was enough stuff on one arm to make a frock for a little girl,' and asked me directly if I did not find such a dress a 'barrier to the people'.
>
> (Jane Addams, *Twenty Years at Hull-House*, 1910)

Moldovan social work educator Vadim chose *Jane Addams' coat* because it is a symbol of wealth and privilege that stands in stark contrast with the poor person's garb. He argues that the social worker who ministers to the poor from the position of power, material well-being and authority does not empower, but relegates the needy to the role of alms-taker, a charity case. Vadim also asserts that Jane Addams' coat can symbolize the potential hypocrisy for the social worker who proclaims to uphold the values of social justice and yet lacks the self-awareness to recognize how their behaviour might subvert that message. The encounter with Tolstoy that is related by Jane Addams in her book, *Twenty Years at Hull-House* (1910), triggered a profound crisis in her, and a reorientation towards a more authentic and socially responsible social work practice – what we would today call a *critical social justice practice*.

Sticking plaster (or bandaid)

American social work researcher Barbara nominated a *sticking plaster* (or *Bandaid*), stating that though the concept is perhaps a bit simple, the object reflects the struggle and ambivalence that she has had for nearly fifty years, despite her immersion in the social work profession in many different roles.

Barbara fears that most of social work's energy and attention goes into 'fixing' individuals, groups and families, yet this has always seemed so inadequate when the need is for more fundamental social reform. This awareness began when Barbara was in graduate school in the 1960s and met community organizers for the first time. Students in that track were disruptive and interrupted lectures to say that people should be engaging in rent and garbage strikes, rather than having their thoughts, motivations and behaviours examined and 'treated' by social caseworkers. The community organization students were very rude, but she thought they were right!

This inclination caused much difficulty for Barbara over the years, because she was always straining to fix the injustices and/or dampening rules that get in the way of needed change – whether it is within an institution (psychiatric hospitals, social service agencies, or universities), or involving community or policy change. Her behaviour was often seen as inappropriate, anti-establishment and insubordinate, although she was nice enough to keep her jobs: 'but it seems that most of us who are still alive or at least employed, sold out in many small and sometimes large ways. Not a comfortable position.'

Think about …

You are in town on a Saturday and recognize a young person that you are working with, and you wonder if you should go over and say hello or walk past without acknowledging them.

Is there a dilemma? If so, what is the nature of your dilemma? And what do you do?

What might make a difference to the nature of your dilemma? Consider your own boundaries on your day off and the young person's right to confidentiality, given you are not sure who might know their situation.

Origins of value conflicts: Personal, professional and structural

The dilemmas that social workers face are usually associated with conflicts in values. These stem both from *within* the profession because of the elusive, complex and contested nature of social work and its purposes; and also from the friction *between* various social systems. These seismic zones are illustrated below (Figures 3.1 and 3.2) where the overlapping edges represent the areas of regular conflicts in values.

Figure 3.1 depicts the three main functions of social work, all legitimate and essential to the social work role, but not sitting comfortably together. Ethical conflicts frequently occur within the 'overlap' zones.

Figure 3.2 represents the four different social systems that are at play in all social work encounters – the social workers themselves, the people they work with, the organization that employs them, and professional oversight and allegiance. Each system experiences different kinds and levels of power and influence, all of which influence decision making and can generate conflict.

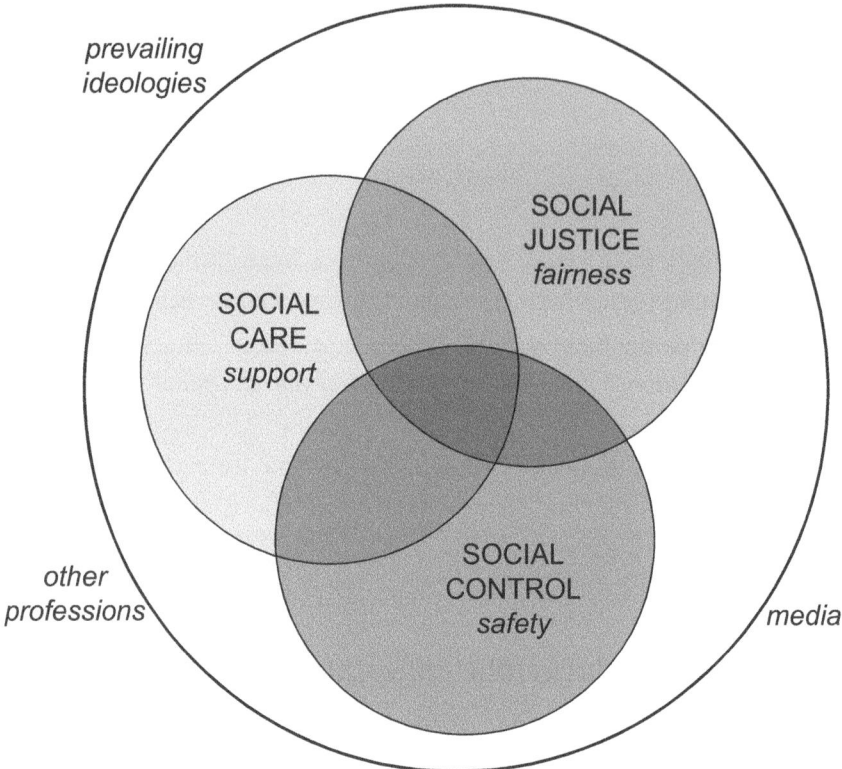

Figure 3.1 Social work's reason for being.

The factors that impinge most on these systems are shown at the edges of the circles.

Some conflicts play out within the individual as they try to determine which of two or more values should triumph when each would lead to a different course of action; for instance, whether to vote for a leader of a party with whose principles you agree, or whether to vote for a leader who seems more likely to win the next election. These conflicts can be difficult to resolve, but they need not involve other people. Other value conflicts arise between your own and those of other people – colleagues, service users, the management of the agency, the law, etc. These situations are more complex because of the number of variables involved and because of the power dimension (see Chapter 4); some moral players in these conflicts are more powerful than others, so it is not necessarily the 'best' (most ethical) outcome that is achieved, but it might be the one that carries the most weight.

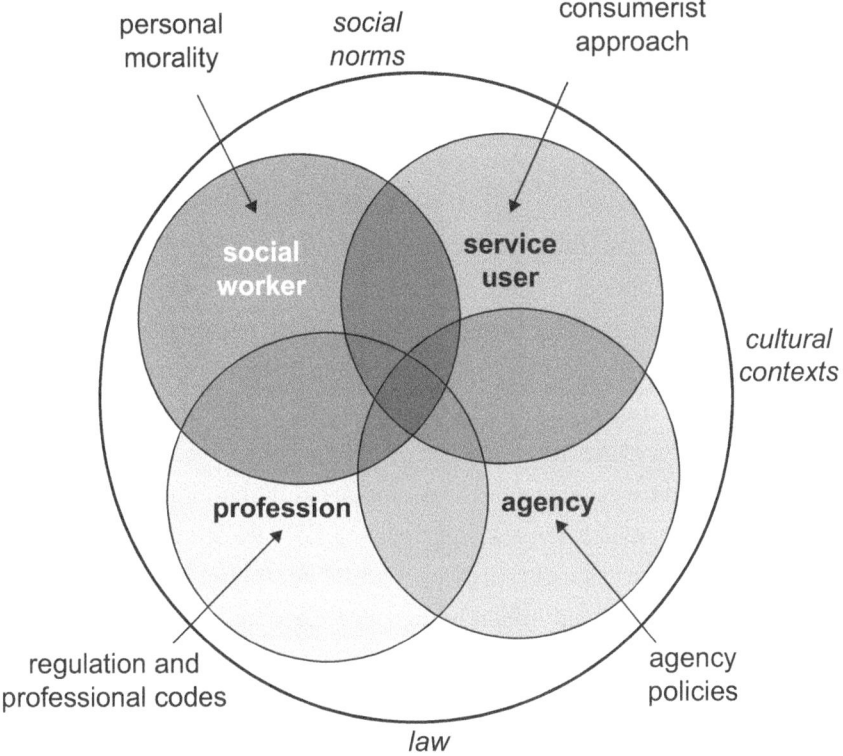

Figure 3.2 Social work and social systems, adapted from Doel et al. (2010).

Let us consider the different circumstances that can give rise to these conflicts in professional settings.

Get a life

A common conflict is the struggle between meeting your own needs and meeting those of others – that is, the value you put on your own needs and the value you place on others'. For instance, your work phone rings just as you are about to finish for the day. Do you assert your own needs by ignoring it, or bend to the need of the caller by answering? The overshadowing of domestic responsibilities by professional dedication has become a TV cop cliché, but it does illustrate a real clash between the value given to domestic life and the value given to work. At the far extreme of this continuum, Das and Kulkani

(2006a: 82) describe the ultimate sacrifice of a social worker who lost her life fighting a powerful lobby of builders in India on behalf of her clients.

Mind a gap

A daily conflict for some social workers arises from the distance between their own lifestyle and their services users', illustrated in the introduction to this chapter by the story of Jane Addams' coat. Economic differences might be evident not just in daily living conditions, but in opportunities such as foreign travel. This gap can feed feelings of guilt. There are parallels with the gap between the wealthy West and the rest of the world: how is it possible, ethically, to buy a plane ticket to a foreign holiday in the knowledge that the cost of that ticket would save the lives of many children in a famine-ridden foreign country (possibly the one you are flying to)? Like our current attitudes to nineteenth-century slavery, perhaps a future generation will look back to our present behaviour with moral repugnance. There is a universal cognitive dissonance that acts as a kind of self-medication against the true horror of these appalling inequalities.

The gap is not just an economic one. A social worker might wonder how their severely depressed service users would feel if they saw her partying at a club when an hour or so earlier, she had been empathizing with their trauma and distress. Is this compartmentalization a human dilemma or an ethical dilemma, and is this distinction a useful one (Das and Kulkarni 2006b: 92)?

Earn your crust

At the height of the radical social work movement in the 1970s, a phrase was coined – 'revolution on the rates' – that poked fun at the moral ambiguity of Marxist social workers drawing their monthly pay packet from the very system they were apparently intent on overthrowing. After many decades of neoliberal economic policies, it is currently 'radical low-tide', but there are nevertheless plenty of value conflicts for social workers in organizations that from time to time compromise notions of good practice in social work (Dolgoff et al. 2009). One of the authors, immediately after qualifying in social work, found a job that was in an agency where they felt the practices to be oppressive to service users, and the agency's systems impeded rather than facilitated good practice. However, the job paid their salary and it was far from home. Even so, the conflict in values and the difficulty in making any significant changes led them to resign.

We must ask ourselves: *Do social workers work 'at' or 'for' their employing organizations?* To what extent, then, should a social worker's priorities and the way they work be determined by the role as it is defined by the employer? How far from the individual practitioner can the power of this decision be removed before it becomes unacceptable, even unethical? For example, social workers working in the market-driven environment of much American mental health practice find that decisions about where they can put their time and resources are determined by insurance companies. The values of accounting are being applied to judgements that were once professional and, if they wish to earn their crust, social workers must accept them.

An extreme example of the value conflicts concerning social workers earning their crust can be found in the 1978–9 strike in various local authorities in the UK – part of the infamous 'winter of discontent'. A secret ballot of about four hundred social work staff in one Social Services Department resulted in a wafer-thin majority of nine in favour of strike action. Value conflicts are not usually settled with a vote, not in professional settings, but the dominant organizational model at that time was an industrial rather than the current corporate one. All participating in the ballot had placed their trust in this democratic, majoritarian system and so the result carried *moral authority* even for those who had voted against. There was some compromising, with those against striking permitted to staff a rota for a team responding to severe emergencies. There was collective trust that this team would respect the terms of 'severe emergency' and not continue to work normally. Certainly, everyone was counted as 'on strike' and therefore made the collective sacrifice of loss of salary.

The conflicts were common ones about long-term and short-term value: ought the short-term suffering of service users deprived of a social work service (and the hardship for social workers and their families caused by loss of income) outweigh the long-term benefit of a properly rewarded profession? These complex considerations were summed up in the beginning of this chapter by social worker Barbara's notion of the sticking plaster.

Square a circle

In traditional societies, social workers often find their 'new' adopted professional values clash with the families from which they come and with the communities where they are placed – for example, the presence of extremely stigmatizing social attitudes to homosexuality and people with HIV in the Republic of Georgia (Doel et al. 2016). In India, clients are likely to accept bribery as a way of life and it is the only way some officials earn enough to live, whilst social workers are likely to consider it their moral obligation to fight bribery (Das and Kulkarni 2006a: 82). Should social workers refuse to offer bribes, even if this will prevent their clients from gaining the resources they need and the clients themselves accept bribery as acceptable?

The norms in social democracies are possibly in more harmony with social work values than these examples from Georgia and India; nevertheless clashes between social attitudes and social work values, and between individual social workers and service users, can feel like trying to square a circle. How should a social worker respond when a service user uses racist language? Social workers can feel conflicted between the values of non-judgemental acceptance and those of challenging discrimination. They might also find it difficult to judge the balance between risk to the relationship as a result of a challenge, and risk to their integrity by colluding with racist values (more on risk in Chapter 7).

Walk this way

Is it better to make your own worse decision or another's better one? Social workers often have a strong sense of what would be best for their service user, but offering opinions conflicts with the professional values of self-determination. Offering solutions is a form of judgement and this can be detrimental to the service user's own decision-making capacities. On the other hand, a direction offered at the right moment can prevent the service user making costly mistakes, perhaps helping them to avoid a potentially destructive relationship. Of course, there are occasions when social workers must take full control of decision making on behalf of other people and are given legal powers to do so, emphasizing the social control function as shown in Figure 3.1.

Plug a hole

One of the central tenets of social work is that it is a holistic discipline in which practitioners work with the individual in the context of their family, community and broader society. Social workers are educated to understand the socio-political reasons for individuals' circumstances – the relationship between public policy and private experience and, ultimately, the links between poverty, health and social well-being. What moral obligations does this knowledge confer? At what level of intervention ought the social work take place and how does 'good' social work take account of the charge of applying sticking plasters to one problem at a time, when the problems themselves are so often related to public policy? There are constant value conflicts when the people who are eligible and could benefit from social work far exceed the resources available. What are the ethics of social triage?

Meet the neighbours

From the 1970s to the 1990s, British social workers worked in large public-sector Social Services Departments led by a director who by law had to be a qualified social worker. Social workers can now find themselves in multi-professional settings where professional values might be interpreted differently from one professional grouping to another, and close proximity means that value conflicts are more likely.

A classic tension is that between medical and social models of practice. For example, a medical model of obesity would consider the biological and psychological factors that lead an individual to become overweight, while a social model would consider the link between poverty and obesity and the unregulated policies of the food and drink industry, the effects of advertising, and environmental factors that inhibit walking. The medical and social models of obesity are not incompatible, but there are value conflicts about blame and responsibility.

The growth of inter-professional education means that students are likely to come into direct contact with different professional cultures and the values that support them. The hope is that with early contact will come understanding and accommodation (CAIPE 2012).

> ## The big picture
>
> You are living as a social worker in a country which has an increasingly authoritarian government. It has ramped up the rhetoric against minorities, is cutting public provision and has severe measures to limit any opposition to its policies and power. Draconian laws are in place that limit free protest and, increasingly, any person or any organization that opposes the government is named as an 'enemy of the people'.
>
> Social work is relatively new in your country and it is not a 'protected' profession (that is, it has only limited recognition as an independent profession in the state's laws); you and your colleagues have spent two decades working to establish social work as a respected profession, through your country's Association of Social Workers.
>
> There are some members of your professional association who openly oppose the government; they use social media and join the nightly anti-government demonstrations. They see the government's actions as in direct opposition to social work values. One of these social workers has been charged with 'obstructing the road' – she had not taken the precaution of wearing a hood or other disguise and a facial recognition camera had identified her. She now faces a court appearance and a fine equivalent to a year's salary. Another social worker has been arrested and beaten up by the police.
>
> Some members of your professional association argue that it is necessary to engage with the government agencies; otherwise, all the good work to establish social work as a recognized (and therefore powerful) profession will be undone. They do not publicly criticize the government and do not join the demonstrations. These social workers and the ones who join the demonstrations are at loggerheads about the direction in which the Association of Social Workers should go, and there is now a split.
>
> What would you do? Would you be vocal about your opposition to your country's government in the hope of bringing fundamental change, or would you work with it to try to preserve what advances you feel you have already made?
>
> For the social workers in the country in question, this is not a hypothetical choice.

Four responses to value conflicts

When working with value conflicts that involve you and others, what options do you have? Let us consider a typography of response and then illustrate by means of an example dilemma. Note that these four responses are presented with no moral weight – in other words, we are not suggesting that any one response is more ethically 'correct' than the others:

- Compete: The conflicting value systems are seen as irreconcilable, the one a threat to the other. This leads to assertive, competitive behaviour in order to establish a dominant set of values.
- Compromise: Attempts are made to settle the conflict by pragmatic moves to a convergence ('halfway between the two') or a compromise that takes something from one value and something from the other and melds them.
- Concede: As with competing, the values are seen as irreconcilable; one of the parties in the conflict gives way and accepts the others' values.
- Avoid: There is an agreement, usually implicit, to pretend there is no value conflict by turning a blind eye, or delaying tactics, sometimes called 'kicking into the long grass'.

Ethical dilemma 3: Two 'lives' – the story of Charlotte and Daniella

Charlotte is a social worker working with a family services agency. She has strong views about abortion, believing that it is morally wrong; indeed, she considers it to be murder. Daniella, one of her service users is pregnant and wants to terminate the pregnancy.

1 How ought Charlotte respond to Daniella's desire to terminate her pregnancy?

First, let us examine what choices are open to Charlotte using the Compete, Compromise, Concede, or Avoid framework:

- *Compete* by promoting her own principles: Charlotte could allow herself to be led by her beliefs. This means challenging Daniella's decision, explaining why termination is wrong and advising her against it.
- *Compromise* by seeking a balance: Charlotte could disclose her own beliefs to Daniella, discuss the case against termination and suggest that she seeks advice from others who can offer the alternative case.
- *Concede* by keeping quiet: Charlotte could choose not to disclose her own beliefs and let Daniella make her decision alone.

- *Avoid* by opting out: Charlotte could ask her agency to provide a different social worker for Daniella on the grounds that she cannot offer balanced advice.

Let us consider the ethical dimensions involved in these choices. The main conflict, for Charlotte, lies between her desire to assert her own needs (not to inflict pain on herself by acting contrary to deeply held beliefs) and her belief in principles of self-determination that allow others to come to their own choices, based on a balanced discussion of the options available. In an extreme case, Charlotte might not feel that there is a dilemma, because when a human life is at stake (the foetus, as she sees it), compromise is not possible and that, though Daniella does not realize it, Daniella's moral interests are best served by keeping the baby.

However, Charlotte does face a number of difficulties if she pursues this position. First, is Charlotte working in a country that sanctions abortion through law? Charlotte might ask how the 'murder' of a foetus can be right in one part of the planet and not in another, possibly in places with common borders. An additional conflict for Charlotte is that she is a member of a profession – social work – which sanctions self-determination. In Daniella's case, this means the rights of women over the rights of the unborn.

There is also an ethical dilemma concerning self-disclosure. On the one hand, there is a good argument that Daniella has a right to know whether her social worker has a view and, if so, whether it is strongly held; on the other hand, Charlotte has rights to privacy and we would not normally find it acceptable for a social worker to be asked, for instance, to disclose their religion.

What we learn from Charlotte and Daniella's situation

What is interesting is that the decisions about whether to compete, compromise, concede, or avoid are not confined to the Charlotte/Daniella situation. Although this particular dilemma and clash of beliefs (between what is brutally over-simplified as 'pro-life' and 'pro-choice') is a common and readily accessible one, it also points the way to ethical dilemmas at a general level. Whatever the specifics of the situation, the dilemma is frequently whether to *compete* (to enter the race and assert your own beliefs and ethical position), to *compromise* (to recognize the various ethical positions that are possible and to aim for a pragmatic resolution that either takes them all on board or charts some middle or third course), to *concede* (not to assert your own beliefs, to 'park them'), or *avoid* by circumventing the dilemma and finding a way of not having to face it.

2 Is Charlotte's moral ground changed if she works for an agency that promotes the rights of the unborn?

Let us consider Charlotte's wider world. She has chosen to work for 'Life', a charity in the voluntary sector that promotes the rights of the unborn. Does this affect the ethics of the options that are available to her, such as those described in the previous section?

Certainly, by choosing to apply to work at 'Life', Charlotte knew what would be expected of her as an employee of the organization. She knows that her own ethical choice (if it is to 'compete' with Daniella's) will be supported by her employer. We might suppose that if Daniella has approached 'Life', she knows what to expect, but this is not necessarily the case. Perhaps she has been referred there by a health professional who shares the same belief system (that others might describe as prejudices) as Charlotte and is hopeful that 'Life' can persuade Daniella to follow what the health professional considers to be the right course of action. Perhaps Daniella is feeling equivocal and wants someone to tell her to keep the baby and that is why she has chosen to go to 'Life'? For instance, if you are canvassing for a political party, no one would reasonably expect you to present a balanced view by also advancing the policies of other parties.

3 Charlotte's life circumstances are very different from Daniella's. Does this have an impact on the 'moral landscape'?

Charlotte comes from a comfortable, middle-class, white British home. She has had a relatively privileged background – her parents are wealthy and have given her a stable, loving upbringing. She excelled academically and she was head-hunted for a well-paid, relatively low-stress job; instead she chose to become a social worker, following a sense of duty, a desire to repay her good fortune, and also to work at something she saw as ethically demanding. Being honest with herself, she recognizes a lot of guilt, too, arising from her self-awareness of a fortunate life. Charlotte has had a number of relationships and is always careful to take precautions against pregnancy, but she knows that if she became pregnant in a situation where she did not want to remain in a relationship with the father, then her parents would support her, emotionally, practically and financially.

Daniella was brought up in care. Her mother has learning difficulties and she has not seen her for two years. Daniella is dual heritage and has never known her father. Her life is described in the substantial case notes as 'chaotic' and as 'living from hand to mouth'. Nineteen years old now, she has already had one pregnancy termination. She has few social supports and drifts on the edge of a drug-using group that commits low-scale crime to fund its drug use.

Does the contrast in the lives of Charlotte and Daniella give either of the two any 'moral authority' in their encounter? Charlotte has education and training; Daniella has lived experience. Can Charlotte advise a person whose life story and current circumstances are in such stark contrast to her own? Does it make a difference that the child that Daniella would bring into the world will have such different life chances to a child of Charlotte's? What is right for one is not necessarily right for another – an example of *moral relativism*?

Charlotte is aware that these two lives – hers and Daniella's – are a world apart. Except they are not: Unknown to anybody but a few close friends, Charlotte works as a dancer in a nearby town at a nightclub, ironically also called 'Life'. She has always been fiercely independent from her parents and does not accept financial help from them, and she finds that her social worker salary at a voluntary agency does not fund the lifestyle that she wants to maintain. Moreover, Charlotte gets a kick from her work as a dancer and, having recently decided that she is not bisexual but lesbian, she has found it a surprisingly good way to meet partners.

One Friday night a new woman starts work in the club. It's Daniella.

4 What, if any, ethical dilemmas arise from Charlotte and Daniella being colleagues at the nightclub?

Does Daniella's response to this revelation alter the moral landscape? Might she feel that it brings Charlotte closer to her own situation and, rather than seeing Charlotte as a toff, she now thinks of her as someone who shares some part of her own lifestyle? Alternatively, might Charlotte be sullied in Daniella's eyes; at least she, Daniella, has little alternative to this work, but Charlotte has the education and background to better herself.

Whatever Daniella's response to the revelation that Charlotte works in the nightclub, it doesn't change the fact that she *does* work there – so can Daniella's response affect the fundamental ethics of the situation? And are the ethics changed if, for instance, Daniella's attitude alters from one of moral repugnance to one of moral respect, once Charlotte has the opportunity to discuss her situation? In terms of *virtue ethics*, Daniella's view of Charlotte's character might be significantly altered by this encounter in the 'Life' nightclub. At another level, however, it feels that the rights or wrongs of Charlotte's behaviour should be a constant and not flip-flop according to how Daniella chooses to view the situation.

5 Does Charlotte's second employment bring her profession into disrepute?

Ought Charlotte to have informed her employer that she is working at the other 'Life'? Her employer might claim that she is bringing the agency into disrepute, alongside the social work regulator's concerns that her night-time job also brings the profession into disrepute. However, what is meant by 'disrepute' in these circumstances – does it just mean going against the norms – and who is doing the disreputing? Charlotte might claim to have taken reasonable precautions by taking up her second employment in another town, using an alias in the club and not talking about her day job.

Does the nature of the dancing affect the judgements – if it includes pole-dancing or lap-dancing, for instance? Does the state of dress or undress have a bearing? Are Charlotte's motives material to the discussion – is it relatively more acceptable if economic circumstances forced her to find other employment, as opposed to her finding thrills from the work or, even more 'culpable', a route to make sexual contacts? Or, if there *is* a transgression, does this stem from the failure (dishonesty?) of not informing her social work employer that she has a second job? If that is the case, should she, then, have informed 'Life' (the nightclub) of her employment as a social worker at the voluntary organization, or is that different? What if Charlotte makes more money at the nightclub than from the voluntary agency – does that make social work her secondary employment, something that provides her with pocket money?

Does your view of Charlotte's employment at the nightclub change depending on which of these two situations pertains and, if so, why?

1   Charlotte has no idea that there could be any ethical problems in working at the nightclub and just decided that's what she wanted to do.
2   Charlotte has asked herself all the questions posed above and, having weighed the possible answers, has come to a considered decision that it is ethically acceptable for her to work at the nightclub. She can explain her reasoning when asked by her supervisor at the social work agency.

There is no difference in the outcome (Charlotte.1 and Charlotte.2 end up working at 'Life' the nightclub), so *consequentialist* ethical reasoning would support the view that your perspective ought not to be influenced by this information. However, *virtue ethics* would see good in Charlotte.2, someone who is exercising moral judgement and making a decision on the basis of it. However, a cynic might consider that she is merely more expert than Charlotte.1 at rationalizing what she wants to do and dressing it up in ethical reasoning.

Charlotte and Daniella get to know one another better at the nightclub than they ever did in the voluntary agency and Daniella confides in Charlotte that she is HIV positive.

6 What ought Charlotte to do with the knowledge that Daniella is HIV positive?

Daniella has not informed the nightclub that she is HIV positive. The nightclub has strictly ruled that there should be no sexual contact between the dancers and the clientele, so no risk is posed to the customers or other dancers. However, Daniella confides to Charlotte that she has not informed her partner with whom she is having unprotected sex. Daniella has found stability and happiness for herself and her baby (she was convinced by the Life charity's promises of help if she didn't pursue the abortion) and she is afraid that her partner will leave if he finds out that she is HIV positive.

What are Charlotte's moral obligations at this point? She has discovered this information not as a social worker but as a dancer – Daniella is both service user and co-worker. Charlotte is aware that there would be no baby without the support and persuasion from the social work agency; looking back, would the knowledge that Daniella was HIV positive have influenced her advice? Charlotte might wonder why Daniella made this recent revelation, perhaps speculating that at some level Daniella wants to be advised to inform her partner, with a hope that Charlotte can provide enough support to help Daniella to sustain the relationship. Or did it all come out after a night's work and several vodkas, with Daniella now adamant that Charlotte should just forget it?

In the meantime, Charlotte has decided to tell her supervisor Francis about her work at the nightclub.

7 What ought Charlotte's supervisor, Francis, do with the knowledge that Charlotte is working at the nightclub?

In Chapter 2, we looked at different models of ethical discourse and you might briefly want to look back to pages 24–31 before reading on.

With these in mind, we will consider four alternatives for Francis:

Francis.1 subscribes to a *duty-based, Kantian* system of ethics.
Francis.2 is a *utilitarian*.
Francis.3 bases his judgements on *virtue ethics*.
Francis.4 bases his judgements on *care ethics*.

How might the different Francis's come to each of their decisions about what to do, and how might these decisions differ?

A composite, eclectic Francis, or a Francis who is just not really aware of his moral reasoning, might draw up a list of factors to consider. We have started a checklist that you can add other factors (see Figure 3.3). What might each one tell us about Francis's ethical stance?

Francis is a *moral agent* in this situation; in other words he is a person with values that inform his actions. The beliefs and opinions that spring from his values will influence his judgement about what to do. We consider these possible beliefs in Figure 3.4.

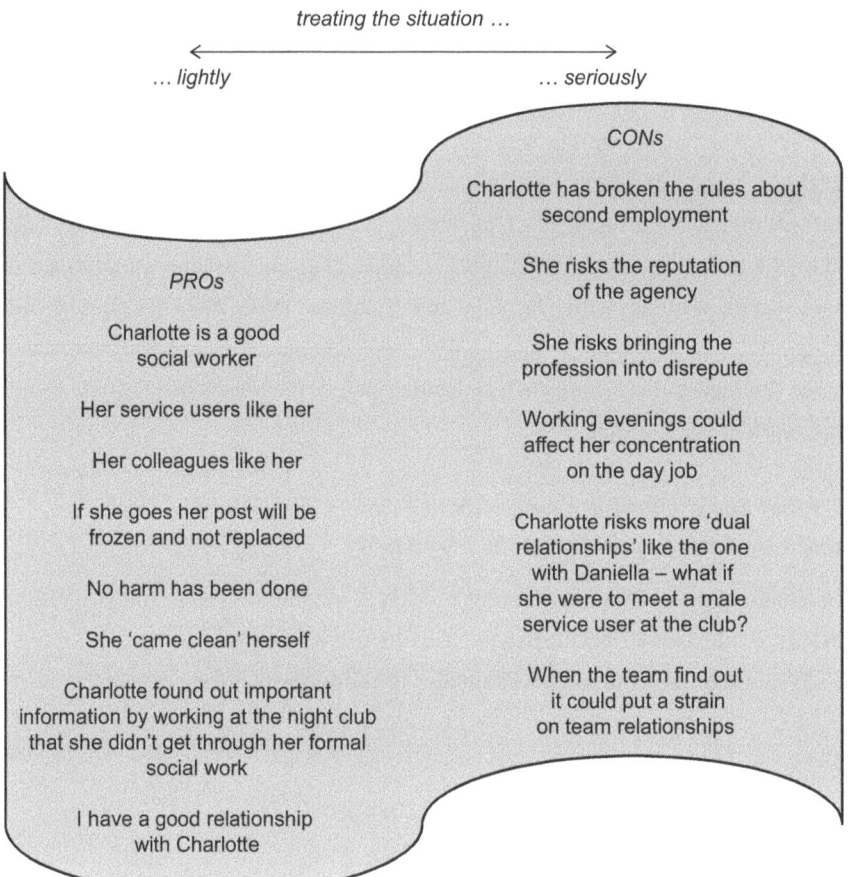

Figure 3.3 Pros and cons (1).

Francis is a person with certain life experiences and these, too, will influence his judgement of what he feels he ought to do, with the knowledge that Charlotte has an evening job at the nightclub. For example, consider what bearing these different life histories might have:

Value Conflicts amd Choices 59

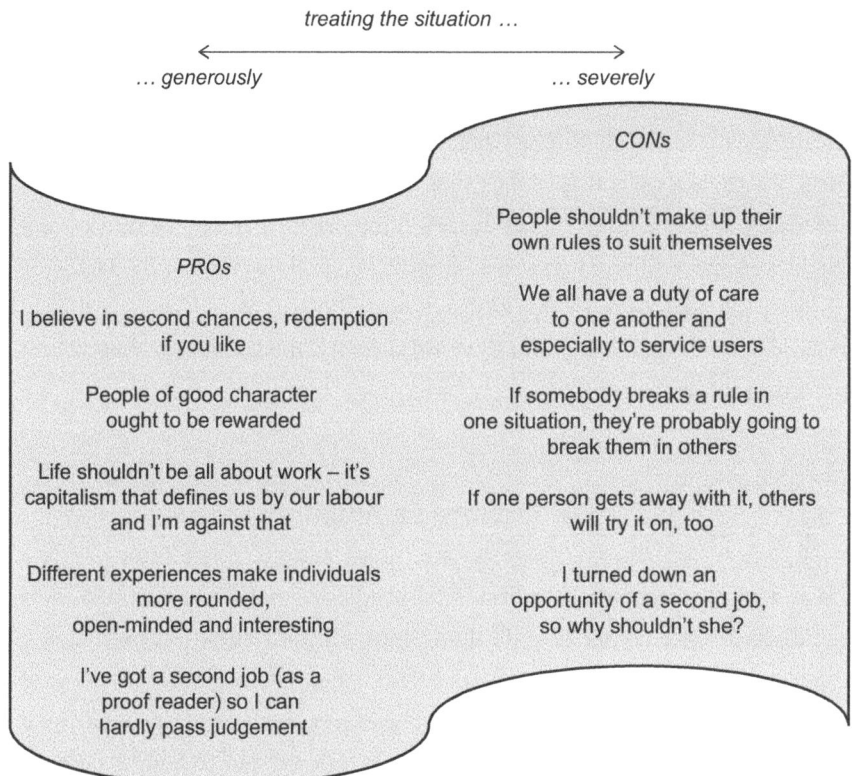

Figure 3.4 Pros and cons (2).

Francis has recently returned from four years living and working as a social work manager on a small Pacific island where everyone knows everyone, most people had two, three, or more jobs and *dual relationships* such as Charlotte and Daniella's were commonplace, indeed inevitable.

Francis is experiencing an acrimonious divorce from his partner, who left him to go and live with the owner of a nightclub.

From an ethical point of view, *ought* these different life histories influence the path that Francis chooses? We have evidence that, right or wrong, they do: Charlotte's situation, working as a dancer in a lap-dancing club in her own time, was used as one of the scenarios in a research study of professional boundaries (Doel et al. 2010: 1889). The responses ranged from a social work manager who would expect the social worker to face disciplinary action and likely be sacked, and another manager in the same city who would talk it over in supervision and give her a light telling-off for failing to disclose it (so, these different Francis's *do* exist). We don't know how these widely different conclusions were reached, nor what value conflicts each Francis might have tussled with, but we can speculate that the different outcomes emanate from differing values and ethical positions, even if these were not made transparent. Might we expect different responses depending on the gender of the manager? (In fact, the managers in this research were both male.) *Moral relativism*, an understanding of the moral world heavily mediated by context and circumstance, is the reality.

Alternative paradigms

The strategies of compete, compromise, concede, or avoid derive from a Western paradigm of value conflicts, as do the various ethical frameworks presented in Chapter 2. There are entirely alternative worldviews: for example, the *surrender* principle suggested by some First People cultures, such as indigenous North American. Surrender – the ability to let go – is fundamental to holistic cultures, where value conflicts are subsumed in the community's solidarity and the will of the individual is gifted to a collective wisdom. Superficially, this looks like 'concede', but it stands in contrast to the Western notion of concession which is an individual's choice in the face of another often more powerful individual. *Surrender* is a collective experience, often enacted through ritual in ceremonies that promote a sense of one-ness at a spiritual rather than a material level (Some 1997). This 'letting go' arises in cultures where there is a high level of empathy and interdependence, not only human, but also animal and natural (Rifkin 2009). *Surrender* has parallels with Western notions of suspending judgement, with a similar release of creativity. *Surrender* is also one way of looking at the collective decision to 'let go' to the will of the majority vote in the social workers' strike described earlier in this chapter.

The African notion of *ubuntu* is another alternative to Western ethical paradigms (Olusa 2023). As the word's meaning suggests – *I am because we are* – *ubuntu* is based on a collective idea of ethical living, in contrast to the individualized ethics of Western philosophies.

However, when non-local cultures meet, surrender and *ubuntu* become more difficult, as there is no singular authority to embrace a collective letting-go. Even so, *empathy* can enable communities with contrasting values to understand each other and to learn from one another. In practical terms, this would mean a local service placing sufficient value on the needs of a minority population that it adapts to meet these needs, rather than requiring the minority population to adapt to the service.

Viewing value conflicts through the prism of an alternative paradigm stimulates us to consider different kinds of value conflict, ones that at first seem tangential to professional life but touch on it nevertheless. For instance, in a child's early schooling, what ought to be the relative value placed on playfulness and on formal learning? This conflict in values, between those that emphasize the child as a creative and inquisitive social learner and those that emphasize early years' schooling as the foundation for numeracy and literacy skills, will have a direct impact on a school social worker working with the children and staff in that school.

Guidance from codes, standards and principles

The IASSW/IFSW joint *Statement of Ethical Principles* (2018) clearly recognizes the dilemmas that social workers face, due to value conflicts:

- The fact that the loyalty of social workers is often in the middle of conflicting interests.
- The fact that social workers function as both helpers and controllers.
- The conflicts between the duty of social workers to protect the interests of the people. with whom they work and societal demands for efficiency and utility.
- The fact that resources in society are limited.

Would it help if there were a clause in the professional code of practice that gave guidance about when a question of personal conscience took precedence over professional code? Would it be right to allow individual practitioners to excuse themselves from certain situations, ones that they see as morally compromising them? For instance, in the example dilemma earlier, should Charlotte be allowed to suggest that she should not work with Daniella because she did not feel able to offer 'neutral' advice?

In terms of clashes between the value of a personal life and the value of work, the IFSW/IASSW (2018) *Statement of Principles* asserts that 'Social workers have a duty to take necessary steps to care for themselves professionally and personally in the workplace and in society, in order to ensure that they are able to provide appropriate services.'

Conclusion

In Chapter 1, we introduced you to the wise professionals. How might they respond to the discussion on value conflicts? They are likely to be clear that there is no Answer with a capital A, no easy algorithm to apply. Indeed, the wise professionals probably see personal beliefs, professional codes of practice and religious creeds as crude attempts to simplify situations and to line them up against a slide rule of value judgements. However, they are equally unlikely to find satisfaction in an approach that is so flexible that it judges each and every situation as it stands, with no regard to any fixed points.

Perhaps the wise professionals can suggest some fixed points, some 'compass points', not ones as specific as 'abortion is right' or 'abortion is wrong', but ones that can be applied to each and every situation to help us decide what they mean from one case to another and, therefore, what actions suggest themselves after careful interrogation of the circumstances. How about these:

- What is fair in this situation?
- What is generous in this situation?
- What is kind in this situation?

At first glance, fairness, generosity and kindness seem to be rather general, even slippery, concepts – but therein lies their strength. If you think of any act – personal, political, or both – and apply the principles of fairness, generosity and kindness, we can say with reasonable certainty that they would have changed events for the better. This is not to suppose that there are not circumstances when it is right not to act with fairness, generosity and kindness: an undercover agent for the French Resistance in the Second World War might regularly have to act against these principles in their personal conduct, though might reasonably argue a higher-level 'fairness, generosity and kindness' that motivated their individual contrarian acts.

In Charlotte's case, the wise professionals could reasonably argue that the suggestion that Charlotte be permitted to absent herself from work with Daniella because she did not feel able to offer 'neutral' advice would satisfy the notion of fairness, that it would be generous to Charlotte to allow her not to be in that situation, and that it would be kind to Daniella to let her have access to someone with no strong moral opinions about abortion. Wisdom would suggest that we test these principles further. In the case of value conflicts, these wise professionals are leaning, thus far, towards an *ethics of care*.

Think further about …

… a recent decision you have made that has an ethical dimension. This might be in your personal or your professional life. Apply the framework we introduced on page 51 and examine the choice available to you and the course of action you took using the Compete, Compromise, Concede, or Avoid framework:

- Does it help you to a better understanding of the decision you made?
- Does it confirm your decision? Or, in retrospect, would this understanding move you towards a change in your decision?

Ethical dilemmas with twelve people

Vadim Moldovan (Jane Addams' coat)

I wandered into social work after emigrating from the Soviet Union to the United States, studying at Columbia University Business School, and driving a cab in New York for four years. Never looked back.

With the Master of Social Work degree, I worked for ten years as a psychiatric social worker. With the PhD in social work, I joined faculty at York College of the City University of New York and my main professional focus at the time is education, professionalization, and legitimization of social work in Moldova and other post-socialist countries.

Barbara Friesen (Sticking plaster, or bandaid)

I worked first as an 'orderly' in a state mental hospital in the US, then as a social worker in another psychiatric hospital, helping some of the patients prepare for a life outside the hospital, especially those who had been interned because they didn't take care good care of their medical needs, such as diabetes. Eventually, I became a social work researcher, and previously headed the social work Research Center at Portland State University in Oregon.

Further reading

Parrott, L. (2014), *Values and Ethics in Social Work Practice*, London: Sage.

Reamer, F. (2024), *Social Work Values and Ethics*, New York: Columbia University Press.

Tedam, P. (2024), *Anti-oppressive Social Work Practice*, London: Learning Matters.

Thompson, N. (2020), *Anti Discriminatory Practice: Equality, Diversity and Social Justice*, London: Red Globe Press.

4

Power

Introduction

This chapter introduces different types and sources of power and the notion of empowering social work practice and self-determination. Power is inherent in all social work practice as it is based on procedural and legislative expectations and requirements. However, it also comes from the power and lack of power that each person in a working relationship holds and feels. A case study helps the reader to recognize ethical dilemmas associated with power and to identify the power held by all those involved: social worker, the person with lived experience, service provider and colleagues, whilst also reflecting on a range of possible empowering responses.

Ethical dilemmas in twelve objects

Lappieskombers (quilt)

South African social work student Marla reflects on the empowering nature of quilt-making and its connection to social work:

> Each piece of the *lappieskombers* (quilt) is beautiful but when they are sewn together, they become something yet more wondrous. Good social work is multi-professional and I see the pieces of the quilt as the coming together of many people to empower service users. Each piece of material already possesses the potential to be something beautiful, someone just has to unite it with the other pieces. We are the thread that links service users to other professionals and with each other, but the service user – like the panel in the

quilt – already possesses the real beauty, all we need to do is to show them the personal power they have inside of them.

Marla reflects on the importance of professionals working together, symbolically represented by the *lappieskombers*. The quilt can also represent the coming together of many experts by experience, too. The AIDS Quilt is more than a symbol – it is a real quilt that memorializes and celebrates the lives of people who have died of AIDS-related causes. It is the largest piece of community folk art in the world, with individuals, groups and organizations contributing their talents to making the 50,000 panels. Quilts, large or small, are an artistic display of solidarity, the visible and tangible product of empowerment.

Think about …

… Your practice educator on placement, or manager at work, asks you to work through your lunch break to complete an administrative task for a sick colleague to meet required deadlines. They are aware that you had arranged to go for a walk with a friend, as you need a break for your emotional well-being and to manage your stress. This is not the first time that this request has been made to you this week.

Is there a dilemma? If so, what is the nature of your dilemma? And what do you do?

What additional factors might make a difference to the nature of your dilemma? Consider if it alters your thinking if it were a personal appointment, or agreed prayer time, or if areas for development had been raised with you about managing your time or engaging with the team.

Power

Power is an emotive word that can create a picture of a master and servant; of the strong person influencing, nay manipulating, the weaker person to do their bidding; the wealthy man controlling the poor, powerless, opinion-less working-class population; the abusive partner, or the corrupt government.

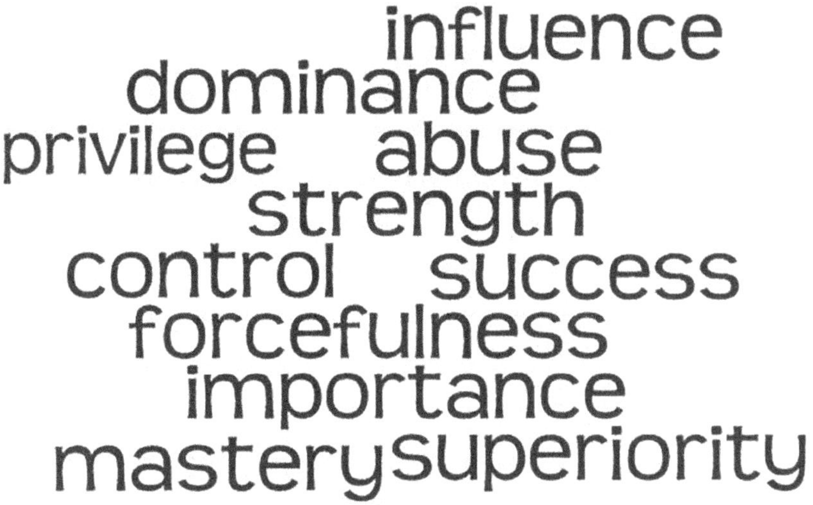

influence
dominance
privilege   abuse
strength
control   success
forcefulness
importance
mastery superiority

Figure 4.1 Words associated with power

As Figure 4.1 illustrates power often has negative connotations that imply control and enforcement of views or actions by one person or agency over another. Instead, consider from a strengths-perspective the definition of power as: 'the ability or capacity to do something; the capacity or ability to act in a particular way to direct or influence the behaviour of others or the course of events' (Smith 2008: 1).

If read positively, power can be used to motivate, change and influence yourself and other people, a core social work value. It is this patchwork quilt of social workers and people with lived experience coming together that gives us the combined power of our profession. Considering the definition further, we can see that Smith (2008) reflects that power comes from both internal and external directions. You have an internal strength and self-determination that you can access to critically analyse external prompts and make up your own mind – a powerful skill. Yet the definition also acknowledges the external influences which can further motivate and enhance your internal strength to facilitate change.

We would develop that further to say that our power comes from the ethical expectation that we first engage with people to find empowering solutions, rather than apply legal mandates. Indeed, Beckett et al. (2017) remind us that social work power often comes from legislative roles and mandatory working where people do not want us in that role. Ethical dilemmas can arise from the practice dilemma of how to empower a parent who steadfastly refuses to share how a baby received non-accidental injuries to enable a long-term plan to be developed: do you react to that reluctance to share openly and honestly and fast-track to adoption, or do you use your power to engage the parent to explore what led up to such an incident so that you can support them to change? Whilst you may not be able to rehabilitate the baby to the care of the parent(s), you might be able to place with grandparents and have open contact with the parent as a positive outcome.

Tedam (2024) is right to emphasize that social workers need to be aware of power within their role, as they hold, wield, use and experience power in their daily interactions with people with lived experience and other professionals. She goes on to assert that it is only by understanding this power that social workers can critically reflect on how they use power productively and also challenge power effectively. So, whilst this chapter is based on a positive reading of Smith's definition of power, and views social workers as inclined to use power to engage and motivate, there remains an understanding that negative experiences of power may predispose people with lived experience to be reluctant to engage with service provision. Indeed, Thompson (2024) reminds us that whilst legislation gives social workers the power to undertake a task, it is a *duty* that requires us to do so. As such we should exercise our power with care. Whilst it is recognized that some social work roles require an element of care (looking after people, helping people) and control (acting to safeguard the person, their family, friends and society), Thompson (2024) continues to advocate the importance of partnership working and empowerment as a norm, even where care and/or control is required.

Types of power

Professionals have the power to change people's lives. However, social workers can use that power to impose change or to empower people with lived experience to change and as a social worker, you will face the ethical dilemma of how you intervene and how you use power within your daily practice. To develop an understanding of the influence of power on motivation, French and Raven (1959) provide five classifications of power, which remain pertinent: *legitimate*, *expert, referent, reward* and *coercive power*. These forms of power can be used to both motivate and to repress (Foucault 1991): it is your responsibility as a social worker to use power wisely and ethically (Weber 1922).

Legitimate power (sometimes referred to as positional power) can be seen to be the authority invested by an agency through procedure or role. As a social worker, you will have legitimate power by remit of your designated role, which is set out in the legislation of the country or region that you work in. This power can be used to the person's detriment – that is, an authoritarian role that instils fear and demotivates – or to empower them, where you acknowledge the power and seek to share it to motivate and engage.

The big picture

In his famous letter to Bishop Creighton, Lord Acton wrote, 'Power tends to corrupt, and absolute power corrupts absolutely' (Acton 1887). Whilst Acton's letter was a challenge to papal infallibility, this sentence rings true in contemporary society where religious, political and business leaders alike are held to account for their unethical actions whilst in a position of power. The belief that they see themselves as above the law or impervious to society's rules, social norms and accepted ethical behaviours defies belief at times. It is often only the actions of the less powerful standing against them (or 'whistleblowing' – in itself a power-laden term, often used derogatorily, see Chapter 8) that alert society to unethical practice so that they can be held to account. In the last decade alone, 'Partygate' (where British Tory MPs broke their own Covid lockdown rules), US President Trump's multiple convictions of using his power to quash stories about his actions, and tax evasion by companies such as Amazon, Apple, Facebook, Google, Netflix and Microsoft show the effect of power in corrupting ethical decision making.

The common adage from a Spiderman comic 'with great power there must also come – great responsibility' (Lee 1965) was preceded by a range of similar religious and political statements that very much apply to your role as a social worker. You will have power and authority: use it wisely and ethically.

By contrast, *expert power* can be seen to be the power that comes from professional experience. This becomes practice wisdom, a combination of theoretical knowledge and the understanding that arises through its practical application (Samson 2015). Expert power creates a respect for your developing professional wisdom and your support and advice can motivate people with lived experience to engage with service provision and address change in areas for development.

Referent power is the power afforded by respecting and admiring a person, also associated with *virtue ethics*. This is the respect that the social worker gains through their appropriate use of legitimate and expert power and their professional approach. Respect is earned rather than attached to a specific role or position. The stronger the referent power that you develop through a positive, empowering approach, the greater the influence that you can have on a person's life. Equally, if you fail to act with professionalism and integrity (as discussed in Chapter 5), you are less likely to be taken seriously and may lose the opportunity to engage and motivate for change.

Reward power comes from the provision of a perceived positive outcome, such as a material benefit or an honour. The ultimate reward in social work might be withdrawal – no further involvement. Developmental rewards are enhanced self-confidence and self-esteem and an emotional reward could be the joy of improved relationships with loved ones. Recognition for one's achievements is related to self-confidence and self-concept, and you can use reward power to improve motivation to engage with service users.

Finally, it is important to be aware of *coercive power* as it can be used by social workers where an action is enforced, for example, the control and use of a court order to require an action such as detainment or removal of children. In social work, this should always be seen as the last resort and after careful interrogation of the impact of such actions on all involved, using an ethical framework of deliberation. It is important to remember that even when using coercive power that the wishes and feelings of people with lived experience should be wholly taken into account, and everyone treated with respect in a difficult situation. Of course, the hope for empowering engagement is not always achieved, but it is important to leave the door open for non-coercive engagement in the future.

As a social worker, it is important that you are aware of each of these types of power, and that you reflect on the impact that they can have on the people with whom you are working and adjust your practice to reduce inherent power differentials.

Dimensions of power

It can be helpful to understand the dimensions of power (Lukes 1974; Foucault 1991). Power can be argued to be a form of social interaction and as such *how* you intervene is important to reduce the power differential (Allen 1998). First, you can exert power *over* a person, which is where your perspective is dominant. Whilst this authoritative role can be effective in the short term to exert control, there is a risk of significant harm, and it is neither an effective nor empowering way to work with people in vulnerable circumstances, who are already feeling powerless. Secondly, you can '*do to*' people – often considered the 'care' side of social work. When applying for a social work course, students often cite that they want to 'help people' and want to solve people's problems. This kind of caring can, of course, take account of people's wishes and feelings, but if it is a rush to 'save' or 'rescue', it can be experienced as disempowering (Karpman 1968).

Whilst *doing to* can enable people with lived experience, it is working *with* them that empowers them. The power differential is reduced as you listen, respect and give action to people's wishes and feelings, to support them to make changes. This is not a question of supporting unrealistic solutions; instead, it is about creating realistic boundaries with openness and honesty regarding your role and expectations. When working with someone, you will be required to ethically negotiate solutions that enhance their experiences and outcomes, yet remain in the remit of service provision expectations. It is they who have lived their own life, making them 'experts by experience' and social workers must listen to this experience and welcome it. In addition, people with lived experience are not subject to professional accountability, so they are free to focus on their own needs and wants flexibly and creatively, whilst social workers must balance many other considerations, including their professionalism (reputation and livelihood) which might lead them to focus on rules and procedures.

As a social worker, you will use your professional and personal identity, social work knowledge and skills, your legal mandate to intervene and your understanding of your use of power to work with people with lived experience towards change. It can be helpful to consider these questions:

1. How do you *feel* about using the authority and power of the social worker?

2. When is the use of power *right* in social work?
3. How do social workers exert more *subtle* forms of power in their role?
4. How does your *identity* have an impact on your use of power?
5. Can you feel *powerless* as a social worker?

Individual practitioners can feel themselves to be far from powerful. This can stem from a lack of authority to bring about the changes you want and the absence of resources to meet the need you have identified. Furthermore, the complexity of people's situations can be overwhelming and leave you feeling powerless to act, particularly at the start of your career. It is helpful to remember the significance of critical thinking and regular supervision. Power requires accountability, which means that the decisions that you make ought to be subject to transparent review, as part of the ethical process, as will be discussed in Chapter 7.

Oppression, equality and social identity

Power is a socially ascribed attribute, where some of these attributions, related to gender, ethnicity, class, age, ability, sexuality, etc. carry higher social status than others. Most service users are highly disadvantaged, and the notion of 'equality' can ring hollow. Life experiences, life opportunities and life expectations are often, though by no means always, very different from the social worker's (Tedam 2024). An important question to ask yourself is: *do I see myself in the person I am working with?* There is no right or wrong response to this, but asking the question is the first step. In Western societies, social norms, rules and laws are constructed by and to the advantage of older, white, wealthy men. Indeed, people living in poverty are often powerless as they lack confidence to self-advocate and feel voiceless (Narayan 2010). The Black Lives Matter and Me Too social activist movements demonstrate the fact the impact of being minoritized not does not depend on being a 'minority' – men making up only half of the global population and white people comprising roughly 15 per cent.

Social identity is always relevant to an understanding of practice and ethical dilemmas; sometimes it plays its part on the sidelines and other times it is centre stage. Ethical social work recognizes and acknowledges social identities (gender, race, class, etc.) without making assumptions about what these identities might mean, either to the person we are working with or to the society that nurtures or shuns them. Ethical practice understands stereotypes without stereotyping. To achieve nuanced practice might mean accepting that, at some *existential* level, we are all victims, all perpetrators, all accomplices, as the existentialists remind us (de Beauvoir 1947/1986). You have status and power through your role as a social worker, and what impact does your *social identity* have on your power? How does the social identity of the person you are working with signify, in terms of differences and similarities to yours? Socially ascribed power is very complex in practice, with individuals often occupying multiple identities, referred to as *intersectionality* (Crenshaw 1989).

Freire (1968) and Foucault (1991) both asserted that the powerless and oppressed must play a role in their liberation by voicing their wishes, feelings and opinions, as seen in the movements cited above, but that ultimately it is those in power who are able to choose whether to share power. For change to occur, the relatively powerful must be willing to rethink their way of life (including their relative economic power) and examine their own part in oppression, if true liberation and power-sharing is to occur. Arguably, it is our duty as social workers to fight injustice and strive for a more equal society. Indeed, Feldman (2019) argues that social workers should fight on a relational basis with service providers and policy makers who sustain poverty-based powerlessness. As moral agents, we can impact social care service provision and the lives of vulnerable people, so we have a duty to contribute to, and construct, as moral a world as possible. Indeed, Fook (2023) argues that we should reflect on our own perceptions of power and powerlessness in relation to our identity and our role, to deconstruct and reconstruct our understanding of self and location within society to identify the power that we do hold, before turning our lens to supporting the people with whom we work to empower them to do the same. Sadly, however, not all social workers agree with the sentiment that it is our duty to fight social injustice, instead focusing solely on the individual vulnerable person. It is helpful to take a moment to reflect on whether you can support and empower the individual vulnerable person if you do not advocate against the oppression they are experiencing.

It is helpful to consider ideas from moral philosophy, especially *Kantian* notions of the moral worth of each person, although it is important to recognize that a Kantian equality can also be used to justify a very unequal economic status quo, if it is not allied to notions of *redistributive social justice* (Rawls 1958). Nevertheless, in this Kantian idea we have a *qualitative* notion of equality, not a quantitative one. This equal value is not without practical difficulty. It means, for instance, treating with an equal moral worth those persons who have beliefs that would condemn large numbers of humanity to a violent death, or who have committed unimaginable crimes against children. There is a difference, then, between the person and their behaviours and/or beliefs.

Empowering practice

Empowerment is not necessarily seen as a fair and equitable redistribution of power, as that may not be viable in contemporary society. However, it is rooted in self-help, advocacy, self-advocacy and cooperation, and is a multifaceted approach that takes account of community, organizational, group, interpersonal and individual issues and requires a critical thinking lens to identify oppression and inequality, as well as solutions to address them (Adams 2008). Empowerment in social work practice provides a practical means to redistribute power to vulnerable people within society on an individual basis, although it needs to be done within a context of fighting for social justice too (Fook 2023).

On an individual basis, empowerment can be seen to be supporting a person to take control of their own life and develop skills that enable them to manage future challenges, thus reducing recidivism and the need for future social work involvement. It is firmly located within modern models of intervention, for example, restorative practice (Wachtel and McCold 2001) and a strengths-based perspective (Rapp 1988). It is the dimension of doing *with* the individual so that you are taking their expertise and knowledge as a foundation to work from, thus sharing the power to act. Empowering a person with lived experience does not mean abandoning service provision parameters, instead it means sharing knowledge to support them to make an informed and realistic decision. Foucault (1991) effectively argued that knowledge is power (Bacon 1597) and similarly Howe and Hill (2024) reflect that power comes from knowing what will happen to you and having control of your own destiny, which empowerment and working in partnership facilitates.

The concept of empowerment, however, is not without critique. Fook (2023) argues that as social workers we must critically reflect to ensure that our notion of empowering is not in itself disempowering. For example, when a substance misuse worker enables a person to ask a family member for help without checking if the family member has the emotional, practical and physical ability to provide this support. Potentially this can disempower both the person and family member, 'setting them up to fail', and leave both parties deflated and diminished.

Self-determination

A key element of empowerment is facilitating self-determination. Smith (2008) argued that whilst external influences impact people, there are internal motivators that can mediate against these external factors. Self-determination is a principle based on the belief that individuals should have every opportunity to guide and direct their own lives, which means making their own decisions. Self-determination is valued as a moral good, not least because people are generally the best judges of what is good for themselves, but also the process of making these decisions for oneself is a *good* in itself. Imagine that you were told you *had* to study a specific subject at a given university: you might feel less engaged or even just not bother. Apply that to how a person with lived experience might feel in working with you. Beckett et al. (2017) argue that self-determination provides dignity and that unless embraced robustly can be in danger of being meaningless; it is therefore beholden on social workers to use their power to facilitate self-determination wisely. This will enable the people with whom you work to take ownership of decisions made by them about their own lives and be more engaged with the process: a great start towards positive outcomes.

Deprivation of self-determination

Inevitably, there are social work powers that violate the principle of self-determination, most notably the loss of liberty in a compulsory admission to mental health hospital and the removal of a child from its parents against their will. Where is the moral threshold at which point a social worker is justified in departing from the principle of self-direction to safeguard and protect? A libertarian would likely say 'never', whilst *duty ethics* might suggest that kindness is more important than the overriding of the person's wishes and feelings. The point at which unwanted intervention is generally justified is when a person's actions threaten the welfare of self or others. This, of course, requires a judgement in itself. It can be helpful to reflect on:

- What might justify intervention when a person's actions threaten only their own welfare?
- If the choice is available, do you block the harm via a paternalistic intervention or restore the choice via an educative intervention? Can you do both?
- Is a restoration of the person's autonomy feasible?

It is right to do everything possible to preserve the identity of a person's self, particularly when a basic right, such as freedom, is being removed. Self-determination relies on a sense of self, yet social workers find themselves working with some people where this identity is distorted, fading, or has been assaulted by others. It is, therefore, a great challenge to make self-determination meaningful when there is an absence or confusion of self.

Ethical dilemma 4: The medication

In this scenario, we consider the respective power and powers of mental health social worker, Nathan and Humerah, a South Asian woman who uses a wheelchair and has experiences bouts of severe and enduring mental health problems. She has lost count of how many social workers and community psychiatric nurses have been involved over the years. Nathan became Humerah's social worker just two months ago. He is a white, gay, able-bodied man so, apart from being the same age as Humerah, in many other respects they are quite different.

Humerah has recently stopped taking her medication (not for the first time) and her mental health has deteriorated. The first ethical dilemma to consider is what ought to be the balance between the social worker's power to intervene to ensure Humerah takes her medication and Humerah's right to refuse it. First, let's consider Humerah's perspective.

1 What power does Humerah have in this situation?

Humerah has the power of *self-determination*. She can decide whether to take her medication and how to engage with Nathan. However, perhaps she feels relatively powerless in society and with her social work involvement over the years due to the multiple changes of staff. Perhaps she sees stopping taking medication as a means of control.

An empowering approach would be to take Humerah's wishes and feelings into account, where preventative solutions and coping strategies are identified *with* her that take account of her own understanding of her health, what triggers the crises, and how she perceives her needs. This might lead her to start her medication again, and it might not.

However, Nathan has apparently more power, both in terms of his social location and in this situation. Let us consider his role as social worker.

2 Does Nathan have the power as social worker to determine the impact of medication on Humerah?

Social workers need to use other professionals' expertise to inform their decision making: so, although Nathan has the legitimate power to enforce the decision regarding the risk of significant harm, he likely does not have the expert power to determine the impact of medication on Humerah.

3 Does Nathan have the power as social worker to come to a decision?

Nathan might take a consequentialist approach to consider the impact of medication on Humerah. For instance, he knows that the effects of long-term medication and over-medication can be worse than the illness itself and they can mask the person's own mechanisms for recovery. On the other hand, there are situations where the medication remains essential to maintain a person's stable mental health. Medication may enable Humerah to function well and gain self-confidence and achievement. So, first there is a practice judgement about which of these two possibilities is, on balance, the more beneficial for Humerah.

4 Does Nathan have the power as a social worker to bring his personal and professional values to this situation?

The bringing of self into social work has long been debated. Relationship-based social work (Hennessey 2011; Ruch et al. 2018) advocates the importance of self to bring about an authentic relationship. However, is the application of personal values to professional decision making an inappropriate assertion of power?

If Nathan's value base is 'medication at all costs' and he takes an authoritative approach to exert legitimate power over Humerah, this restricts his ability to have an ethical discussion 'with himself' (as well as Humerah), thus resulting in the negative use of coercive power, devoid of critical reflection on the ethics of the dilemma, and Nathan probably not even seeing it as 'a dilemma'.

If Nathan's value base is to respect Humerah's wishes and feelings, then a duty ethics response might be unequivocal in supporting her decision making – but this ignores Nathan's professional duty as a social worker to work within a legal and procedural structure. It is for this reason that agencies have clear policies and procedures as well as accountability through management structures, so that personal values can be considered in a broader context.

5 Does Nathan consider the needs of the community over Humerah's right to choose?

Nathan could approach Humerah's refusal to take medication from a utilitarian perspective and consider the greater good. Whose danger is the greater?

Whilst Humerah has the right to make an unwise decision in terms of her own well-being (in the UK enshrined in the Mental Capacity Act 2005), if it places the community at risk of significant harm, should Nathan honour or disregard Humerah's wishes and feelings in relation to her medication?

6 Does Nathan have a duty to hear Humerah's wishes and feelings irrespective of all of the points we have reasoned with so far?

Even in the most difficult of situations with a person in the most vulnerable of situations, a virtue ethics perspective would emphasize the need for social workers to act with ultimate respect and compassion for the individual. In Humerah's eyes, Nathan has no referent power, as she has no respect for his job title, following multiple social workers' unwanted and largely unsuccessful involvement, and they have very different identities to build on at this early stage in their relationship. An open communication style that truly listens to Humerah's views and attempts to explore the context for decisions may not change the situation immediately, but the respect shown may start to reduce the power differential and begin to develop the relationship. Furthermore, the ability to implement some of Humerah's wishes and feelings may begin to engage her for future work to be undertaken.

7 How does Nathan empower Humerah?

Nathan judges that once Humerah is in recovery, he has a better opportunity to empower her to have her voice heard in potential future episodes. He has a conversation with Humerah to ensure that he is aware of what she would like to happen if she again stops taking her medication. Humerah tells Nathan that she would not care what she had agreed to when she was well. Nathan accepts this and, likewise, Humerah accepts that Nathan and the professionals will make decisions for her when required to do so. Humerah sums it up as 'they just need to take control – and that's not to give up control forever.' Temporary shifting of power is important for Humerah: she wants to remain in control of decision making until she is unable to. As a result of this working with her proactively to reduce the power differential, Nathan has a better understanding of her wishes and feelings and they are both able to respect this agreed plan. Both Nathan and Humerah feel that their work together has been ethically sound.

Guidance from codes, standards and principles

The IFSW (2018) Global Statement of Ethical Principles makes clear links between integrity and professional use of power, which includes: 'not abusing their positions of power and relationships of trust with people that they engage with; they recognize the boundaries between personal and professional life and do not abuse their positions for personal material benefit or gain.'

Power is inherent in all social work interventions and working with integrity underpins every social work code of ethics. Whilst it is essential to know how your own code of ethics applies to power, the British Code of Ethics (BASW 2021) acknowledges the importance of and understanding of the inherent power in the role: 'Social workers need to acknowledge the impact of their own informal and coercive power and that of the organisations involved.'

It goes on to outline the importance of empowerment:

> Social workers should promote and contribute to the development of co-produced policies, procedures and practices that are anti-oppressive and empowering. They should seek to understand people's beliefs, values, culture, goals, needs, preferences, relationships and affiliations but be prepared to offer respectful challenge when necessary.
>
> Social workers should recognise their own prejudices, ensuring that they do not oppress any person or group. They should ensure that services are offered and delivered in ways that are appropriate for the people who will use them.

The Irish Code of Ethics (IASW 2023) provides clear explanation of the importance of being emotionally intelligent in practice to reduce power differentials:

> Social workers, in focusing on individuals, families, groups, and communities in which they live, will be aware of the potential power imbalance in the relationships that follow. Social workers will strive to use their power appropriately within such relationships and will place special emphasis on the consideration of and promotion of service users' views (or the views of the service user's legally appointed representative) in all decisions that are related to the quality of their lives.

Conclusion

This chapter has asked you to consider power within social work on a personal and professional basis and its relationship to making ethically sound judgements. Different types of power were presented and how to work with people to reduce power differentials. We considered how power can be used positively to motivate the people we work with to address areas for development. However, we also recognized that power can demotivate or even intimidate people, and that there are ways to avoid this. The chapter considered empowerment not just as an individual activity to facilitate self-determination, but one that includes campaigning for social justice. As social workers, we may not be in a position to eradicate societal oppression and inequality, but we can aim to resolve the power dynamics in our day to day work.

Think further about …

… a situation in which you were aware of your power in your work.

- What kind of power was it? Consider French and Raven's (1959) typology: *legitimate, expert, referent, reward,* or *coercive power*?
- In what ways did you aim to share this power? Were you successful?

… a situation in which you felt relatively powerless.

- What was it that made you feel powerless?
- What did you do in response to this feeling?
- What would you have liked to have done?

Ethical dilemmas with twelve people

Marla Louw (*Lappieskombers* – quilt)

When I donated the *Lappieskombers* (quilt) I was a third-year social work student at the University of Pretoria in South Africa. I was also the Chairperson at the University of Pretoria Student Social Work Association.

I studied to become a social worker because I have a passion for people from all walks of life. Also I have a personal story that will inspire and help people believe in a better tomorrow. My inspiring story involves a very rebellious teenager from divorced parents, one that got involved in very destructive activities. Still, regardless of all the cards that were dealt, I managed to stand up out of my situation and make a better life for myself.

Further reading

Fook, J (2023), *Social Work: A Critical Approach to Practice*, London: Sage.
   Chapter 4, on power, and Chapter 8, on empowerment, are useful chapters to develop your critical reflection on the concept of power.
Smith, R (2008), *Social Work and Power*, Basingstoke: Palgrave MacMillan.
Tedam, P. (2024), *Anti-oppressive Social Work Practice*, London: Learning Matters.
   Chapter 3 is useful on power and powerlessness.

5

Professionalism

Introduction

This chapter will consider what constitutes professionalism, and consider both personal and professional ethics and how they impact professionalism. Professional behaviour is often associated with competence in social work knowledge, skills and values. However, it is also related to wider ideas such as social justice, anti-oppressive practice and appropriate use of power. The notion of professional integrity will be explored, in tandem with an ethical dilemma that asks you to consider your own professional integrity in the light of a gift.

Ethical dilemmas in twelve objects

Black bin bags

British social worker Mark reflects on the rights and wrongs of the use of black bin bags in his early social work practice:

> In the 1990s, our social work practice included using bin bags to transport children's belongings as we took them into care. A few of the team didn't drive and would take children into care on the bus, sitting at the bus stop in the rain with a couple of children and any number of bin bags. Thirty years into my career I reflect now with a sense of shame at this practice – how unprofessional and disrespectful it feels of the children and their things.
>
> However, I can also view these black bin bags positively. Our social work team raised funds through ceilidhs (traditional Irish or Scottish community events involving folk music and dance) and the like in order to stock a food

cupboard (this was before 'food banks'). At Christmas, people would leave with donated children's presents. One Christmas Eve, we were about to close up when a woman arrived and hesitantly explained she was a single parent with five young children and had nothing for the children for Christmas and no food. She'd been hoping for a miracle and had promised the children that this year they would have a present each. She'd never been in a social work office, but an emergency loan for food had been refused and she was desperate. We were able to provide some food and presents from the cupboard – her profound thanks made it all feel even more inadequate. Still, she left very pleased and relieved. I watched her go back into the street, black bin bags swinging at her side on a long walk back to the tower blocks. I drove home for Christmas crying.

The mother had been so appreciative, but it had felt such a limited piece of work in the face of her family's needs. Contrast that with other times when parents were angry and aggressive, yet the work felt valuable. Where do we find validation for the work that we do? Though I drove home with a sense of despair that day, more than 25 years later, I look back at that Christmas Eve as a social work moment that I can now value.

Think about ...

... on a home visit, you are offered a drink: do you take it?

Is there a dilemma? If so, what is the nature of your dilemma? And what do you do?

What might make a difference to the nature of your dilemma? Cultural etiquette in Britain would suggest you accept the offer of a drink of tea or coffee. How about a slice of cake to go with it? We are having lunch, do you want some? I've bought you a bottle of whiskey. Let me give you a lift home. Let me fix your car for you. Where do you draw the line?

Does the nature of the visit make a difference? Consider different responses in relation to visiting someone where you are closing the case, a parent where you are increasing the intervention level (perhaps moving from child in need to child protection, or considering care proceedings), a foster carer, an assessment to assess a person's capacity to stay in their own home, or sharing news that service provision has been agreed/withheld.

Professionalism

Koehn (1994) argued that professionals have expertise and knowledge in their field, are trustworthy, have autonomy over their work, yet keep the person with lived experience central so that neither the professionals' expertise nor procedural and professional requirements eclipse the service user's wishes and feelings. We can apply this to social work professionalism and consider perhaps that it is 'knowledge, skills, values *and* accountability' (Thompson 2024: 195). However, it is also about addressing social justice and inequality and can therefore be considered virtue ethics-based (Beckett et al. 2017). The provision of Christmas presents is a common, virtue-based task undertaken by social workers and often considered an important part of professionalism through social justice of ensuring all children wake up to Santa having visited (where they celebrate Christmas), yet our social work value-base may recoil at the necessity of the use of black bin bags rather than respecting children with lived care experience have the right to be moved with dignity. Being considered to be 'unprofessional' (Webb 2017) can be a grave insult and provoke feelings of failure for a social worker, where professionalism is valued highly and considered a non-negotiable foundation of social work practice.

It can be helpful to stop for a second and reflect on what you feel makes social workers *professional*. You may have considered the ability to apply theory to practice, a skill base that includes communication, empathy, informal and formal assessment, written, analytical, cultural competence, and organizational skills, and a social work value base that includes anti-oppressive, anti-discriminatory, person-centred and respectful practice. You may also have considered the ability to use supervision, critical reflection, emotional intelligence and procedures to ensure that you complete the role expected of you; this, coupled with motivation and commitment to supporting vulnerable people with lived experience to enhance their outcomes whilst also protecting and safeguarding those at risk of significant harm, makes you professional. It is no mean feat: being a social work professional is complex and the fear of appearing unprofessional is often used as a motivational stick to drive social workers towards adhering to *conventional* professional ethics and behaviour (Webb 2017).

However, professionalism can be seen through different lenses (Koehn 1994). Radical social work posits that by becoming a cog in a bureaucratic machine we not just continue but condone a 'value-poor, punitive and authoritarian' role (Fenton 2019: 43), with both the individuals and the community we work with and within. Indeed, Fenton suggests a move beyond organizational professionalism towards occupational professionalism, which requires placing the person with lived experience first, very much a Koehnian approach to true professionalism. This can be achieved by working in partnership to empower people (as will be discussed in Chapter 6) and through critical thinking, so that application of policies, procedures and established practice norms can be seen as guidelines to apply ethically to any given situation dependent on the person's needs.

It is perhaps rather sad that placing the person first is considered 'radical', yet it is the basis of this book – that is, critical thinking about your ethical position to enrich your practice with people with lived experience. Professionalism in social work *must* be fluid, subject to constant critical reflection and review, so that we are able to continue to adapt, to remain relevant, and to keep the person with lived experience central to our service provision.

Personal and professional ethics

Professionalism and ethics are bound up in many ways, not least by the question of who has the power to define what is or ought to be professional behaviour, and who determines and enforces professional standards. In addition, professional ethics are impacted by personal ethics and prevailing social, political and agency-based influences, and so are often socially constructed (Gergen 2000).

Personal ethics

Personal values and ethics are shaped by our social, cultural, individual and educational experiences. As children, we share common values with our parents and, perhaps, our community, which are then developed further by our educational experiences and our friendships through shared experiences and values. As a teenager, then as an adult, we are exposed to wider influences that continue to shape our values and ethical base, which can be influenced by various media and changing social groups. At its most extreme, a person's ethical base can be manipulated or groomed in a cult or through some forms of 'radicalization'. However, most adults develop a sense of identity that conforms within the prevailing social ethical base.

The big picture

An interesting ethical dilemma arises where refugee boats try to cross the Mediterranean Sea or the English Channel. We know that this puts lives at risk, as many migrants have already died attempting to cross the waters, yet we fail to have checks for boats being seaworthy or positive alternatives to avoid the need to make the journey using illegal crossings that benefit ruthless profiteers. Furthermore, we reject refugees who do make the crossing safely, or place them in inhumane conditions, in the name of migration rules that are inherently unjust due to an ideology that is based on racism and capitalism.

Reflect on this for a moment to consider how society is encouraged to value some lives differently and where immigration policies stand in relation to the ethics of social justice.

What are your personal ethics on this and what do you do to support or fight this?

Often the first step to developing professional ethics is understanding your personal values and ethics, so time spent reflecting on them is time well spent.

Professional ethics

Professional ethics consist of the set of values that are purportedly shared by members of the same profession, often gathered into a code to which members of a profession are expected, even required, to subscribe. Countries where social work has legal standing and where there are professional social work associations have their own national codes of ethics. Whilst examples are referred to throughout the book, this is not an exhaustive list, and it is recommended that readers access their own national social work association for clarity on specific applicable codes of ethics. Banks (2020) critiques reliance on codes of ethics as being too prescriptive, which in turn can facilitate social workers being duty-based and rule-orientated rather than virtue-based. During the Covid pandemic, where a flexible, creative and responsive social work intervention style was necessary, she found that it created a space for virtue ethics that enhanced practice for health and social care professionals (Banks 2024).

Many countries' social work Codes of Ethics have a presumption that the professional's behaviour *outside* their work role ought to be subject to greater scrutiny than someone who is not in this trusted position. This position has strong links with virtue ethics, as it poses the implicit question: *can you be a good social worker if you are not a good citizen?* From this perspective, for example, drink driving might be considered not as the conduct of a private individual but as that of a member of the social work profession and as such the etiquette of that profession is breached.

Nevertheless, other ethical frameworks present potential counterweights to virtue ethics. Principlism draws from the notion that ethical positions should be guided by a set of principles; so, a consequence of drink driving would, as with any citizen, be possible prosecution, but loss of employment might be considered disproportionate and therefore unfair.

Redemptive ethics would reframe the question thus: *can you be a good social worker if you are not **always** a good citizen?* In other words, does one bad act in the street write you off forever? Can I not mend my ways and change? Rather than lose my job, would a reflection on the behaviour that takes account of possible causes and future actions be a more progressive and productive route than job suspension or loss?

A further perspective on the clash between personal and professional ethics can arise when working with a person with lived experience. For example, a social worker holding religion-based or rights-based personal values, might be challenged when faced with supporting a person through the decision-making process of a termination of a pregnancy. Similarly, homophobia can be religion-based (but, we would argue, never rights-based), but can this be true to the social work ethical base of social justice and respect for diversity?

Social workers are required to engage with continual professional ethical development, and this is bound to have an impact on their personal ethics. As part of your social work education, you may find yourself exposed to alternative values and be required to explore the foundations for those professional ethical codes which quite naturally may trigger critical thinking in terms of your personal ethics and values.

Social Work England's Professional Standards set out six core indicators of professionalism:

Professional standards

- Promote the rights, strengths and well-being of people, families and communities.
- Establish and maintain the trust and confidence of people.
- Be accountable for the quality of my practice and the decisions I make.
- Maintain my continuous professional development (CPD).
- Act safely, respectfully and with professional integrity.
- Promote ethical practice and report concerns.

(Social Work England (SWE 2019) https://www.socialworkengland.org.uk/standards/professional-standards/

Reflect on these indicators:

What would it mean in practice for you to act professionally within each indicator?
What ethical basis are you acting on with each one?

Social work ethics are entrenched in the Professional Standards as social justice is required to promote rights and ethical practice, and professional integrity is required to establish and maintain trust, be accountable, maintain Continuing Professional Development (CPD) and to act safely and respectfully.

However, it is worth reminding ourselves here that ethical dilemmas occur, even within our Professional Standards. When we consider issues such as confidentiality versus the duty to protect, the right to self-determination versus the best interest of the person, or the importance of cultural competence and respect versus potentially culturally abusive or oppressive practice, we are starting to consider that it may be difficult to both promote 'rights' and 'well-being'. Here the importance of critical thinking, supervision and reflective discussion are central to 'address issues that arise from ethical dilemmas' (SWE 2019: Section 3.7).

Personal and professional identity

Before considering how you develop your professional identity, it is worth reflecting on your *personal* identity, your social location, in relation to Burnham's (2012) 'GGRRAAACCEEESSS':

> Gender, Geography, Race, Religion, Age, Abilities, Appearance, Culture, Class, Ethnicity, Education, Employment, Sexuality, Sexual Orientation and Spirituality.

From here you will begin to understand the complexity and intersectionality of personal identities that make you who you are (Crenshaw 1989).

Professional identity is equally complex. Reflect on your professional identity:

- How does your personal identity from GGRRAAACCEEESSS impact your *professional* identity?
- Does being a student impact your social work professional identity?
- How does being an apprentice impact your professional identity?
- Does qualification as a social worker change your identity?
- Do you identify as a specialist social worker – children, adults, or another? Does this make a difference to your professional identity?
- Is your professional identity bound up with what you want to achieve as a social worker?
- Do you think social work professional identity is more or less significant in making you who you are as personal identity?

Social work is a gendered profession, with a predominantly (although important to reflect not exclusively) female working population. As such, the professional identity of social work is inevitably woven with the personal identity of women in a patriarchal society (Webb 2017). Whilst this will vary from culture to culture, the traditional Western identity of woman as carers locates social work's professional identity as perhaps *less*, in terms of status, than other professions – for example, those centred on accumulation of wealth or power – and this has an impact on the status (or relative lack of status) of social work. Indeed, the historical foundations of social work began within faith-based and class-based benevolence supplemented with informal, community-based support for vulnerable people, and was considered to be an unpaid and unvalued woman's role within a patriarchal society (Hill et al. 2018).

However, it is also a profession whose identity is developed from colonial ideas of subjugation and oppression of indigenous populations, where white, male values were impressed upon communities irrespective of existing societal values and ethics. Colonization is still felt in contemporary social work, with white privilege impacting social policy, social work knowledge and informing practice norms (Bhatti-Sinclair 2022). It is important as social workers to be aware of the impact of societal norms on our professional identity and practice, which warrants critical reflection to prevent unthinking acceptance of the status quo: 'Any study of social work in totalitarian regimes shows the grave risks to human dignity and human rights which can follow when social workers owe blind allegiance to the employer and forget their humanitarian values' (BASW 2020: 5; also, see '*Yellow star*' in Chapter 8).

Chapter 3 reflected on social work values and ethics that contribute to the development of your professional identity. However, identity is also intrinsically linked to the role that we undertake as social workers. Social work professional identity comes from an understanding that we will protect and safeguard vulnerable people, but also that we will empower and support people to be independent. A shared understanding of this role is important in developing a professional identity, and a sense that other social workers and employers of social workers share these goals sustains our identity, as a kind of professional *ubuntu* (see Chapter 3). Professional social work identity in Australia has been found to develop through socializing with other social workers to develop a sense of belonging and feeling connected (Long et al. 2023). The researchers found that where social work values and the employing agency's values align, it is possible for social workers to develop a sense of professional pride, have confidence in their social work knowledge, skills, behaviours and values, and feel as though they to fit in with the organization.

Indeed, professional identity develops if there is conformity to professional norms (Webb 2017). Professional identity is nurtured through the development of traits located within the professional codes of ethics and where social workers measure themselves and their professional identity against the development of their knowledge, skills, behaviours and values (Wiles 2017). Professional identity may start in the classroom as part of social work education, but it is undoubtedly developed and nurtured within practice. Social workers develop professional identity through strong personal values, empathy and self-awareness, but this needs to be supported through positive supervision (Shlomo et al. 2012; Long et al. 2023). Furthermore, professional identity for qualified social workers in Northern Ireland was found to be centred around social justice, to empower service users, with social work values forming the core (BASW 2020).

Professional identity is composed of expectations, rules, procedures, policies and expectations that social workers adhere to (related to duty ethics), alongside a code of ethics focused on care and kindness (related to virtue ethics). This is important because it gives social workers a sense of collective belonging, which can boost confidence and well-being. It builds social worker resilience (Wiles 2017; Long et al. 2023), an important social work attribute in a challenging landscape of lack of status, reduced budgets, increased workloads and staffing shortages. However, we should also remind ourselves that shared professional values do not necessarily lead to shared actions: Doel et al.'s (2010) research showed very different actions being proposed by people with supposedly shared professional values.

Professional integrity

Integrity is concerned with honesty and moral compass and is central to the notion of professionalism. The very term 'integrity' suggests a clear line between the rights and wrongs of social work, effectively simplifying it to an obvious route to be taken. However, as is the theme of this book, ethical dilemmas rarely provide neatly packaged responses. Instead, working with people often creates dilemmas with multiple right answers, some wrong answers, and a good selection of grey areas that are dependent on both the individual circumstances and the social, legislative, procedural and political context.

As such, professional integrity remains vague and open to interpretation. When reflecting on professional integrity, and rights and wrongs, one might acceptably argue that listening to the wishes and feelings of a person with a lived experience before supporting them to make an informed decision demonstrates professional integrity, whilst making the decision for them lacks that integrity. However, it may be less clear about how to act with integrity where they have expressed a wish to take an unsafe but informed decision and have capacity to do so, yet family members are clear that it places the person at risk and have threatened to sue the agency if this happens, and other professionals feel unable or unwilling to take a position as they feel the situation is not in their remit. In this case, the professional decision is unclear, and integrity could be seen as taking the time to reflect carefully before making a decision.

Professional boundaries establish safe and supportive relationships, build and maintain trust, ensure minimum standards, set limits to service delivery, and minimize misunderstanding (Cooper 2012). However, our professional social work ethics require us to reflect further on every situation to ensure a nuanced and individualized approach within established boundaries to ensure professional integrity.

Ethical dilemma 5: The gift

Regina is a social work student in a hospital team. She is supporting Donna, a terminally ill patient who has returned home between treatments. During a home visit, Regina has been talking about a wedding invitation she has just received with an '80s theme and sharing her anxiety about finding the right outfit as a busy and cash-strapped student. As Regina is leaving, Donna slips a package into her hands and shuts the door quickly. Regina is busy and does not open the package until the next day. She is stunned to see a pristine Vivien Westwood dress in her size. It is perfect for the wedding, but she cannot accept such a gift from a service user … or can she? Regina puts the dress on a hanger in her wardrobe to think it over. Regina recognizes that whether to accept Donna's gift or not is an ethical dilemma. Will her professional integrity be called into question if she takes gifts from people with lived experience despite procedure stating that she should not do so? Consider the following questions from an ethical perspective.

1 What questions might Regina be asking herself?

Perhaps make your own list before reading on.

Regina may have asked herself these questions:

1. Did I give a wrong message by talking about the outfit?
2. Did Donna think I was dropping hints? …
3. In fact, was I unconsciously dropping hints?
4. Is Donna's gift a thoughtful gesture, an act of simple kindness?
5. Why would she give me such a beautiful dress?
6. How does Donna's gift make me feel?
7. Should I have opened the package immediately?
8. Should I tell my practice educator about the gift? Or ask another student for advice?
9. What is the agency's policy about accepting gifts?
10. How much did the dress cost?

A clear element of professionalism in this example is the critical reflection on a complex situation. It is only by considering the different perspectives that impact our decision making (as will be discussed in Chapter 7) that we can be truly professional. Considering this further, behind these factual questions lie some ethical issues that are also worthy of consideration.

Motivation: *Ought the meaning behind the gift, and the act of giving, have a bearing on what Regina should do?*

All social acts have meanings that include overt, stated ones and others that are covert, sometimes not even known to the person doing the deed. Cynics tend to look for underlying motives and view most behaviour as selfishly driven; naïve opinion denies the existence of this Machiavellian world, accepting meanings at face value. For some, no matter what the consequences of the gift, if Donna's intentions were good and she had no maleficence in the deed, then it is a good act, in accord with *virtue ethics*. Does Regina need to take into account Donna's intentions when deciding what to do about the dress?

Timing: *Ought Regina have made an immediate response, or was she right to take time to reflect?*

Regina has accepted Donna's gift by default. She felt joy and wonder at merely seeing a Vivien Westwood dress, imagining trying it on for five minutes. She has been unable to concentrate for thinking about it and her practice educator, Ron, has asked if she is ok as she seems distracted. She wanted to tell him, but now she is too embarrassed and terrified that she might fail the placement because of her actions. Does the power differential shift and have an impact on her decision making as time has passed?

Impact on others: *Ought Regina consider how others will feel about this?*

We could look at Regina's dilemma through the lens of Regina and Donna's working relationship. Over the last few days, Donna may have experienced the pleasure that comes from giving. Regina feels she ought to take the path that is most respectful of the relationship, an *ethics of care* approach in which emotions are not the enemy of reason, unlike some ethical frameworks. Donna did not seem to want thanks or recognition as she swiftly shut the door. She is terminally ill, and she may feel that being kind is helping her through this stage in her life. If Regina returns it now, she can explain in measured tones that, touched though she is by the gift, she has given it some thought and, on balance, regretfully feels it is not right to accept it. She can outline the agency procedure that prohibits gifts from service users, however kind. However, this may create displeasure and disappointment for Donna and leave her feeling diminished. Should Regina base her decision on the largely *utilitarian* notion of greater good?

Scale: *Ought it make any difference what the dress cost?*

If Donna gave Regina a bar of chocolate would these same ethical considerations apply? A home-baked muffin? A theatre ticket going spare? A prize she won at a raffle that she can't use? A dress for a wedding? … Are ethical considerations just about scale, then, and if so, at what size does a gift become ethically unacceptable: somewhere between the raffle prize and the dress or somewhere beyond the dress? This would be considering the principle of *proportionalism*.

Rules: *Ought Regina follow the agency's protocols whatever they are and whatever the consequences?*

If Regina's first instinct is to access the agency's gifts policy and to follow its proscribed procedure unthinkingly, she would be subscribing to a *duty-based* system of ethics in which she interprets the right way to act as equivalent to following the agency's protocol, no matter the outcome. The procedure would likely be to return the dress, and arguably the one most likely to uphold professionalism in the eyes of most Code of Ethics.

Power: *How ought Regina to reflect on the impact of her own status?*

So far, Regina's ethical approaches have largely neglected an analysis of power (see Chapter 4). There is inherent power in the act of giving and receiving: in this case, it is Donna who has the power of gifting and Regina the power of accepting or rejecting.

Regina ought perhaps to consider the impact of her status as social work student. With status comes power and the impact of words casually spoken (the musing over the '80s wedding in phatic conversation) might invest Regina's words with legitimate power (French and Raven 1959).

Regina might consider the economic power and how this might alter the ethics dilemma and her decision making. Donna is financially comfortable whilst Regina suffers from student poverty.

Do any of these points change the dynamic in the gift transaction and should they? At some point a decision must be made. Should Regina seek support from her practice educator?

This was a complex ethical dilemma for Regina as a social work student and we would always advise seeking support and advice from a practice educator or line manager where there is an ethical dilemma. However, seeking advice is not abdicating your own responsibility to think things through: ask for support with your own perspective to facilitate further ethical debate. A key part of professionalism is accountability and knowing when to seek support and advice.

The week after receiving the dress, Regina summons up the courage to seek out her practice educator, Ron, and ask his advice about what she ought to do. Increasingly, she is feeling that she should not accept the gift. Ron laughs and tells her to keep it, but this leaves her feeling that his ethics are compromised. She sees him differently, less respectfully, than before. Increasingly, as the days pass, Regina feels she has been complicit in a decision that she now judges to be wrong and against her sense of professional integrity. She feels she was influenced by a more powerful person, Ron. She respects him and she reflects that she was prejudiced by his expert and referent power (French and Raven 1959), so took his advice despite her reservations.

2 How should Regina respond to Ron's advice?

The practice educator's role is one of mentor: to model professional social work and impart their practice wisdom to enhance your knowledge and skills. Arguably here, Ron's response lacks professionalism: he laughed at Regina's serious request for support and advice, he did not critically reflect on the situation, and he offered advice (instruction?) that was counter to the agency's policy.

If you do not feel that advice adheres to professional social work ethics, your own moral reasoning can be a powerful asset, especially when the advice is coming from someone in a more powerful position. You should reflect on whether it is appropriate to talk to your tutor or Ron's line manager, and what is your ethical position on whistleblowing (see Chapter 8), and how it affects your ability to remain professional.

Regina now realizes that she was not seeking Ron's opinion but his *approval* for the decision she had already made – to return the dress.

3 How might Regina return the dress?

The only way to retain professional integrity in this situation is to facilitate an open and honest reflective discussion directly with Donna. Regina visits Donna and outlines her gratitude and delight at seeing the dress, reflecting that it has brought her great happiness to see such a quality vintage dress. However, she explains the procedural requirements and that she is unable to keep it, but thanks Donna for her kindness. Regina draws on her professional communication skills (Beesley et al. 2023) and ensures that she is open and honest, is clear in her position and her reasoning for the position. She ensures she allocates plenty of time to the visit to listen to Donna's response. Consider the five possible responses by Donna below. What ought Regina do and say in respect of each of them?

1. Oh, you've got it all wrong. It's for one night, I want it back, and dry-cleaned too. I just thought you would look amazing in it. Don't you like it?
2. You know, I wondered whether it was the right thing to do. But that dress was just so right for you I couldn't resist it. It's been in my wardrobe since I was friends with Vivien and she was going to throw it away. It will only

go to a charity shop soon ... Would it make things better if you bought it off me?
3. You have been an amazing social worker, I could not have asked for more over the last few weeks. You have given me a joy that is priceless. I'm sorry if it has put you in an awkward position. But, the dress is not really a gift as such, more of a thank you from an admirer, a recognition and praise of your time. I hope that means you can accept it – it'd make me feel a lot better actually.
4. Why've you taken a week to say this? You could have spoken to me sooner; I thought we had a good relationship where we could be honest with each other.
5. How come it was OK when you brought me your Nan's homemade cake last month?

It is often not the mistake (if mistake it is) that you are judged on, but how you respond to your mistake that makes you professional. If Regina acknowledges how Donna feels, owns her hesitation to raise it with her, apologizes and seeks to restore their working relationship and move forward, she has shown integrity. What is interesting is that, though Regina might demonstrate integrity, Donna might still feel unhappy about the decision.

Convenience ethics

Ron's easy answer and quick laugh suggests that he was acting from a position of convenience – that the easiest thing to do is to keep the gift and not to cause a fuss. It also seems 'convenient' in that Ron has not had to think through the issues. However, equally 'convenient' is to blindly accept agency policy. If Ron's laughter meant 'no-brainer, agency policy says you can't keep it', we should also feel uneasy that he seems not to be willing or able to really think about the issues involved. We should always be suspicious of *convenience ethics*, whatever decision they point to.

Whilst we can't go back in time, to the moment a dilemma arose, we *can* learn by imagining alternative scenarios in situations, where you consider how you could have responded and the potential outcomes, so that if faced with an ethical dilemma that challenges your professionalism in the future that you are prepared and more able to approach it with integrity. Perhaps the greatest learning from this in relation to professionalism and professional integrity is to avoid prevarication, which is different from reflection, and not to avoid decision making.

Guidance from codes, standards and principles

The IFSW (2018) Global Statement of Ethical Principles provides 'an overarching framework for social workers to work towards the highest possible standards of professional integrity'.

Professionalism and professional integrity underpin every social work code of ethics. Whilst it is essential to know how your own code of ethics applies to professionalism, the British Code of Ethics (BASW 2021) states that social workers' professional integrity is required:

> Social workers have a responsibility to respect and uphold the values and principles of the profession and act in a reliable, honest and trustworthy manner.

It continues to cite the principles as:

1. Upholding the values and reputation of the profession.
2. Being trustworthy.
3. Maintaining professional boundaries.
4. Making considered professional judgements.
5. Being transparent and professionally accountable.

The Canadian Code of Ethics and Guiding Principles provides a clear explanation of professionalism in practice:

> Value 5: Preserving Integrity in Professional Practice
>
> Social workers maintain high standards of professional conduct and are honest, responsible, trustworthy and accountable to service users and to colleagues in their own and other professions. Social workers adhere to the values and ethical principles as laid out in this Code and the ethical standards of their provincial or territorial regulatory body. Accountability to the public includes registration with the profession's regulatory body where provincial or territorial regulatory legislation exists.

(CASW 2024: 16)

The Canadian Code of Ethics continues with the following principle:

> Social workers demonstrate integrity in professional conduct by:
>
> 5.1.1 accurately representing themselves (e.g. educational qualifications, professional registration, professional designation, professional experience, cultural identity, etc.) within the context of a professional relationship;
>
> 5.1.2 making true, honest, and accurate claims regarding the nature and scope of service and past or anticipated service outcomes;
>
> 5.1.3 taking appropriate action where a breach of professional practice and professional ethics occurs consistent with the Code, the standards of their provincial or territorial regulatory body;
>
> 5.1.4 informing service users of any factor, condition or pressure that affects their ability to practise at the earliest opportunity;
>
> 5.1.5 advising service users, colleagues, and employers as early as possible when services will be interrupted or terminated and facilitating a referral to another service provider or program;
>
> 5.1.6 registering with relevant social work regulatory bodies in jurisdictions where they engage in social work practice or use the title 'social worker'.
>
> (CASW 2024: 16)

These principles are typical of most national codes. However, they illustrate the often generic content, which leaves them open to interpretation. Where rights and wrongs are considered, there is common agreement that professional integrity is a right, but that 'right' can be subjective. This is helpful, as having to act in a specific, prescribed and regimented manner would limit social workers' ability to be responsive, flexible and creative. It is important to support people with lived experience in ways that are tailored to their particular needs and that empower them to help themselves. However, flexible interpretation of these principles can create a range of different notions of professionalism and integrity. For example, if we suggest that social workers should be diligent, what might the word *diligence* mean?

- 'Careful and persistent work or effort'. Oxford Languages https://languages.oup.com/google-dictionary-en/
- 'Constant and earnest effort to accomplish what is undertaken; persistent application and endeavour; industry, assiduity'. Oxford English Dictionary

- 'An individual's effort toward holistic development in mental, moral, physical, and social dimensions, as indicated through … Motivation, Concentration and Assimilation, Conformity and Citizenship, Discipline, and Responsibility' (Bernard and Schuttenberg 1995).
- In Buddhism, diligence is seen as 'the right effort' which is explained as nourishing but not draining.
- In law, due diligence can be argued to be either a robust amount to facilitate good practice, or is about doing just enough to prevent legal proceedings through negligence.

Irrespective of which of these definitions or ideas that you subscribe to, it can be seen that diligence can be interpreted subjectively. Diligence remains the ethical realm of the individual social worker and subjective to reflection on the rights and wrongs that apply to any given situation. This use of *duty ethics* – to require social workers to be committed to a high standard of practice – remains dependent on subjective analysis.

Conclusion

This chapter has discussed social work professionalism. First, we located the importance of understanding both your own personal and professional identity. We then considered how professional ethics relate to ensure ideas of professionalism and professional integrity. There are core traits that every social worker should strive to demonstrate, through their practice, cognisant of notions of professional boundaries that help with ideas of right and wrong in practice. However, there are also many situations where the complexity of the ethical and practical dilemma requires personal reflection and subsequent discussion with a peer, mentor, or supervisor and with the persons involved.

It is these complex dilemmas that help to make social work *a profession* and not a technical or rational job. Social workers must be capable of critical thinking and ethical debate to explore a multitude of possible outcomes, each one with its own kinds of impact on the people who experience social work directly. Social workers in touch with their ethical base and moral compass will be better placed to be professional.

Think further about …

… a recent example of a situation where you would have liked to make your decision more promptly.

- What made you prevaricate?
- What were the consequences (positive and negative) of your prevarication?
- Did it affect the quality of the decision and your sense of professionalism?

… a recent example of a situation where you relied on *convenience ethics*, as you now understand it from your reading of this chapter.

- Why did you resort to convenience? What might you do differently now?
- How did convenience decision-making affect your sense of professional integrity?

Ethical dilemmas with twelve people

Mark Fraser (Black bin bag)

> I started working as an unqualified social worker with children with disabilities – residential care with teenagers – and found it both rewarding and also very challenging. After a few years I left to travel and while studying Buddhism in the Himalayas we had an audience with the Dalai Lama. 'We don't need Westerners living here as monks and nuns,' he said. 'We need you all to go back to your own countries and be social workers or teachers. Give to your communities. That is the greatest work.'
>
> That is what I did. I returned home to qualify as a social worker and have worked in different roles with children and families ever since. I am now a practice development worker. Social work is an amazing privilege. It really is the greatest work.

Further reading

Burnham, J. (2012), 'Developments in Social GGRRAAACCEEESSS: Visible– invisible and Voiced– unvoiced', in I.-B. Krause (ed.), *Culture and Reflexivity in Systemic Psychotherapy: Mutual Perspectives*, London: Karnac.

Fenton, J. (2019), *Social Work for Lazy Professionals*, London: Red Globe Press.

Long, N., Gardner, F., Hodgkin, S. and Lehmann, J. (2023), 'Developing Social Work Professional Identity and Resilience: Seven Protective Factors', *Australian Social Work*. DOI: 10.1080/0312407X.2022.2160265.

The Social Work Podcast (n.d.), Social Work Ethics https://www.socialworkpodcast.com/Barsky_ethics.mp3

Wiles, F. (2017), 'What is Professional Identity and How Do Social Workers Acquire It?', in S. Webb (ed.), *Professional Identity and Social Work*, 35–50, Routledge.

6

Working relationships

Introduction

This chapter focuses on the notion of relationship-based practice, both in direct work with service users and co-working with colleagues and other professionals and boundaries that exist within that role. Relationship-based practice is commonly practised in social work, where working in partnership is paramount. However, it is not without dilemmas. This chapter explores ethical and practical dilemmas that can arise within working relationships, and how to reflect on them to come to a point of action. The case study asks you to reflect on ideas of relationships with a birth mother, foster carers, prospective adoptive carers and the professionals involved.

Ethical dilemmas in twelve objects

Jigsaw puzzle

Lithuanian social worker Žaneta uses the idea of a jigsaw puzzle to develop our notion of relationship building.

> When I work with people, and children in particular, they are like individual pieces of a puzzle who may not seem to 'fit' in; through my social work, and in particular my groupwork, I start to see a larger picture, how they might all fit together; and they begin to see it, too. By making connections we are making one whole puzzle picture – relationship building is both a frustrating and a joyful process!

Think about …

… When you arrive you at a meeting, you realize that one of the professionals at the table is a neighbour with whom you are in a dispute.

Is there a dilemma? If so, what is the nature of your dilemma? And what do you do?

What might make a difference to the nature of your dilemma? Consider how you would feel if they disagreed with your professional opinion in the meeting. What difference does it make if this is only likely to be a one-off professional encounter or something more long-term?

Working relationships

Working relationships come in a variety of shapes and sizes. As a social worker, you will be working with a wide variety of people whose identity, needs, experience, engagement and personality will vary and will impact the nature of the relationship, as well as their lived experience, particularly of oppression or discrimination. As we discussed in Chapter 5, it is important to be aware of your personal and professional identity and how that impacts your ability to act ethically and professionally. It is important to be aware if your religious beliefs or gender-critical views are impacting on your ability to engage with other people respectfully, as micro-aggressions are often undertaken subconsciously, but can have a devastating impact on working relationships. You will often work with people in very vulnerable circumstances and at the most vulnerable times in their lives and power differentials will be evident (Chapter 4). Irrespective, a collaborative approach should be taken within all working relationships so that everyone feels informed, involved, valued and respected: this fundamental ethical perspective forms the basis of social work practice when the pieces of the jigsaw fit together: 'Principles of social justice, human rights, collective responsibility and respect for diversities are central to social work' (IFSW 2018).

Arguably, an ethical relationship is based upon honesty and trust, respect, equality, mutual consent, effective communication, understanding, empathy and compromise. However, it should be noted that conflict is likely to arise in relationships, as they are complex and are dependent on open communication (Beesley et al. 2023). This should not prevent you from working ethically. However, it may make it more challenging on both a personal and professional level.

Another picture

Ryker and Yara have recently met and are 'talking', which means a lack of commitment to each other as they are in the early stages of developing a potential relationship. Ryker feels that he is ready to progress the relationship further to make it 'exclusive' and is upset when he hears that Yara has been talking to a range of other people, both men and women.

There are a number of issues raised here:

- Yara has not been open that she is bisexual.
  - This lack of communication leaves Ryker feeling that Yara did not trust him to discuss it.
  - Ryker feels that Yara has not been respectful to him by sharing her sexuality.
  - He feels that he has lacked the ability to make an informed decision.
  - He is now unsure if he can trust her moving forward.
  - He knows that he often becomes quiet or withdraws rather than work through conflict.
- When Yara has shared her sexuality in the past, the relationship has ended quickly. She was waiting to assess if Ryker was empathic enough to support her. She is upset that he feels this way and wants to share her perspective and past experiences with him.
- Yara feels that Ryker has not communicated his change in feelings to her and that he has not given her the opportunity to consider her own feelings in the light of this new information.
  - She feels disappointed that he is judging her.
  - She knows that she can communicate this as anger as a defence mechanism.

Ryker and Yara can end the early-stage relationship here.

However, instead they can discuss their feelings in an open and honest manner so that both are heard and so that they can together decide if the relationship is viable. By listening to each other, they are able to strengthen their mutual understanding and develop tools to navigate future conflict in relationships, or even to prevent them from occurring in the first place. Their future is together.

We navigate personal relationships all the time. Reflect on your own relationships, with family, friends, or partner and consider how you are honest, respectful, equitable, communicating, understanding, empathic, and able to compromise. Which of these skills can you transfer to working with service users and which skills do you need to develop further?

Obviously, it is challenging to discuss an ethical approach to working relationships without considering *relational ethics*. Boszormenyi-Nagy (1987) suggested that relational ethics is based on mutual respect, engagement, parity of knowledge (both in respecting the knowledge that each party brings to the relationship and in ensuring all parties are fully informed), shared accountability, acknowledgement of uncertainty and the development of an environment that nurtures the relationship: by working in partnership, a collaborative approach can be taken that harnesses strengths and identifies problem-solving solutions. An excellent example of relational ethics in practice is the *ubuntu* philosophical approach (see Chapter 3). In contrast to the dominant Western approach of capitalism which prioritizes power, wealth and individuality, *ubuntu* argues for a collective response that takes account of all individuals' wishes, feelings and needs (Mayaka and Truell 2021). Taking a relational-ethics perspective in social work allows for a more creative and flexible response that recognizes the service user as a person and an individual rather than responding procedurally with a one-size-fits-all approach and draws on the strength of family and community to support the individual or group.

Relationships with service users

Social work is relationship-based, as it constitutes an engagement in meaningful relationships at the interpersonal level (Hennessey 2011; Ruch et al. 2018), which can involve conflict, difficult choices and moral ambiguities. Indeed, Hollinrake (2019) rightly points out that humans are complex, and as such we need to be aware that service-user needs are individual and deserve a person-centred approach. Banks (2020) recommends that relationship-based social work professionalism should be *virtue-based* and advocates professional integrity, trustworthiness, compassion, honesty, warmth and competence to engage and work in partnership. Furthermore, Thacker et al. (2019) argue that working in partnership with service users facilitates professional curiosity, which in turn leads to more robust relationships, assessments and interventions that safeguard vulnerable adults. In Chapter 2, we introduced Biestek's (1961) seven principles for 'the casework relationship', and it is worth revisiting them in our present discussion:

- Purposeful expression of feelings
- Controlled emotional involvement
- Acceptance
- Non-judgemental attitude
- Client self-determination, and
- Confidentiality.

However, we also need to be cognisant that people's responses to situations will be individual and influenced by a range of factors, some of which we are not aware. This can cause conflict, even where we are not aware of it. Parker (2024) reminds us that people and situations change and that, when working with people, we need to be aware of this and take a critically reflective approach. Conflict resolution that places the service user first can engage them to work with service provision, so from both an ethical and a practical perspective, it is the right thing to do.

Terminology can be an ethical challenge, where terms such as 'disguised compliance', 'hostile relationships', 'difficult', 'non-engaging', 'uncooperative', 'non-compliant' are loaded with judgements that the person is not engaging openly and honestly. It is ethically beholden on you as the social worker to be empathic and try to resolve the conflict, even where that feels difficult. It can be helpful to remember Karpman's (1968) drama triangle, where the service user may be stuck in the role of victim and locate you as persecutor or rescuer, a situation where you need to change the narrative to a collaborative partnership for problem solving. Ferguson et al. (2021) recognized that working relationships in social work can often be based on anxiety and confusion which lead to mutual hostility, and that social workers should break the cycle with compassion and calmness.

A practice dilemma that has a negative impact on the service user's outcomes can be where a social worker assumes that their angry response means a lack of engagement, where it can be a sign of frustration and not necessarily disengagement. Do you take behaviour at face value and respond accordingly as it is their choice on whether to engage? Or do you see the social worker role as understanding and addressing lack of engagement, even when the service user indicates that it is not what they want, as part of relationship building and positive outcomes? Finally, how long and hard do you try before you acknowledge that they are not yet ready to engage. Whilst we hope you consider the latter correct, we must acknowledge the importance of respecting people's wishes and feelings, even where the consequence is an unsafe decision. It is essential that a relational approach is taken, that enables exploration of the person's intent and takes account of social, cultural and life experiences that may have an impact on their initial presentation. Indeed, Beckett et al. (2017) assert that social workers have a duty of realism that requires us to assume the best and that positive expectations inspire the people with whom we work.

Relationships with professionals

Working with professionals is both good practice and embedded in practice guidance (SCIE n.d.; DfE 2023). The joy of inter-professional working is the different perspectives that look at the same issue to offer a range of solutions, which is designed to best work with the service user and meet their needs. However, these differences can also create problems and Thompson (2021) asserts that differences in inter-professional working can come from different values, perspectives, priorities, expectations, norms, financial restrictions, protocols and experiences, and to that we might add organizational and allocation boundaries.

Nevertheless, using Beauchamp and Childress's (1979) ethical principle of justice, it can be argued that inter-professional working has the potential to facilitate a collaborative approach that takes account of a range of perspectives to enable the fair distribution of services through both *non-maleficence* and *beneficence*, determined within a community of practice. Indeed, McAuliffe (2022) states that ethical literacy is developed by being able to justify ethical decision making to a range of audiences, and inter-professional relationships enable this, as they prevent assumptive habits forming. Furthermore, inclusion of service users when working with other professionals aligns with the ethical principle of respect for autonomy.

A practical dilemma in working relationships can be where different professionals have different perspectives on how a person should be treated. For example, whilst a social worker may feel that a young person's offending behaviour warrants a social approach with support to explore the reasons behind their behaviour and change such a narrative, the police might argue for a penal approach. A possible solution here is community service, that both engages the person and provides boundaries for future behaviour. A relational approach advocates that negotiation through open and honest discussion facilitates collaboration even in the face of difference or conflict.

Boundaries

Boundaries 'set limits for safe, acceptable and effective behaviour' (Cooper 2012: 11) and yet often require ethical reflection on complexity, as they must take account of the person, strengths and areas for development, the service provision, the law, your personal and professional values, and the rights and wrongs of social work. A consideration of boundaries is important to strive towards better practice, build trust and understanding, equity of service delivery, reduce the risk of exploitation or abuse, prevent role confusion, empower and build service user independence, and sustain objectivity and focus. In Chapter 4, we discussed the boundaries surrounding professionalism in receiving a gift. Whilst there are some clear boundaries that you should not cross – for example, oppressive practice – a good many are less clear and require reflection and debate to ensure boundaries are maintained. Here, turning to the code of ethics can be helpful to begin a reflective discussion (Parrott 2014).

An example of an ethical dilemma where boundaries can be unclear could be where a social worker is supervising family time and steps in to ensure the children's well-being, but in doing so masks the true lack of parenting skills, resulting in informed decisions being made based on false information. The paradoxical dilemma of protecting the child in the short term but not the long term could be met by coaching the parenting, recording the input, and assessing the development of parenting skills as a result of the intervention. However, if the goal is assessment, then having a dual goal of enhancing the quality of family time can be difficult and requires clear boundaries. Indeed, what a clear boundary is in relation to safe parenting may in itself be subjective: we know, for example, that smacking is culturally appropriate and/or legal in some countries but not others, and where it is not illegal is often subject to ethical debate within society and social work circles. A clear planning discussion with peers or a line manager, or even within the court process, about what constitutes safe-enough parenting in a supervised environment that is also communicated to parents involved will be important. Furthermore, discussion with parents about parenting expectations may create deeper understanding of expectations for parents and norms for the social worker, thus becoming a productive activity that enhances the situation. Consider if there is a parenting 'line' that you would step in for; do you have triggers that you might need to consider if you would subconsciously apply, or is your ethical stance that it is an assessment and you would address the issues afterwards no matter what?

Bringing the personal into social work relationships

Inevitably, you bring your self to any encounter with service users, in terms of your personal strengths, foibles, personality into the engagement, all dependent upon your communication skills (Beesley et al. 2024). For example, the reciprocity of phatic conversation ('hello, how are you?', discussion about the weather, football, or recent social occasions designed to engage them before moving on to the purpose of the meeting) engages service users. However, it is important to consider how reciprocal you can be, or indeed should be. For instance, how do you respond to the service user asking if you have children? On one hand, knowing that you have parenting experience may engage the service user and give them confidence in your ability to assess and understand the situation, but on the other hand, your social work training and qualification should equally equip you with those strengths and provide that confidence. Finding an equal footing can be very useful here, but always reflect if it is the right way to achieve this footing or not. An ethical dilemma is the constant weighing-up of how much of yourself to give to the working relationship where you expect the service user to share openly and honestly their most vulnerable moments.

An emotionally intelligent social worker is aware that some work experiences can trigger strong emotions in themselves, such as anxiety and grief, and also joy and relief – perhaps a confusing mixture of many feelings which can arise suddenly or might be slow to manifest. Social workers' feelings about service users and their situations might be reactive, perhaps associated to the social worker's own value base: anger at the injustice a service user has endured or revulsion at the racist attitudes of another. In contrast, the feelings might have their roots in past experiences: sympathy for a person who reminds us of a previous well-liked and appreciative service user; or overwhelming anger, sadness, or joy where we identify with the person with whom we are working.

The term *transference*, first coined by Freud, is used in psychodynamic theory to describe strong feelings that we transfer from one person or situation to another, often unconsciously, where the present reminds us in some way of the past. A tender relationship with your grandmother might transfer to similar feelings towards an older woman that you are working with, whilst working with a young person who looks like the school bully may transfer feelings of resentment and lack of power. There might be a strong *countertransference* when this person does not respond in the way that is expected, thus leaving you feeling angry, confused, even in some ways betrayed. As a social worker, you are expected to navigate these complexities and their ethical dimension: this requires individual reflection and reflective discussion with others.

Taking this a step further, sexual attraction is hugely important to human life, yet it features little in the social work literature (Bernsen et al. 1994). The question of sexual attraction is probably the one that is most buried, not just in social work writings but in supervision and everyday workplace chatter, because it is considered to be such a taboo topic. There is often blanket collusion in the idea that professionalism is about denying any questions of sexual attraction; however, it is unprofessional *not* to be aware of and *not* to discuss feelings of sexual attraction or repulsion. If there is denial (whether conscious or not), decisions are made with a layer of important knowledge obscured. Professionalism is not about denying the feeling, but it is about declining to act on it. To be emotionally intelligent means to be aware of these feelings and to harness them to your ability to intervene professionally and without bias: 'Self-awareness and self-reflection are crucial to relationship-based practice and are part of the professional expertise that social workers use in practice' (Chard 2019: 103).

An ethical dilemma could be where you are working with a service user whose mannerisms remind you of an ex-partner: do you ignore them, do you embrace them, or do you voice them to another to enable you to work through them, even if means risking their judgement?

Confidentiality

Confidentiality is a basic ethical requirement of being a social worker and forms a clear form of professional integrity and professionalism. We are dealing with people's private and sensitive information about their lives, and it is our duty to ensure that we keep that information safe. However, it does not mean keeping things secret. The ethical perspective here is that of sharing information that needs to be disclosed and not communicating anything over and above that. There is no dilemma in deciding whether to share with a school that a child is at risk of significant harm, yet it can be undertaken ethically. The importance of ensuring that parents are informed when information will be shared cannot be over-emphasized and indeed can be seen to be part of the relationship building required in social work.

It is not uncommon for a young person to say 'If I tell you something, you can't tell anyone.' At this juncture, you face an ethical dilemma: it is important that the young person feels safe to share their feelings with you, yet you cannot promise that you will keep it secret as you are a safeguarding professional and will need to take action if required to do so. The ethical route is to be open and honest with the young person, even if this results in a delay in them sharing the information. Sometimes we have to be patient in our relationship building, but strong foundations are fundamental to their longevity.

Ethical dilemma 6: The adoption

Adam is a three-year-old who has been in foster care with Mr and Mrs Brown for a year and is thriving there despite early concerns about developmental delay. Adam's birth mother, Cassie Cook, had subjected him to unnecessary medical interventions with fictitious illnesses and there remain fears about her mental health.

Edna is the allocated social worker, having been involved for two years with Adam. Despite her hope that Adam would return to Cassie's care and a high level of support and intervention from a range of professionals, a plan for adoption has been agreed. Cassie contests this decision.

1 How might you feel, if you were Edna, about continuing to engage Cassie in Adam's life?

It may be that you consider Adam's perspective and come to the conclusion that either the longer that he has involvement with his mum the better, or that the sooner it reduces, the sooner he can start to engage in the next chapter of his life. Both can be argued as ethically and evidenced-based decisions.

It may be that you consider Cassie's perspective and feel that it respects and values her to ensure that she is a participant in decision making in relation to her son for as long as is viable.

This is an ethical decision to make; you will need to weigh your personal and professional values against agency procedure in ethical, reflective discussion. In a chapter on working relationships, we would ask you to reflect on the impact of rule-orientated versus person-centred social work, with perhaps a *virtue-based* approach being most important here.

In considering this, do you place Adam's or Cassie's needs first? Can you consider both of their needs simultaneously? How will your decision impact your working relationship with Adam, Cassie and the foster carers?

Whilst Edna respects the court's decision to reduce regular family time and contact between Adam and Cassie to facilitate an adoptive match, she feels that it is important that she continues to work with Cassie throughout the decision-making process.

2 How might Cassie feel about continuing to work with Edna?

It is important that Edna has empathy for Cassie and reflects on how she may be feeling and how those feelings may be communicated. Cassie has suffered the loss of a child and the stages of loss can be helpful to consider here to understand if she is expressing denial, anger, bargaining, depression and acceptance (see Kubler-Ross 1969). This will enable Edna to understand and accept Cassie's responses so that she is able to continue to engage her and to ensure Cassie receives support.

3 In what ways could Edna maintain the working relationship with Cassie?

As long as Cassie's parental rights have not been ended through a court order, she would continue to be consulted in relation to Adam's welfare, so issues such as health and education would be developed in discussion with Cassie. This can be undertaken by providing information to her on his well-being and including her in decision making, which can be both on an individual basis and in review meetings. Sadly, if there were a court order in place, this input would reduce significantly and move to updates at pre-agreed intervals.

A second step would be to involve Cassie in planning for an adoptive placement. Whilst it may not be her preferred option for her son, the ability to feel that she has some control within the adoptive placement provision enables her to feel that she has some say in her son's future. The working relationship should continue to be respected despite the statutory nature of the plans for Adam. This would also include involvement in life-story work, where she would be able to ensure that Adam would have access to his family history (Wrench 2024).

Edna has begun searching for an adoption match for Adam and identifies a strong potential match. Mr and Mrs Woods are assessed as being able to meet Adam's needs and they express a strong commitment to enabling annual face-to-face contact between Cassie and Adam in the future. However, Adam's foster carers, Mr and Mrs Brown, belatedly also nominate themselves to be considered as adopters, but express their wish that it would need to be a closed adoption due to their preceding relationship with Cassie and their being local.

4 Who would be involved in decision making about Adam's adoptive placement?

As discussed above, we would advocate that Edna involves Cassie in the decision making for as long as possible – gathering her wishes and feelings is an important way to respect her parental responsibility for as long as she legally has it. In addition, it is hoped that Edna's working relationship with Adam has developed whilst she had been the allocated social worker. An argument may exist that three-year-old Adam is not capable of understanding the nuances of the decision, yet Edna's working relationship with him should enable her to undertake playwork with him that could identify his needs, which could then be applied to her decision making.

We would normally advocate the importance of the foster carers being involved in adoption placement matching, but in this situation Mr and Mrs Brown have a vested interest and could not be seen to be impartial, yet Edna needs their support in assessing Adam's needs to supplement Cassie's knowledge. Collaboration here is important, where Edna seeks Mr and Mrs Brown's views. She assumes that just because they have a wish to adopt Adam does not mean that they will be incapable of expressing their professional, open and honest view of the strength of the match for Adam with them, seeing integrity and *virtue-based* ethics as part of working relationships.

Mr and Mrs Brown's foster-link social worker would need to be involved, as potentially the agency could lose a foster carer couple at the expense of an adoption. Mr and Mrs Woods' adoption-link social worker also needs to be a participant, and it may be that on hearing that there is doubt about the match that they advise Mr and Mrs Woods to also consider other children, placing the Adam match at risk. Nevertheless, it is important for working relationships that their perspective is advocated for in the meeting.

If Adam had health or educational professionals involved, their views would be invaluable in the meeting. As with all decision making (see Chapter 7), Edna's manager would be involved; nevertheless, Edna will be making the recommendation, and her view is important.

Finally, any decision would be considered and ratified by an Adoption Panel; this would include the members of the panel who often include people with lived experience including adopters and people who were adopted as a child, social workers and other professionals. The working relationship here is to ensure a clear and concise summary of the pertinent points so that the panel can make their informed recommendation.

However, there is an added layer of complexity to this situation. When Edna undertook the initial discussions with Mr and Mrs Woods about potentially placing Adam with them as adoptive carers, she thought she recognized Mr Woods, though couldn't quite place where. Soon after the meeting, Edna received a call from her mum. Her mum's friend's nephew is Mr Woods, and she reminds Edna that they played together at parties when they were young.

5 How should Edna respond to this information?

Edna immediately shares this information with her line manager, who helps her to decide that the personal relationship is tenuous and agrees that she can continue to assess if they are a suitable adoptive match for Adam. The manager knows that Edna will put Adam's needs first whilst she assesses their suitability.

At their next appointment, Edna raises the issue and clears the air, so that everyone is clear on the professional basis of the working relationship.

With the advent of the delay as a result of Cassie's contesting the plan for adoption, which coincided with Mr and Mrs Brown also requesting to adopt Adam, the plan has become more contentious and now the personal, albeit tenuous, connection is potentially problematic. The manager determines that Edna will continue to be the allocated social worker. Nevertheless, Edna starts to reflect on her working relationship with Mr and Mrs Woods, as well as her working relationship with the foster carers Mr and Mrs Brown.

6 Consider each of the scenarios and reflect if they might impact Edna's working relationships and how you might respond in Edna's situation.

- Edna had positive memories of Mr Woods.
- Edna had negative memories of Mr Woods.
- Edna has now developed a strong working relationship with Mr and Mrs Woods.
- Edna had a strong working relationship with the foster carers Mr and Mrs Brown.
- Edna had struggled to connect with Mr and Mrs Brown professionally, finding them warm with Adam, but unwilling to work with other professionals.

Cognitive bias is a challenging and impactful problem for working relationships. Whilst we strive hard to identify bias and moderate our behaviours, sometimes we overcompensate or take unwise assessments that are influenced by our feelings about people. It is natural that we will like some people and not all people; professional working relationships are just the same. However, we have to put aside our 'like' of a person and make an objective assessment and decision. In this situation, we would hope that Edna discusses her feelings with her line manager, as accountability and reflective discussion are basic social work skills that must be adhered to. Furthermore, listening to other's views, wishes and feelings within working relationships will compensate for any potential bias.

As such, a meeting of professionals is called to consider the choices and to make a decision. Edna is able to represent Cassie's wishes and feelings, but it is agreed that Cassie will not attend the meeting, in order to maintain adopter anonymity. Furthermore, as the decision involves both the foster carers and the prospective adoptive carers, neither couple are included in the meeting. This is a dilemma, as good practice indicates that all relevant parties should be included in the decision-making process. Do you feel that this is the right decision by Edna from an ethical point of view?

7 What is the dilemma?

The dilemma for those in the meeting to consider is whether to support the application of the Browns or the Woods to adopt Adam.

Everyone agrees that Adam's long-term needs should be put first, and the dilemma becomes centred on relationships. Is an ongoing relationship with the Browns, who have cared for him for such a significant proportion of his life, more or less important than the ability to sustain a relationship with his mum Cassie?

However, the support social workers also have the dilemma of the impact on their working relationship with each couple in the future.

In the meeting, it becomes clear that there is an ethical split between prioritizing the need for continuity and the need for ongoing contact with Cassie. Both are relationship-based, but the relationship for Adam is central to the dilemma.

8 How could the ethical dilemma impact working relationships with other professionals?

In line with *relational ethics,* each person in the meeting should have an equal opportunity to voice their opinion and be heard, whatever status or power they are perceived to hold within the group. Once the nature of the facts has been established, it is important to frame the dilemma. Does each member see the same dilemma or are there different formulations of it and, if so, what gives rise to these variations? It is a practical decision as to which of the two applications should receive the meeting's support, but the reasoning that will now inform the decision making will ensure that the decision is *moral*. A *utilitarian* decision would hold to the primacy of Adam's needs and a consideration of which carers create the last harm and/or greatest good for Adam, by weighing up continuity versus family contact. However, can this decision be taken without any consideration of the needs of the carers?

By displaying professional integrity throughout the meeting, listening to all perspectives and providing a clear, reflective rationale for the decision that is based on her role as Adam's social worker, Edna knows that whilst not everyone will agree with her decision, they will respect the decision. She will not have placed her future working relationships at risk.

It will be difficult for Edna to break the news to the unsuccessful couple, but she knows that to ensure a productive working relationship and to feel that she has been 'true to herself', that she needs to take responsibility for sharing the outcome immediately. She again sets out her reasoning and the ethical process followed in the meeting, and is able to manage their disappointment in a planned way with their link social worker.

Finally, she ensures that she keeps Cassie informed so that she is aware of the proposed plan. This will help to sustain her working relationship with Cassie, which is important both for respecting and valuing Cassie and for Cassie's future with the agency. This will facilitate contact between Adam and Cassie, in whatever form that is agreed.

Reflect on this ethical dilemma and consider how it helps you to consider how you can sustain your working relationships in complex situations.

Guidance from codes, standards and principles

The IFSW (2018) Global Definition of Social Work states that 'social work engages people and structures to address life challenges and enhance wellbeing.' It goes on to assert that the 'participatory methodology advocated' should mean that 'as far as possible social work supports working with rather than for people.'

This locates relationship-based working as central to social work. The British Code of Ethics for Social Workers (BASW 2021) recommends the developing of professional relationships:

> Social workers should build and sustain professional relationships based on people's right to control their own lives and make their own choices and decisions. Social work relationships should be based on people's rights to respect, privacy, reliability and confidentiality. Social workers should communicate effectively and work in partnership with individuals, families, groups, communities, and with public bodies and other agencies. They should value and respect the contribution of colleagues from other disciplines whilst being prepared to offer constructive challenge when necessary.

In this definition, two important points are raised. First, empowering people to self-determination, as discussed earlier in Chapter 5, maintains and develops working relationships. However, secondly, the skills of communication and challenge are equally important parts of working relationships. The ability to provide information, listen to others, negotiate and work through conflict is critical in relationship building as openness and honesty develops trust. The dilemma here is about assessing when to challenge and when to support decisions made by others, as will be discussed in the next chapter.

BASW (2021) suggests that professional relationships can be developed through 'acting with the informed consent of service users, unless required by law to protect that person or another from risk of serious harm', 'providing information to people affected by social work decisions', 'sharing information appropriately', 'using authority in accordance with human rights principles', 'empowering people', 'striving for objectivity and self-awareness in professional practice' and 'using professional supervision and peer support to reflect on and improve practice'. It becomes clear that ethical working relationships are built and sustained by ethical social work practice.

The Aotearoa New Zealand (ANZASW 2019) code is underpinned throughout by the principles of working relationships; it states: 'Whanaungatanga social workers work to strengthen reciprocal mana-enhancing relationships, connectedness and to foster a sense of belonging and inclusion.' Here there is a clear commitment to collaboration and working in partnership to share the power and control (mana) inherent in the social work working relationship, which they achieve through 'respect, kindness and compassion. We practice empathic solidarity, ensure safe space, acknowledge boundaries and meet obligations'.

Conclusion

In this chapter, we have looked at working relationships, both those with service users and with other professionals. Underpinning working relationships from an ethical perspective is the importance of relational ethics. Here, working collaboratively together to share power and negotiate appropriate outcomes is paramount, returning to the social work idea of doing *with* people, not *to* people. The chapter also considered the importance of boundaries, using codes of ethics to guide you and the importance of reflecting on your own personal and professional values to ensure that the use of self in your intervention is measured and appropriate.

Think further about …

… a time when you were asked a question about yourself by a service user that you found difficult to answer.

- What was the question?
- What made it difficult to answer?
- Was there an ethical dilemma in the asking and answering of the question?
- How did you respond?
- How, with hindsight, and having read this chapter, would you now respond?

Ethical dilemmas with twelve people

Žaneta Šerkšnienė (Jigsaw puzzle)

> I came to social work when I started my undergraduate studies in Lithuania. Social work education was relatively new in my country at that point.

During my four years of studies, I didn't find a place where I could realize myself as a social worker. I have practised in various institutions but felt that they were not the right fit for me. When I later started my Masters studies at the same Lithuanian university, one of the social work tutors involved me in groupwork and I felt inspired. At the same time, I got a job at a secondary school with children who have special needs and I also initiated groups where I could teach social skills. I really felt I found my spot and was able to develop strong working relationships.

Further reading

Dix, H., Hollinrake, S. and Meade, J., eds (2019), *Relationship-based Social Work with Adults*, St Albans: Critical Publishing.

Parrott, L. (2014), *Values and Ethics in Social Work Practice*, London: Sage. Chapter 7 is on the ethics of partnership working.

Ruch, G., Turney, D. and Ward, A., eds (2018), *Relationship-based Social Work: Getting to the Heart of Practice*, London: Jessica Kingsley.

7

Decision making

Introduction

This chapter reflects on risk in decision making in social work practice, which includes making decisions about eligibility for services, safeguarding and care planning. Decision making in social work includes both relatively straightforward day-to-day decisions and more complex ethical dilemmas that require significant reflective discussion to ensure any decision best balances the needs of the individual person and society. The chapter presents a model of ethical decision making and considers the importance of professional curiosity in social work practice. It supports and challenges the reader through a case study of common ethical dilemmas about the level of support to offer a family in need, a situation that is often present in social work practice.

Ethical dilemmas in twelve objects

Escher's *Relativity* (sometimes known as 'the Enigma')

Scottish social worker Angie chose *Relativity*, a lithograph by Dutch graphic artist M. C. Escher. It is a series of five prints that depict twisting perspectives, staircases that go on forever and impossible perspectives, with some people seemingly upside down. For Angie, Escher's images reflect the fact that social work is not all it might seem and – depending on perspective – we may all see things differently. She writes:

> The work we do, and in particular [in our decision making], it is so subjective. For me the Enigma [*Relativity*] highlights the multifaceted dynamics in any one situation or person's life. When and from where we walk into this

picture will determine what we see, where we see it, what we perceive to be reality. However, this entrance and timing and observation will always be determined by which of the people and which position they are in on the stairs. The direction is not always so easily determined. We all too often find ourselves as practitioners entering the lives of people in times of crisis and chaos, stumbling down the stairs, but we hope that our work together will result in people once again climbing back upwards.

Escher's Enigma graphically demonstrates the immense number and variety of sensations that can be experienced when confronted with a decision to be made. Untangling what decisions are possible, who ought to be involved and where they are likely to lead us can feel like you are entering Escher's frame.

As you would expect, we do not offer a definite answer (there isn't one, as Escher makes clear), but we do hope to engage you in an enlightening discussion, asking questions and presenting frameworks that will help you to navigate through your own enigmas.

Think about ...

... You accidentally spot your best friend's family on the agency-wide IT system: do you take a look at what is happening to them?

Is there a dilemma? If so, what is the nature of your dilemma? And what do you do?

What might make a difference to the nature of your dilemma? Consider if your best friend asks you to check on her file, as the social worker isn't telling her anything and she felt blindsided at the last meeting as the social worker shared information that your friend should have been told prior to the meeting. Here, your personal and professional values may collide and the dilemma may be about how to move this forward without breaking confidentiality.

Risk in decision making

Risk is the balance of probability of a negative outcome arising from a decision. It can constitute any kind of risk – physical, emotional, economic – to the individual, group, organization, society, or environment. Knight (1921) introduced the concept of risk within insurance, suggesting that some areas of risk were quantifiable, by looking at past behaviours and outcomes, but that some factors will remain uncertain. The desire for certainty and a wish to reduce the anxiety generated by uncertainty can lead to denial of the uncertainty, so that beliefs frequently persist in the face of contrary new evidence, which is likely to be dismissed as unreliable or unrepresentative, and initial impressions structure the way subsequent evidence is interpreted (Fischhoff et al. 1978). Professionals ought to be open about their uncertainties, and continue to express doubt and to see each decision as tentative, made in the midst of uncertainty and met with the best-quality reasoning and judgement available at the time. *Safe uncertainty* is where risk is continually reviewed, remains flexible and is solution-focused (Mason 1993).

The big picture

Data is not very reliable, but one study showed that deaths by terror attacks were about 8,000 globally in 2023 (IEP 2024). That same year saw 33,000 global deaths in armed conflict (AOAV 2024). Though these numbers are horrific, a disproportionate degree of spending is given to anti-terrorism and the armed forces above health, social welfare and education – spending that would enrich society. What is the risk to the world if these areas are neglected?

Increased spending may be able to redress the fact that 'millions of children still died before seeing their fifth birthday' (Unicef 2024) and almost 10 million people died of cancer (GCO 2024), whilst poverty and gender are linked to illiteracy (WPR 2024) and a staggering billion children worldwide have experienced physical, sexual, or emotional violence or neglect (WHO 2022).

Clearly, the impact of fear and power comes into play in risk assessment. Influential voices in the media and in politics create a moral panic that terrorists are an everyday threat; in reality, there are far greater risks than terrorism. Events are thought more likely to happen if they are easy to recall or imagine, sometimes termed the *availability bias* (Fischhoff et al. 1978). We perceive systematic patterns even when there is randomness because we have a yearning for meaning. How might we achieve a bias-free risk assessment and decision-making process in relation to the allocation of funding?

Risk assessment is a common activity for social workers. It is associated with both the *seriousness* of the risk of harm to the individual person, their family, friends, carers, or community and the *likelihood* and *frequency* of the risk of harm; and the balance between all of these. In England, risk to children is assessed through Section 47.1.b of The Children Act 1989 which gives social workers the duty to investigate where they have 'reasonable cause to suspect that a child who lives, or is found, in their area is suffering, or is likely to suffer, significant harm'.

In terms of adults, Section 42.1 of the Care Act 2014 requires assessment of risk and need to facilitate decision-making in relation to an adult who

(a) Has needs for care and support (whether or not the authority is meeting any of those needs),
(b) Is experiencing, or is at risk of, abuse or neglect, and
(c) As a result of those needs is unable to protect himself or herself against the abuse or neglect or the risk of it.

As with Knight's insurance risk assessments, social workers assess situations based on past behaviours and responses to situations, both risks and strengths to develop, and they try to work with uncertainty. Social work assessments attempt to reduce rather than eradicate risk through reflection on practical and ethical dilemmas that balance physical, social and emotional risk (Parrott 2014). However, social work can become risk averse (Featherstone et al. 2018). Avoidance of, or the attempt to avoid, risk is often not based on a consideration of the ethics of the situation, but on self-preservation – which of the 'damned if you do' or 'damned if you don't' is perceived to be the least high profile? Whilst social workers are skilled at predicting what *won't* happen, they are less effective at predicting what *will* happen (Wilkins and Meindl 2024).

However, risk assessments which aim to predict the likelihood of an event happening too frequently ignore the question of *value*. Social workers must, therefore, discover the subjective value that a service user places on their own and other actions, if they are to understand how need and risk are to be weighed in any one situation. Research has found that balancing risk and ethics in decision making is best achieved through supervision, reference to the Code of Ethics, using a decision-making model and reflecting ethically on the decision (Abishevaa and Assylbekovab 2016). The first two allude to the importance of *accountability* in social work, a critical component of professionalism in social work. We must remember that there is also evidence to suggest that social workers can come to very different conclusions about the action to take, even when they ostensibly share common values (Doel et al. 2010).

Professional curiosity

An instinctive approach to decision making and problem solving, described as heuristics, characterizes the reality of much decision making in practice: you are likely to make decisions quickly and unconsciously, often based on your instinctive understanding of the world around you. In social work, you are required to make decisions that require deeper critical thought, and it is beneficial to slow the decision-making process in order to make more consciously formulated decisions.

Part of this approach to decision making in social work is the idea of professional curiosity which requires the desire and ability to explore uncertainty, be that to clarify the nature and degree of risks, or to support a person to explore their own uncertainties. It is exploratory actions and discussions that lead to the development of understanding. Often, it is about just wanting to know a little more about the situation that sheds light on the risks involved. Banks (2020) highlights that whilst an ethics of care (kindness, compassion, altruism) leads the social worker to respect the service user's wishes and feelings, the social work role also requires empathy, an orientation to social justice and reflection, with the result that social workers often need to challenge individuals and the wider society.

Lack of knowledge and skills, as well as a managerial approach to social work, can restrict professional curiosity in practice. Burton and Revell (2018) recommended emotionally intelligent supervision as necessary to develop the skills to explore challenging situations with sensitivity, but not avoidance, and to nurture an awareness of possible emotional 'triggers' for service users. Courage is also required (Dickens et al. 2023).

Ethical decision making

All dilemmas require a decision, even if the decision is to do nothing. Sartre's (1946) moral universe has us all free (or condemned) to choose, depending on how we see each decision-making event, each *singularity*. Dilemmas and decision making are by no means always about binary choices. We understand the dilemmas of difficult decisions as springing not from a choice between two sides of the same coin (for instance, honesty/dishonesty), but as the tension of having to choose between two *different* coins (for instance, the honesty/dishonesty coin and the causing harm/avoiding harm coin) (Joseph and Fernandes 2006). This might include where a social worker inflates the needs and risks faced by a vulnerable person (dishonesty) to present to a funding panel to ensure much-needed services are agreed (avoiding harm). Choosing to avoid harm might incur dishonesty; in other words, one good (avoiding harm) has trumped another good (honesty).

It may be that you have a *duty-based* approach to decision making, where you feel your strongest imperative is to follow the rules. However, this can become confusing and even contentious when you have a duty to uphold the law and implement a procedure, where you perceive they are, at best, contrary to your social work values and Code of Ethics or, at worst, unethical. You may feel that your duty to safeguard the person with whom you are working and/or duty to respect their wishes and feelings, for example, counters a financially orientated procedure within a restrictive legislative basis. Here, the ethical dilemma becomes a matter of determining your priorities: will you make decisions from a value base of preferencing rules or person-centred outcomes? Arguably, both perspectives would contend that they are morally correct and conscientious in their decision making, reinforcing the importance of understanding yourself (emotional intelligence) and an awareness of the sort of social worker you want to be.

However, for many social workers, it is less clear whether to always follow the rules or always make person-centred decisions. Often a more nuanced approach is taken to decision making, that weighs up a number of factors. For example, you could approach decision making from a *principlism* perspective (Beauchamp and Childress 1979), where autonomy (the right to make an informed decision), *beneficence* (placing the welfare of the person central to the decision), *non-maleficence* (creating no harm to the person central to the decision) and justice (awareness of the impact of social oppression and discrimination on the person central to the decision), and ensure that the decision either facilitates fair distribution or challenges unequal distribution of rights. This would mean that participative decision making is central to your work as a social worker, but that decisions are taken in the wider societal context of understanding the person's lived experiences and societal expectations. It can therefore be argued that ethical decision making is best made on a case-by-case basis – *casuism* – that weighs up a range of competing needs rather than an 'always do' or 'always do not' basis.

Participative decision making

As we have emphasized many times, all decisions about a person must be made *with* the person. An ethical approach to decision making must take account of the wishes, feelings, ideas and solutions held by the people you are working with (Banks 2020). This makes practical as well as ethical sense, as it is much more likely to be effective, building on people's innate strengths, problem-solving skills and coping strategies, and developing them where they are diminished or difficult to access and require support. As such, a discussion on risk in decision making is not complete without a discussion about strengths, resilience and safety factors. Indeed, a strengths-perspective (Saleebey 1992) comes from a perspective of resourcefulness and resilience (Howe and Hill 2024).

In order to fully involve service users in decisions about their own lives, they need to be able to make informed decisions, so an open and honest working relationship is key to person-centred decision making (see Chapter 6). Parker (2024) reminds us that social work requires empathy, warmth, genuineness, concreteness and immediacy, *and* also the ability to confront service users with discrepancies and inconsistencies. Interestingly, Reamer and Siegel (2021) frame withholding information as an act of *omission*, whilst reflecting that if it is for the greater good it is an act of *commission*. It is hard to imagine a situation in social work where *omission* would be ethically sound, and any such judgement should be taken with advice. Nevertheless, this is an excellent example of Joseph and Fernandes (2006)'s 'two coins', where one coin is the ethical dilemma of sharing or withholding information which at first sight appears to be simple: be open and honest is a basic social work principle; which would be balanced against the second coin, which is that omission enables you to avoid harm whilst an open and honest approach may cause harm.

Participative decision making creates additional benefit beyond the immediate encounter with a service user. Whether explicitly or not, social workers are coaching service users about how to draw on their strengths and problem-solving skills in ways that they, the service user, can use in future (Marsh and Doel 2005). This will apply not just to any future social work encounter, but more broadly in their lives. Part of the skill of the social worker is to make this process explicit rather than assume that service users will 'absorb' it. We might ask ourselves whether it is, indeed, an ethical duty to be explicit about the teaching and learning that is taking place in a participative method of social work.

Defensible decision making

A further dimension of ethical decision making is ensuring that it is defensible. 'Defensible' should not be confused with *defensive*, which means a focus on protecting your reputation or covering yourself against future investigation. Defensive practice is, indeed, an element of ethical risk management in order to protect both self and service users (Reamer 2023a), but it ought not to be the primary focus. *Defensible* decision making means ensuring that it is justified and informed and based in a practice that follows procedure correctly or, if it doesn't, that you can support a strong ethical defence as to why not. Balancing a participative approach to gathering all the required information, listening to all perspectives, critically reflecting on possible outcomes, ensuring accountability and, of course, recording the rationale for the decision, all are components in defensible decision making. As noted in the case study in Chapter 6, defensible decision making enhances working relationships.

Social workers need also to be able to defend their actions in terms of their professional Code of Ethics (Parrott 2014), without being overly self-critical, especially when external circumstances have limited the scope for good practice (Beckett et al. 2017). This is difficult to achieve if the organizational culture is one of blaming. Finally, let us remind ourselves that decision making should not be driven by management-oriented checklists that make it difficult to maintain a person-centred focus (Fook 2023).

Framework for ethical decision making

Irrespective of ethical philosophy, a model for decision making enhances practice (Abishevaa and Assylbekovab 2016), as it provides structure and process to enable evidence-based and defensible decisions to be made. Put simply, when someone questions your decision making – for example in court, in a meeting or under review – your critical thinking around any dilemmas that leads you to the decision is the clear basis for the response. Weighing up evidence and coming to an informed decision is critical in social work, and a framework will facilitate and demonstrate your ability to do this.

It can be helpful to consider a range of frameworks. Firstly, Barsky's (2019) framework for ethical decision making, which we will apply within Ethical Dilemma 7 later:

1. Identify ethical issue.
2. Determine appropriate help.
3. Think critically.
4. Manage conflict.
5. Plan and implement decision.
6. Evaluate and follow up.

However, Reamer (2024) suggests a framework specifically for ethical decision making in social work:

1. Identify the ethical issues, including the social work values and ethics that conflict.
2. Identify the individuals, groups and organizations that are likely to be affected by the ethical decision.
3. Tentatively identify all possible courses of action and the participants involved in each, along with possible benefits and risks for each.
4. Thoroughly examine the reasons in favour of and opposed to each possible course of action, considering relevant
    (a) ethical theories, principles, and guidelines;
    (b) codes of ethics and legal principles;

(c) social work practice theory and principles, and
(d) personal values (including religious, cultural and ethnic values and political ideology).
5. Consult with colleagues and appropriate experts (such as agency staff, supervisors, agency administrators, attorneys, ethics scholars and ethics committees).
6. Make the decision and document the decision-making process.
7. Monitor, evaluate and document the decision.

Bias

It is helpful to be aware that your decision making may be subject to a range of biases that will require identification, as it is only by recognizing the need for change that you can address it proactively. Forms of bias include:

- Confirmation bias: the tendency to search for and interpret information consistent with your beliefs, knowledge, experience and expectations.
- Conformity bias: a tendency to have your views influenced, or changed, by peer pressure.
- Credibility bias: the tendency to be more inclined to accept a statement by someone we like or respect, and vice versa.
- Framing bias: the tendency to be more inclined to accept a statement by someone who presents it in a reasonable manner, and vice versa.
- Optimism bias: the tendency to expect positive outcomes in interventions.
- Pessimism bias: the tendency to expect negative outcomes in interventions.
- Prejudice: the tendency to bias from conscious or unconscious stereotyping.
- Recall bias: the tendency to recall events based on your own lens rather than factually.
- Repetition bias: the tendency to make assumptions based on previous experiences in similar situations.
- Similarity bias: the tendency to favour (and make assumptions about) people with a similar identity to your own.

Social work is provided within a social context (Pease et al. 2018) where, at least in contemporary Western society, where the socially constructed truth tells us that vulnerable people are less important and should learn to become productive, albeit with the kind help of the profession of social work. Indeed, social work is a gendered profession that is based on being the carer and helper, which can create an unconscious bias that we are the *rescuer* (Karpman 1968). Furthermore, where we have been socialized to see the world from a white, male perspective (even when we are not white, male, heterosexual, or subscribe to the prevailing faith-base), decisions will be made based on that narrative. How, then, do our unconscious biases impact our ethical decision making?

Moral cognition is the notion that we make decisions based on our moral judgements, which are in turn informed by a range of stimuli, including past experiences, social conditioning and personality traits. When making a decision, you will experience unconscious bias in the way that you receive and process information, and in the ethical stance with which you will approach it. For example, if you have an inherently positive bias towards people's capacity to change, you are likely to assume the best, which may be reinforced or eroded depending on the agency's philosophical and practical responses to people. Nevertheless, approaching the situation from a *virtue-based* bias may lead you to ignore key risk factors.

How then do we ensure that decision making is ethically sound if bias is so prevalent? We should be critically reflective to identify, understand and address bias having an unrecognized impact on decision making, seeing this as critical to good judgement and good choices (Kahneman 2012; Banks 2020). Exercises that expose underlying bias – the paradigms we use to explain the world to ourselves – can be very revealing, such as *The Drawbridge* in Doel and Shardlow (2005: 207–9). Of course, you must always be on the alert for bias and prejudice, conscious or unconscious, which is a tendency to favour or reject evidence depending on the person's identity, presentation, or power to ensure ethical decision making. Leigh et al. (2020) provide an excellent example of this, where they critique the phrase '*disguised compliance*' as one that can create bias against a desire to engage with services, when in fact assessing the barriers to engagement would be more productive. Nevertheless, Sicora et al. (2021) identify the importance of intuition in decision making, so this is not to ignore your instincts, but to be cognisant of their existence and their potential impact on your decision making.

Finally, a word of warning from Reamer (2023b): it is important that social workers do not allow their bias to rest unchallenged, as it can lead to moral disengagement where professional decision making can be impaired.

Ethical dilemma 7: The Friday afternoon enigma

Amy and Ollie Dawson have three children: Star aged 6, Keira aged 4 and Sam aged 2. Amy comes to the office late on Friday afternoon saying that she has no food in the house, no money to feed the children and no income until Monday. Fabius is the duty social worker. As a social work student in an English fieldwork office, he is authorised to make a Section 17, Children Act 1989 Child In Need payment of up to £25. This enables Fabius to provide support in circumstances when:

(a) he [sic] is unlikely to achieve or maintain, or to have the opportunity of achieving or maintaining, a reasonable standard of health or development without the provision for him of services by a local authority under this Part;
(b) his [sic] health or development is likely to be significantly impaired, or further impaired, without the provision for him of such services; or
(c) he [sic] is disabled. (HMSO 1989)

However, whilst Section 17 provides a legal duty to assist those 'in need', the assessment of need is a discretionary social work task. It can be argued that Star, Keira and Sam could be considered to be in need, as a lack of food over the weekend would be detrimental to their health.

1 What decision needs to be made here?

The decision is: should Fabius provide a £25 payment to Amy to support the children's well-being and health?

For some social workers, making payments is an ethical issue but not a dilemma because they either *always do* or *always do not* support families on a Friday afternoon, based on their own value system that prioritises consistency.

If you are a social worker who always does, you might be employing the *Kantian categorical imperative,* treating everyone with an equal regard, and how you would want to be treated; or you might be adhering to *virtue ethics* with the person that you want to be being a kind, generous person. You might consider the principle of *fairness*, avoiding prejudice or bias in decision making; or you might argue that without food the children are at risk and emphasize the principle of the primacy of the children's needs (UNICEF 2024).

What might explain the social workers who see no dilemma in this situation because they *always do not* offer support? Consistency, again, but a less common stance, we might suppose, and one that stems from beliefs that might be associated with the political right, of libertarianism, a greater good interpreted as safeguarding limited funds and encouraging independence.

We might also consider that both kinds of social worker – those who *always do* and those who *always do not* are *rule utilitarians* though in diametrically opposing directions. Indeed, a procedural approach (always the same response) can be a reaction to the sense of arbitrariness of the social worker who assesses the situation purely on its merits, with the risks of bias as noted earlier in the chapter. It can also become an example of *convenience ethics*, if the decision is always the same, whether thumbs up or down, there is no time needed ('wasted' in some people's estimation) to weigh the situation.

However, for some social workers, there is a decision to be made on the back of a dilemma: a practical one of how to assess the risks in the situation. Ethically speaking, this is a *casuist* approach, a weighing of circumstances case by case, facing each family's request on its particular merits and taking into account all stakeholders' views, from the extent of the family's immediate needs, to the size of the overall budget from which their funds will be taken, to society's responsibility to care and/or to set boundaries.

Fabius falls into the *casuist* camp. He wants to assess the situation and come to an informed decision. He is aware that this will take him longer than a Yes/No rules-based decision, but he feels that he has to balance the agency's limited funds with the risks to the children.

2 How might Fabius decide whether to give the family assistance?

Fabius gathers information. He shares the information with his peers and they reflect on it together. They agree that the balance of decision is close, a difficult call, and decide to discuss it with their manager.

Make yourself a balance sheet: what factors would suggest the payment should be made? What factors would suggest not? Think of your balance sheet as a pair of weighing scales and keep adding factors to one side or the other to keep them in balance. Make the decision difficult for yourself – learning comes from ambiguity and balance, not when it is obvious what you should do.

3 Would Fabius benefit from using a decision-making framework?

This in itself could be considered a practice dilemma. The choice to use or not use a framework may be based on his experience and confidence but also his preferred practice style: if his dominant style is *activist*, he may prefer to head straight in; but if his preferred style tends to *reflector*, he may prefer to spend time thinking the decision through first, so a framework may be helpful for him (Honey and Mumford 1992).

Try applying Reamer's (2024) framework outlined above. Reflecting on this will give you insight into your own skills and areas for development.

Fabius himself decides to use Barsky's (2019) framework of ethical decision making. Even if takes a bit more time, he feels that it will be a better, more ethical decision, whilst also enabling him to demonstrate defensible decision making.

Identify the ethical issue

The first step is to clarify the ethical problem and what decision is required to be made. At this stage, you should identify all the people with a stake in the situation and gather all perspectives to identify what the dilemma is. This might often involve not just the service users, but also involved family, friends, or carers. It requires understanding of the relevant legislation and agency policy and procedures. However, it should also take account of personal and professional values and the relevant Codes of Ethics. You should also establish the facts and identify opinions, so that you have a clearer understanding of the dilemma. This should lead to the development of open questions to be answered in relation to the ethical dilemma.

Fabius asks open questions with Amy to understand her perspective and develops a working relationship with her by showing her respect and empathizing with her situation. However, he feels that he is not quite getting the full picture. He uses his professionally curiosity to discover that the family live in abject poverty, that Amy is a proud woman who has been trying to survive on food banks and limited income (even further reduced due to benefit changes). She is mortified that she needs to ask for help. He assesses the risks as being that the family having exhausted all avenues of support and their strengths as a resilience to survive on little.

Is there even an ethical dilemma here?

Consider how you feel about this: do you feel that she should receive the support as the family are clearly in need, or do you believe that service users' stories need to be verified?

After meeting with Amy, Fabius continues to identify the ethical issue by checking the case notes and finds that when previous financial assistance has been provided, that Amy has later admitted that she spent the money on drugs.

How does this impact the ethical dilemma?

Would this be different if she had later admitted that she spent the money on alcohol, a more socially acceptable drug?

You may feel that *what* Amy spends her money on shifts the ethical issue and may also feel that track record demonstrates the degree of future integrity. Equally, you may feel that there is still no ethical issue, the past is in the past and you need to consider the children's current needs. When considering Maslow's (1943) hierarchy of need, food is one of the basic physiological needs that must be met before any others can be addressed, and therefore that the principle ethical issue is that Amy might not meet her children's basic needs if she were to spend it on anything other than food.

What if she spent the money on heating instead of food?

Here you might consider that this is also a basic need, but she lied to the social worker, would that lie impact your identification of an ethical issue?

What if she spent it on phone data rather than food?

In contemporary society, considering the big picture, digital poverty can be added to the hierarchy of need as meeting both safety and belonging, so technically above the need for food, so consider again if it impacts the identification of an ethical issue.

2 Determine appropriate help

The second step is to develop an understanding of the appropriate people to be involved in the decision-making process. Barsky (2019) states that collaborative decision making enhances outcomes, and so it is beneficial. Here a Koehnian (1994) perspective on professionalism is recalled, locating the importance of working with the person with lived experience and their family, rather than excluding them and assuming that your supervisor or co-worker's expertise is more valuable.

However, this stage is also about identifying the right person for the job, so that where specialist advice is required ensuring that it is identified and sought – for example, engaging the teacher, drugs worker, or legal expert – to become involved in the decision-making process.

Fabius is aware of Amy's perspective: she would not have asked for help if she were not desperate; and he accesses the procedure. However, he reminds himself that Barsky advocated a collaborative decision-making process and asks colleagues for their perspective in the team room. He is given a response by an *always do* social worker and an *always do not* one and so remains unclear about the impact on his decision.

Does this help at all?

It may not give Fabius an answer, but it does assist in his thinking, as he is clearer on both perspectives, moving him closer to a decision.

However, a colleague overhears the discussion and chooses to offer their practice wisdom: information based on practice and experience rather than an evidence-based knowledge (Doel 2023: 170). This is often an excellent source for informed decision making, but it is important to remember that validation and verification of the source needs to be considered. They tell Fabius that they know the family and share their opinion that Amy's uncle can afford to give them this money rather than relying on the state. They provide 'local knowledge' that the uncle has the nickname 'Deliveroo' as he often sends food parcels to family members in need.

- Does this mean that appropriate help could be sourced elsewhere?
- Does this change the ethical issue considered above?

- Do you feel that the state should intervene as Amy may get support from her uncle, but is in need right now?
- The ethical issue becomes what constitutes *appropriate help*, is it the service for whom you work or is the family's local networks?

Whilst you will consider this in the context of your own country's or region's social policy and legislative context and service provision's procedures, it can be helpful here to consider the recent shift in the UK to a stronger emphasis on family support in decision making (Samuel 2024).

Should the decision be delayed whilst family members' perspectives are sought to develop greater understanding of appropriate help?

Should the decision be made today, but this be applied to future support to the family?

3 Think critically

The third stage is to critically reflect on the situation. Barsky (2019) recommends a mindmap that identifies a plethora of responses to the ethical dilemma. This then facilitates a process of evaluating the strengths and weaknesses of each option so that you can determine the best solution. This can be undertaken using a range of ethical lenses:

- *Justice*, considering how all involved can be treated fairly;
- *Rights based*, considering how all involved people's rights can be respected;
- *Utilitarian*, considering a solution that will provide the most good and least harm for as many stakeholders as possible;
- *Common good*, considering a solution that most benefits the community rather than the individual;
- *Virtue*, considering your personal and professional values and ethical perspective and the Code Of Ethics, and
- *Duty of care*, empathically considering the impact on the relationships within the situations.

Killick and Taylor (2024) recommend to first agree a goal with the service users, before considering options to achieve the goal.

We return to the original discussion with Amy, where Fabius had assessed that the family had exhausted all avenues of support. However, this has been supplemented with further information that has made the situation more enigmatic.

Fabius makes a mental mindmap and quickly weighs up the decision to give or not to give the financial support. However, he also weighs this up from different ethical perspectives:

- *Justice*: he feels that in order to ensure justice and treat Amy fairly, that he should provide the payment;
- *Rights based*: he has listened to Amy, accessed procedures and heard different perspectives in the team room and feels that he is balancing risks and rights in providing the payment;
- *Utilitarian*: he feels that providing the payment will support Amy and her children and that a one-off payment will not be detrimental to the agency;
- *Common good*: this is the only ethical stance that is contrary to his other ethical perspectives. He is aware that reliance on payments can be deemed contrary to a functional society, but he counters this with a social value of social justice for all in society, not just the whole;
- *Virtue*: he consults his Code of Ethics which align with his personal and professional ethics, that Amy needs the payment to ensure that her family are not placed at risk for the weekend, and
- *Duty of care*: he feels that providing the payment will provide respect and value to Amy and may engage her to work with services next week to assess if her family's situation can be enhanced in the longer term.

Overall, Fabius determines that the ethical decision is that Amy should be provided with the support.

4 Manage conflict

The fourth stage is the one where problem solving occurs, and your role may change from facilitator to mediator and advocate to ensure that all involved accept the identified and agreed solution.

Fabius presents his conclusion to the manager and advocates for Amy. As he has clearly critically reflected and come to an informed decision, the manager (who is usually an '*always do not*' person) agrees the payment. However, the manager states that it can only be in the form of a local supermarket voucher and will state exactly what Amy can and cannot buy.

Fabius feels that vouchers take away Amy's right to choose and that empowering her with the right to make an unwise decision should be facilitated. He advocates that they should take account of Amy's frequent use of food banks and show her respect through money to enable her to have a freedom of shopping. The manager reminds Fabius that they are a children's service and that, whilst they recognize that food bought would also be shared by the parents, the payment is to ensure the children's basic needs for food are met.

- Whose rights are paramount here?
- Do you feel that cash is an appropriate payment method, or do you feel that a shop voucher or provision of food is more appropriate?
- Does Fabius have the right to determine how he provides support?
- How far can Fabius argue with a line manager?

In any decision-making process, there will be different views and competing needs that need to be considered. It is here that negotiation and compromise skills are employed: whilst the manager is an '*always do not*', the compromise reached is that they will provide support but that it must be in the form of a voucher.

5 Plan and implement the decision

The fifth stage is where collaboratively you determine who is doing what to resolve the problem and implement the decision.

Fabius returns to talk to Amy and is anxious about sharing his manager's decision that he will provide support, but that it will be in vouchers.

Do you feel that his anxiety about sharing this with Amy informed his responses here? Or is he transferring his values and views to assuming how Amy will feel and what she will want?

He is surprised, and a little relieved, to realize that Amy is grateful for anything and happily accepts his proposal. However, she then asks if a different supermarket could be provided. Amy goes on to share that when she shops at the named supermarket, that drug dealers stand outside and demand to take the voucher from her. She reflects that this would put her at risk and begs for a specific supermarket voucher to be provided.

How would you respond to this request?

Would it change your decision making if it you knew that changing vouchers is an arduous and slow task when you know that the relevant admin person is currently walking towards their car as they have a weekend away booked?

Here Fabius suddenly must consider competing needs: does the need to ensure Amy is safe beat his need to be kind to a colleague who he knows works hard and, if he is honest, looks after him well but may withdraw this treatment on such a request? For example, does the greatest good count as himself and his colleague, or Amy and the children? Or does he throw his hands in the air and say, I have argued and resolved the problem, this has to be enough? Or does he simply reflect that it would be unethical to ignore new information at this stage just because a decision had already been made? Fabius returns again to the earlier stages of the ethical decision-making framework, where he identifies that thinking critically enables him to manage the conflict.

Can you think of any ethically located solutions to this problem?

Fabius talks to Amy further, where he is open and honest that getting new vouchers is tricky as the office is closing now and they identify a solution that whilst not ideal results in Amy feeling heard and supported. This person-centred approach further engages Amy, and she agrees to visit Fabius the following week to enable a fuller assessment to be made.

It is important to recognize that as social workers, we may not always be able to make the preferred decision or meet everyone's wishes and needs, but the use of a framework shows the informed and ethical decision making which can in turn engage for future practice.

6 Evaluate and follow up

The sixth and final stage is the evaluation of the outcome, which includes identifying strengths that the person with lived experience has used and/or developed so that they are able to transfer them for use in future challenges. It also includes reflection on the cause of the problem and if wider challenges to issues of social justice should be made to work towards preventing or reducing future dilemmas, a 'lessons learnt' approach. Killick and Taylor (2024) remind us that looking back with hindsight and new information is not helpful in terms of blame and defensive social work, but can be helpful to enhance our own future practice. The task-centred model also emphasizes the importance of workers and services users reviewing their work together in order for them *both* to learn from the experience and enhance future encounters and decision making (Marsh and Doel 2005).

O'Sullivan (2010) suggests that a sound decision is one where processes have been followed correctly (but what is 'correctly'?) and an effective decision is one where the outcome is optimal, so evaluation can be dependent on the evaluation criteria. A final ethical thought relates to whom the success is measured. Is it for the person themselves? In which case, it may have very different criteria than if measured against nationally set performance criteria.

Fabius was able to support the change of supermarket voucher and Amy visits the following week, which enables an assessment to be initiated. The recommended support plan, which is developed in partnership with Amy, empowers her to access a free nursery place for Sam, which is it is hoped will stimulate social interaction. In addition, Fabius suggests to Amy that she might join a local women's group that he can recommend. It aims to enhance members' self-confidence and self-esteem and can provide social support for Amy and her family. This ultimately leads to Amy being supported to join a Women's Rights Group, that she hopes will increase social awareness of poverty and enable her to support other families and mums in similar situations. As a result, Fabius no longer needs to be involved, but feels that Amy has made a significant difference to the family's well-being, and she feels safe to ask for aid if she needs it in the future.

If Fabius had not supported the family and worked collaboratively with them to make these decisions, a preventative approach would not have been taken and the family's situation could have deteriorated. The extra time taken was not, then, 'wasted'.

Did Fabius have a moral obligation to support Amy?

Was the long-term benefit of supporting Amy worth the short-term risk of misuse of financial support?

It is always important to be reminded that there is seldom a definitive right or wrong – discounting clear examples of abuse and safety – yet how comprehensively do you interrogate *other* possibilities with *philosophic scepticism*? To what extent do you rely on something you might call your intuition, without being explicit about this? Practice wisdom and intuition should not be discounted, but instead the basis for the intuition ought to be interrogated and embraced to enable sense making that informs decision making (Sicora et al. 2021).

Guidance from codes, standards and principles

The IFSW (2018) Global Statement of Ethical Principles declares:

> 5. Promoting the Right to Participation
>
> Social workers work toward building the self-esteem and capabilities of people, promoting their full involvement and participation in all aspects of decisions and actions that affect their lives.

This same Statement also reinforces the importance of defensible decision-making:

> 9.7 Decisions should always be informed by empirical evidence; practice wisdom; and ethical, legal, and cultural considerations. Social workers must be prepared to be transparent about the reasons for their decisions.
>
> 9.8 … Social workers and their employing bodies foster and engage in debate to facilitate ethically informed decisions.

The British Social Work Code of Ethics (BASW 2021) states that:

> Social workers should recognise that people using social work services have the right to take risks and should enable them to identify and manage potential and actual risk, while seeking to ensure that their behaviour does not harm themselves or other people.
>
> Social workers should support people to reach informed decisions about their lives and promote their autonomy and independence, provided this does not conflict with their safety or with the rights of others. Social workers should only take actions that interfere with peoples' civil or legal rights if it is ethically, professionally and legally justifiable.

Ethical decision making is a fundamental requirement of every Code of Ethics, and Australia's (AASW 2020: 11) has a whole section dedicated to decision making that can be helpful to consider.

The social work profession acknowledges that ethical dilemmas may arise when a social worker will make a choice between alternative courses of action, each of which is supported by moral considerations and each of which may result in an outcome that is, in some way, undesirable. Noting that all ethical decision making occurs within the context of managing power relationships, ethical decision making is the systematic, reflective process by which such dilemmas can be resolved.

Ethical decision making can be complex. It requires time for critical reflection and will involve all those with an interest in the outcome of the decision. Social workers will be aware of their own worldview, moral, cultural, historical, political, religious, spiritual, societal and professional values and biases and the possible influence of these on their professional judgements.

There are a number of general principles that guide sound, rigorous and reflective decision making, including:

- having comprehensive and as relevant information as possible on the matter about which a decision is being made
- observing appropriate confidentiality and duty of care requirements
- identifying the risks and benefits to each of the parties affected by the decision
- documenting the issues considered and the decision-making process and outcomes.

In pursuing ethical outcomes social workers will be able to:

- articulate their decision-making process
- demonstrate clearly the factors considered
- provide justifications to make themselves accountable for their decisions.

Conclusion

This chapter has discussed decision making in an ethical context. We have considered the idea of risk as an important component in many decisions taken by social workers, both in severity and frequency. We have reflected on the impact of the risk on the individual and the people and community around them. We asserted that weighing the risks of *omission* against those of *commission* can help allay an aversion to taking risks, common in social work as in other professions. The chapter illustrated the importance of avoiding convenience and short-cuts in decision making, by working participatively with service users and colleagues within an ethical framework that helps make explicit the ethical foundations of the work. This same framework can nurture defensible decision making.

Think further about ...

... a situation in which you were conflicted about the right decision to make:

- Did you have an intuition about what the right decision was?
- How readily did you expand on this gut feeling to explore other possibilities?
- Did you consult with others (both those involved and anyone who wasn't involved) to understand their perspectives?
- If you came to a decision, with hindsight do you think it was the right one (or perhaps we should say the best one available in the circumstances)?
- If not, what other decision would you now take? Would you make your decision in a different manner?

Ethical dilemmas with twelve people

Angie McLaughlin (Escher's *Relativity*, sometimes known as 'the Enigma')

I had been qualified just three years when I donated Escher's Enigma to the 'Social Work in 40 Objects' project. Prior to this I had worked in the social care sector for around ten years. My experience includes working with older people, children and families, young homeless people in supported accommodation, forensic learning disability, and adult learning disabilities, all in Scotland. I enjoy problem solving, I embrace change, being a creative and dynamic thinker who likes to think outside the box.

Further reading

Barsky, A. (2019), *Ethics and Values in Social Work: An Integrated Approach for f Comprehensive Curriculum*, New York: Oxford University Press. This second edition reviews and updates the originally presented model of ethical decision making.

Killick, C. and Taylor, B. (2024), *Assessment, Risk in Decision Making in Social Work*, London: Sage.

Parrott, L. (2014), *Values and Ethics in Social Work Practice*, London: Learning Matters. Chapter 4 on being accountable, and Chapter 5 on managing risk, are good chapters to access.

Reamer, F. (2024), *Social Work Values and Ethics*, New York: Columbia University Press.

8

Rules, disobedience and whistleblowing

Introduction

The social work mission to challenge oppression and fight for social justice creates ethical dilemmas in terms of the social worker's role as an agency employee and member of an established profession, working within a system that is inherently oppressive. This is especially important since the ascendance of neo-liberal policies, such as austerity, culture wars and 'poor-blaming', are a direct challenge to core social work values. The climate crisis also poses challenges that are germane to social work. This chapter explores the tensions and dilemmas created by these competing tenets, offering a better understanding about how and why rules might be disobeyed.

Ethical dilemmas in twelve objects

Yellow star

> English social work educator Jo chose the *Yellow star* as a symbol of the Holocaust and a stark reminder of the risk of how 'caring' professions, including social work, can become caught up in ideological frameworks that serve only to breach fundamental human rights. Jo reminds herself that the profession's roots are deeply uncomfortable, from a Victorian ideological and moralizing discourse about who is deemed 'deserving' and 'undeserving', and the influence of the eugenics movement, with concerns about 'lunatics' and the 'feeble-minded' breeding. In Nazi Germany, social workers were required (alongside other professionals like social pedagogues) to submit documents to court detailing 'concerns' they had about children and young people, namely those seen as delinquent, disabled, mentally ill, or not racially

pure. Social workers and other caring professions also worked in institutions, where the killing of those with disabilities, mental ill health and those of so-called 'impure ethnicity' was commonplace. It would be easy to think such practices were in the past, but in Australia, Aborigine children as late as 1970 were forcibly removed from their homes and placed with white families.

Jo reminds us, through the *Yellow Star*, of the moral responsibility to rebel, and also of the great moral courage needed to do so.

Think about ...

... A family shares that they live in poverty despite claiming all available benefits, so they are now also working part time. You are aware that this is against benefit claiming rules and that your agency has a policy that you must report them.

Is there a dilemma? If so, what is the nature of your dilemma? And what do you do?

What might make a difference to the nature of your dilemma? Consider your responses if you see that they each have the latest iPhone (that you can't afford), or you observe that the children are given what there is whilst the parents do without.

Duty to obey; duty to rebel

Is it ever right to disobey the law and does it make a difference whether the society is totalitarian or democratic? In some political philosophies, the duty to civic obedience is dependent on the government's commitment to promoting the 'common good' (Plamenatz 1938); and the corollary is a duty to overthrow a government that is not promoting the common good. However, it is far from straightforward to decide what is 'common' or 'good' about the 'common good'. The seventeenth-century philosopher John Locke explored the nature of *tacit* consent; that, for instance, by travelling in a country you tacitly accept its laws. By working in an agency, do you tacitly accept their policies? Political obligations are not absolute: for example, the Nuremberg defence ('I was only following orders') was disallowed:

Our ultimate obligation to obey the law is a moral obligation and not a legal obligation. It cannot be a legal obligation, for this would lead to an infinite regress – since legal obligations derive from laws, there would have to be a law that says we must obey the law. What obligation would there then be to obey this law? If legal obligation, then there would have to be another law ... and so on. If there is any obligation to obey the law it must, ultimately, be a *moral* obligation.

(Singer 1973: 3, emphasis added)

'Just Stop Oil' activists would claim that the severity of the climate crisis justifies direct acts of disruption and law-breaking; indeed, they might look back to social activists like the Suffragettes who broke laws and suffered imprisonment, yet are now regarded as heroic.

So, it is no longer 'why ought I to obey the law?', but 'when ought I obey the law?' and 'when do I have an obligation *not* to obey the law?'

Protocols, procedures and policies

Utilitarians' views of obligation are merely forward-facing, in terms of what has the best consequences, whereas most people see obligations as having some backward-looking relevance to previous undertakings that might or might not have been given.

Rule utilitarians develop general rules to govern behaviour designed to produce happiness for the greatest number of people using rule-of-thumb principles. Protocols are the playing fields on which action takes place and, from an ethical standpoint, we ought to ask whether the field is level and designed to arrive at a fair decision? The fairness of protocols is often called into question. For instance, the protocol for UK General Elections can see a political party obtain a large majority of seats in Parliament on a minority of the vote.

A problem with protocols is the potential to replace ethical thinking with a step-by-step routine in which the players turn to a manual for instruction, rather than reflecting with their 'wise professionals' (see Chapter 1). Moreover, the manual is often not capable of the precision needed for each specific case. The danger is that social work loses its moral agency to procedural expertise – the power that accrues to procedural expertise lies with the rule-makers rather than the profession. Balancing the benefits of routines that provide stability and standardization of service, with the discretion and flexibility of professional autonomy, is a challenge to any public service, social work in particular. Policies forged in the heat of a public inquiry can have unforeseen consequences that outweigh the initial benefits; for example, a 'no touch' policy can result in an impoverishment of relationships with long-term harm to the quality of social care.

Moral panics

A moral panic is an 'exaggerated or misdirected public concern, anxiety, fear, or anger over a perceived threat to social order' (Krinsky 2015: 1); a panic often occurs after a so-called 'moral crusade' launched by moral entrepreneurs guarding the moral barricades runs out of control (Goode and Ben-Yehuda 2009: 67). There are countless historical examples of moral panics that can take hold of large groups of people, even whole nations, usually aimed at a minority group: Catholics in the Popish Plot (1670s), Jews in the French Dreyfus Affair (1890s), people with HIV-AIDS (1980s), young people in general in the ecstasy scares of the 1990s, and, more recently, migrants. Moral panics, like economic bubbles, are a regular if volatile feature of social life, flaring and collapsing with no apparent rhyme nor reason. In recent years, the flames of moral panic have been fanned by the notion of 'culture wars'.

Social workers work with the kinds of marginalized groups that are targeted in moral panics. Should social workers use their position to stand in solidarity with threatened minorities? How resistant is the profession to policies that increase inequality and deepen poverty in democratic regimes?

Moral panics are often seen as unfathomable episodes, but perhaps they tell us something of more fundamental significance. Clapton et al. (2013: 197) suggest that 'many of the anxieties that beset social work are best understood as moral panics.' Indeed, a social worker can become caught up in a moral crusade not as a bystander but as an active moral agent, such as during the 1980s hunt for 'satanic cults' in the UK, when a belief that devil-worshipping covens were ritually abusing children had devastating consequences. Social workers 'rescued' large numbers of children from their families even though evidence for organized cults was never established. The panic which followed the 'Baby P' case in England led to an enormous spike in referrals and large increases in care order applications.

What ethical position, then, ought social workers pursue in the face of moral panics? There are at least two aspects that pose a dilemma for social workers. The first is whether to play an active part in opposing the specific victimization of the targeted group. Social work's moral mission to work for social justice and to empower marginalized groups would suggest that the profession ought to bring its authority to bear against the moral panic. For instance, the city of Sheffield mobilized as a 'City of Sanctuary' against the moral panic confronting the Syrian, Afghan and Iraqi migrants attempting to cross into Europe. Social media, often accused of feeding these panics, in fact enable 'folk devils' (Cohen 1972) to defend, build allies and hit back. Choice, competition and fragmentation of the contemporary media can mobilize opposition to moral panic. The question for social workers is how actively they ought to be involved in City of Sanctuary-type movements and should they be involved specifically *as* social workers? We would argue yes: international migration is a significant social issue and social work must respond. Any *social* issue is a *social* work concern. The clue is in our name.

The big picture

A further dilemma for social workers is more nuanced and concerns social work's role as a critical commentator on social policy and social anxieties (Ungar 2001). Social work has a duty to be aware of the subtext of social phenomena such as moral panics. What obligation, then, has social work in exposing this subtext and acting on it? As an example, this is the gist of the message that 'greets' the traveller on boarding many trains in the UK:

> *24 hour CCTV is in operation for your safety and security. Please read the safety notices displayed in the carriages. Do not leave luggage unattended. If you see any suspicious behaviour please report it to the on-board staff immediately.*

This is not, in itself, a moral crusade nor yet a panic, but it does provide the steady background hum of threat and fear from which panics arise. The public space of the train is presented as one of danger, not sociability; other people are potential killers, not providers of social protection. What purpose does this constant drone of fear serve? Sociologists like Cohen (1971) have pointed to its role as a diversion to sustain the status quo. Whilst the populace trembles at the remote chance of death by terrorism, the actual deaths by inequality are

> ignored ('Stark inequality [in the UK] kills more than 200,000 people early a year'). Some social workers might see this kind of knowledge as 'political' and therefore not part of professional practice. However, if your service user's life is cut short by 'stark inequality' and your profession's statement of ethics requires you to promote social justice, how can it be right not to act on this knowledge? No longer, therefore, the dilemma of *to do or not to do*, but the challenge of *how*?

Can a moral panic ever be used for good? Would the greater good justify the moral panic? For instance, a moral panic around the dangers of people with schizophrenia killing random people in the community might bring about better resources for mental health services. However, moral panics cast people as non-virtuous – untrustworthy, dangerous, or vulnerable to harm – in order to invoke fear. The deliberate stirring of fear is wrong, so it is difficult to cast the engineering of a moral panic as a 'good', whatever the motivation and the outcome. Practically speaking, from a *consequentialist* point of view, it is impossible to predict the direction and destructiveness of a moral panic.

Sometimes fear and anxiety in the social realm is backed up by 'evidence' from the scientific sphere:

> One day we hear about the danger of mercury, and run to throw out cans of tuna fish from our shelves; the next day the food to shun may be butter, which our grandparents considered the acme of wholesomeness; then we have to scrub the lead paint from our walls. Today the danger lurks in the phosphates in our favourite detergent; tomorrow the finger points to insecticides, which were hailed a few years ago as saviours of millions from hunger and disease. The threats of death, insanity and – somehow even more fearsome – cancer lurk in all we eat or touch.
>
> (Rabinowitch 1972: 5)

This paragraph, written fifty years ago, is surprisingly current.

Moral guardians

The creation of a moral panic may be unethical, but can a moral crusade ever be justified and, if so, ought social workers lead them? In more general terms, might social workers be seen as moral guardians of society?

A social work community that is under-confident, searching for its identity and in need of a guiding light might be well served by a notion of moral guardianship. In which case, what aspects of social work and public policy should be 'moralized'? Social work's predecessors used public anxieties over dangers to children in late Victorian England to create the NSPCC and the Children's Charter (Clapton et al. 2013). Should social workers campaign about the dangers of internet grooming of children and assume a position of moral guardianship of those children?

If we were to consult the wise professionals, they would likely be cautious about moralizing a particular aspect of social work or public policy. To claim moral guardianship is to assume the high ground and, too often, 'pride comes before a fall.' It is one thing to aspire to moral guardianship and another to claim it publicly and openly. This might be an instructive example of honesty not being a good; by the honest act of claiming moral guardianship, it is lost.

In Chapter 1, we were casual about the distinctions between ethics, values and morals, but perhaps those differences now reveal their significance. A strong, transparent position on ethics – that social workers should work to the highest ethical standard – does not provoke the qualms that arise from claiming the moral high ground or moralizing practice. The moral high ground suggests superiority, and moral crusades invariably require their corollary, their own 'folk devils'. Can a moral crusade on behalf of children at risk of being groomed through internet sites escape demonizing the perpetrators? A crusade needs enemies as well as a mission.

The wise professionals would respond to a moral panic the way they have been responding to the dilemmas in this book. They would stand to the side of the panic with the aim of seeing it for what it is, its subtext and its social meaning. They would defend the victims of the moral panic, even if at the same time they would condemn the actions of some groups that are the target of the panic (such as paedophiles). They would make allies of individuals and groups who similarly seek to douse moral panics, such as the City-of-Sanctuary movement mentioned earlier. The wise professionals would want social workers to be active in these social movements *as* social workers; in this way, social work begins to reshape its own identity, makes itself known to its public, and takes hold of its own future.

Moral luck

The journeys we have taken through the stories and dilemmas in this book have been predicated on a belief in *agency* – the power of individuals and groups to make choices that, in turn, make changes. It is a very human need to know that we can and do make a difference and that there are patterns in events that improve our choices with experience.

However, in the equation between intended cause and random outcome, it is likely that people overestimate the significance of the former. The tipping point, the *one-way-or-the-other*ness of events is less under our control than we like to allow. More often than we care to admit, whether there is a good or poor ethical result is dependent on 'moral luck' (Williams 1981). Let us consider examples from social work to consider four kinds of moral luck identified by Nagel (1979).

Resultant luck

Two social workers each want the best for their service user: one makes a decision to support the service user to remain in their own home, and the service user thrives happily; the other makes the same decision with their service user, who suffers unhappily. Like Kant's (1784) 'jewel shining by itself' – is a good act a good act by virtue of the good intention, untouched by any notion of moral luck? In the moral world as it exists, rather than the one Kant would have for us, the social workers will likely be judged differently dependent on the outcomes. Again, if both social workers uncharacteristically completed the wrong paperwork, only the one with the poor outcome is likely to face blame.

Circumstantial luck

Two social workers qualify together with distinction from the same course: one takes up employment in a well-run, well-resourced agency and has the opportunity to perform exemplary practice; the other is employed by an organization which has covert corrupt practices in which the worker becomes unknowingly complicit and this results in the loss of their professional licence. Had that worker been employed in the same agency as their fellow graduate, they would have practised exemplary social work.

Is it easier to be ethically minded, in your professional practice as well as your personal living, if you are fortunate enough to live in a corner of the globe where there is plenty?

Constitutive luck

Who we are and the kind of person we are is largely a matter of luck: so, one social worker is considered courageous in their actions whilst another is perceived as cowardly. Why would the actions of the first social worker be judged morally superior to the latter, given that the first has the good luck to be blessed with courage and the latter has not?

Causal luck

The 'problem' of *free will* centres on just how much control we really do have over our actions. If free will is necessary for us to be considered morally responsible for our actions, then the question of how much free will we can exercise is important when weighing moral responsibility. How responsible any social worker can be judged is circumscribed by how much they were able to exercise free will.

In short, people's actions depend much more on moral luck than we admit, yet we are inclined to assess the moral quality of their actions as though moral luck were not a factor (Nelkin 2013). Many people accept that the link between actions and consequences are hard to pin down, but at least we can and ought to be judged on our intentions; yet to what extent does the nature of intention (benevolent, spiteful, etc.) depend on moral luck? Nagel (1979: 68) came to the conclusion that 'in a sense the problem has no solution.' In the end, we are left with a series of events 'which can be deplored or celebrated, but not blamed or praised'. Perhaps this morally neutral world would be an improvement on the rush to judgement, which is more characteristic of the moral world that has been constructed.

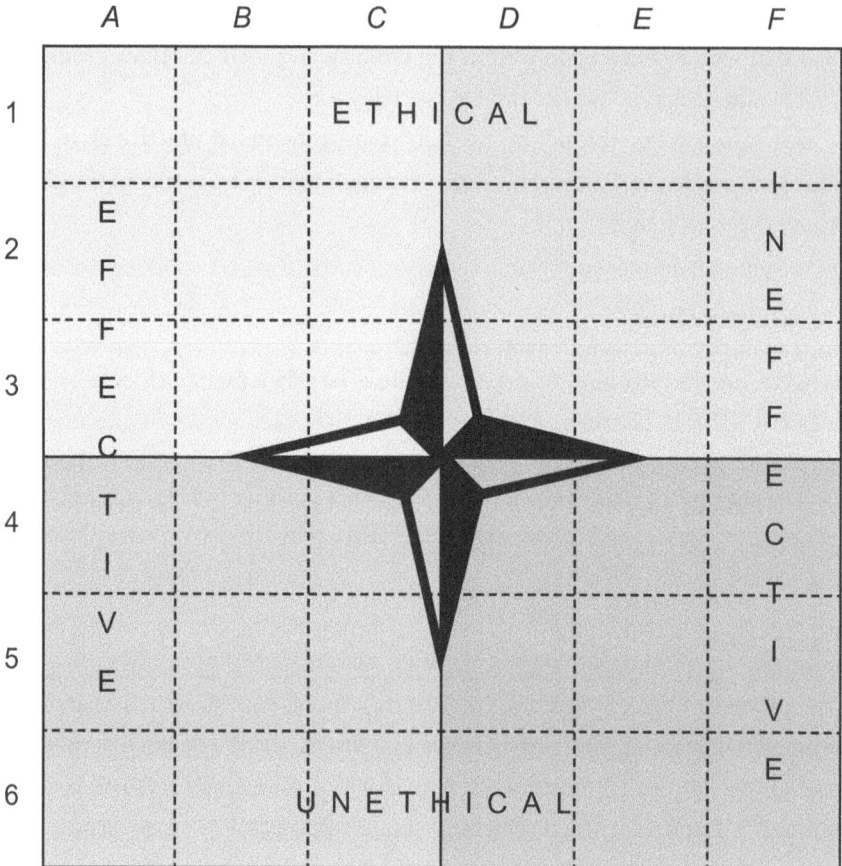

Figure 8.1 Moral compass, adapted from Doel 2010: 97.

Moral compass

A problem might not have a solution, as Nagel (1979) suggested but, still, there might be *better* ways of looking at a problem. Is it possible, then, to devise the equivalent of a compass to guide us around the moral landscape, a way of tracking towards 'ethical north'? (see the object in Chapter 2).

Above is a grid (Figure 8.1) charting two dimensions of practice. The north–south axis is the degree to which an action or situation is ethical; west–east is the degree to which it is effective. Of course, both of these terms – 'ethical' and 'effective' – beg exploration. We hope that the dilemmas in this book have helped with the ethical dimension and, undoubtedly, the effectiveness axis is not divorced from the ethical (can ineffective practice be ethical?) The professional compass aims to help its owner delve into these two dimensions in order to achieve a greater understanding of the possible choices. Wherever on the grid you decide your particular dilemma lands, the aim is to reflect on how you might edge towards the A1 square – to a position that is both more ethical and more effective. What would that look like? Think of the moral compass as the wise professionals in a board game format.

Try using the compass with some of the dilemmas in this book and some of your own.

Whistleblowing

In 2014, Margaret Hodge wrote:

> You only have to look at my Committee's work on everything from GP out of hours services to tax avoidance to see how vital whistleblowers are to protecting taxpayers' money. It is extremely worrying, therefore, that half of workers stay silent about misconduct, possibly because they fear what will happen if they speak out. Government must do more to support those workers.
>
> (Committee of Public Accounts 2014)

Whistleblowing is one form of disobedience, the term given to the exposé of poor behaviour or even wrongdoing, most often associated with an individual or small group revealing what they believe to be poor practices, sometimes even wholesale corruption, in an organization (Ellis 2001; Hunt 1998). Despite legal protection in some countries, such as the UK's Public Interest Disclosure Act 1998 and charities like Public Concern at Work, the act of whistleblowing is likely to provoke strong feelings and many dilemmas, ethical and practical. It is the anticipation of these feelings that can make it difficult and inhibit it from being enacted.

Another perspective on whistleblowing is as a form of disclosure; it is concerned with the handling of information, but in circumstances that are much more exposing than most of the dilemmas of self-disclosure. There are close links, too, with the dilemmas of confidentiality though, again, the whistleblower's stakes are usually higher.

Loyalty is a significant but complex notion with regard to whistleblowing. If the in-group is a collection of people or an organization in whom much energy and trust has been invested, or on whom there is dependency for emotional warmth, safety, a salary, etc., the motivation to ignore its wrongdoings or to try to explain them in the best light is strong: *you don't bite the hand that feeds you*. A *virtuous* social worker is a loyal one. But loyal to what?

Conformity is when individuals feel strong peer pressure (groupthink), even coercion, to alter their beliefs and behaviour to bring them in line with group or organizational thinking (Janis 1972; Turner and Pratkanis 1998). Social experiments such as Asch (1952) exposed this process, in which the pressure of primed group members, 'confederates', all giving the same incorrect answer led the single genuine participant to give the same incorrect answer in three out of four cases. It takes a strong mind to point out that rather than the Emperor wearing *new* clothes, he isn't actually wearing *any* clothes.

Conformity can lead to complicity or to subversive rebellion, still an act of conformity and as such rendering the person submissive. The subversive act allows the retention of some pride but, because it is unknown to the powerful decision makers, it has no impact on that decision. Cumulative acts of subversion can overturn established powers, but covert nonconformity is essentially a *pragmatic* rather than an ethical response.

Referees blow their whistles to indicate a foul, or the game's end, and the term 'whistleblowing' nicely conveys this sense of *'enough is enough'*. Whistleblowing is usually a definitive and purposeful act taken after deliberation, rather than in a moment's rush. Referees have the advantage of clear rules and they are the recognized authority on the pitch, with sanctions for those who do not respect this authority. However, when a worker cries foul, the rules are often not self-evident. There might be a whistleblowing procedure in the agency's protocols, but the process that has led to the whistle being blown is typically heavy with *doubt*: is there an obvious explanation for the practice that you think is unacceptable, something that you are 'missing'? Are your standards unrealistic in this context? How about your own practice – will it stand up to scrutiny? Self-doubt comes from the worry that once the spotlight is switched on, it will shine not on the practices of others but on your own, that it will be you in the line of fire, rather than those who feel they have been sensible in keeping quiet.

We have advocated *philosophic doubt* throughout this book as a way to connect with your wise professionals, but it is this professional predisposition to subject a hypothesis to critical examination, to doubt it, that can also inhibit blowing the whistle, an act which requires supreme confidence. We will consider *consequentialism* (deciding the ethics of whistleblowing by weighing the consequences) in the later example dilemma.

Decisions about the ethics of whistleblowing are rarely made amongst people with equal power (see Chapter 4 for more discussion about power). In the most well-publicized incidents of whistleblowing – the individual ('a maverick') against the organization – it is always clear who has the most power. The whistleblower is not powerless, nor is the organization against which the whistle is blown all-powerful; often it is the loss of prestige and reputation that most motivates agencies to fear whistleblowing and, reasonably, to defend itself from mistaken or mischievous whistleblowing, aware of the common belief that *there's no smoke without fire*. Power ought not enter the ethical equation in whistleblowing, but it does, with an expectation that the most powerful side will win. Ought the judgement about the likelihood of success be a factor in deciding whether to blow the whistle?

One of the more interesting questions around whistleblowing is *why?* We are instinctively drawn to need to understand the *motives* that lie behind the act of whistleblowing. If an individual is set to gain from an act of whistleblowing, should that influence our judgement of the ethical balance?

> The French government decided to renovate *La Santé*, a notorious Paris prison, after the publication of a whistleblowing diary written over seven years by the prison's chief medical officer. This triggered a parliamentary enquiry. The whistleblower received death threats after the publication of her diaries and has been barred from entering the building ever since.
> (www.theguardian.com/world/2014/jul/21/france
> -la-sante-prison-paris-renovation)

If the whistleblower in the *La Santé* case received royalties from the sales of her diaries (there is no suggestion that she did), would this make any difference to the validity of the claims of her whistleblowing? Does the fact that there were seven years between the commencement of the diaries and the public revelation of their content affect our confidence? Ought the moral character of the whistleblower be relevant to our judgement about the strength of her claims?

The motivation for a whistleblower might be 'to do good'. Interestingly, the term 'do-gooder' has become a term of reproach, even abuse, often preceded by 'so-called'. Is the whistleblower a 'so-called do-gooder' whose self-righteousness leads them to conclude that they are in the right when all around them are wrong? Does the whistleblower have a strongly *deontological* sense of the right thing to do and a duty to do the right thing? The logic that has driven to a disclosure is likely to have been *defeasible*, that is, contingent on various and varying factors, open to refutation and interpretation with an 'all things being equal' conclusion, the best move at this point. The experiences from *La Santé* (earlier) and elsewhere suggest that time passes before individuals decide that something is wrong and even longer before they take action.

It seems that whistleblowers need these characteristics: a loyalty to ideals and standards, a willingness not to conform and confidence to stand alone, an ability to move from doubt to decision and to act on the basis of (strong) probability, courage, a motivation other than self-interest, and a strong internal locus of power.

The media's concoction of the whistleblower invariably lauds or demonizes the individual – think Edward Snowden and Julian Assange – in tune with the general obsession with individuals as heroes or traitors, as mavericks against the system, when the reality is that successful challenges to bad practice are more likely to be achieved through collective action.

Ethical dilemma 8: Stan and the files

Stan is a student social worker on a bachelor's degree course. He has just completed his first placement in a criminal justice setting. He is a confident, able thirty-year-old with personal experiences of caring. He passed the placement, but subsequently he was found to have extensive printouts of service user e-files in his possession. Stan had thought the service user was being discriminated against by the agency and had taken the materials to put before a solicitor. He had taken these at the end of the placement with the permission of the service user, but not the agency. The materials contained a range of personal details including third-party information, such as the home address of the judge in the case (unlikely, it's true, but this actually happened.)

The case involved contested contact (sometimes called 'family time') and custody. Stan's service user was the father, a working-class man receiving benefits, whilst the mother was an affluent professional. Stan argued that it is his responsibility to promote the child's rights to parental contact and his service user's well-being and rights were greater than his responsibility to follow agency procedures. Stan listed a number of instances of alleged discrimination (against himself whilst on placement) and how he had attempted to intervene on the service user's part, but had been told he was wrong, or over-attached, or had deficient assessment skills.

The Fitness to Practise protocol

What are the protocols to balance the rights and wrongs in Stan's case? The programme responsible for the governance of social work education has a protocol to convene a panel to decide a student's professional suitability, their *fitness to practise* (SWE 2019). This covers areas that lie outside practice competence or academic ability and relate to behaviours and attitudes, integrity and values. The Fitness to Practise panel is composed of three or four members drawn from inside and outside the school of social work and includes a representative from an agency that provides social work placements but has not been involved with the student. The members are drawn from a regular pool of people who have training to prepare them for this role. Before it convenes, the panel reads a report prepared by an investigating group and Stan's report in response. The leader of the investigating group and Stan (accompanied by his student representative) are present at the panel to answer questions.

In our fictional reconstruction of Stan's case the usual members have been replaced by a panel of moral philosophers:

- Rose takes a *duty-based* approach with some aspects of *rule utilitarianism*.

- Selina follows the *consequentialist* ethical tradition.
- Spencer is a *virtue ethicist*.
- Rajesh is a feminist moral philosopher who focuses on the *ethics of care*.

[You might want to refresh your knowledge of moral philosophy by turning to pp. 24–31 and the Glossary (p. 209), but it is possible to make sense of what follows without this refresher.]

Beneath the explicit questions that the panel puts to Stan, there are implicit questions – subtext – that relate to their moral view of the world.

As the members convene, Rajesh has a question for the panel itself:

1 Who ought to be involved in judging the rights and wrongs of Stan's actions?
Subtext: 'What is our moral authority?'

Rajesh is concerned about the relational aspects of the case and, before any deliberations can take place, he is keen to explore who gets the right to make the decision about Stan's future. Rajesh does not have the power to change the protocols themselves, but he does have the authority to question whether they are likely to be experienced as fair, especially by Stan, and whether there are other parties who ought to be included.

He notes that service users in general have an interest in the outcome but they are not represented. Although the particular service users in this case might find a voice via the investigating group's report, is Rajesh right to question whether there ought to be a service user educator on the panel to provide the perspective of an expert by experience? If Rajesh feels strongly that the composition of the panel is flawed, ought he continue to participate in it?

The panel, including Rajesh, decide to continue. Stan, his student representative and the leader of the investigating team are invited in. Spencer has a question for Stan:

2 'What was your motivation for these actions?'
Subtext: 'Is Stan a good person?'

Spencer is trying to establish what kind of person Stan is – is he 'good'? If he has acted from good intentions, this makes his actions good, no matter their consequences. Let us imagine responses from three different Stans:

STAN.01	STAN.02	STAN.03
I was keen to see justice done and though I knew it was taking a risk with my own future and career, it was the right thing to do. If I'd known there were other personal details in the case files, I would have tried to remove those.	I felt sorry for the father who was powerless against the education and wealth of the mother. I felt sorry for the kid, too, who really wanted to see his dad but had been cowed by his mother into denying it.	There was no way I was going to get my way other than to take the files. I was angry the way I was being ignored and disrespected by the agency, so I was left with no alternative but to take the matter into my own hands.

How might the different Stan's responses influence Spencer's reflections on whether Stan is a good person? Spencer asks a supplementary question:

3 'How were you found out?'
Subtext: 'Again, is Stan a "good" person?'

STAN.01	STAN.02	STAN.03
Well, I wasn't 'found out' as such. I'd been having qualms and wanted reassurance that I had done the right thing, so I mentioned it to my tutor, expecting to get confirmation, well, hoping – but it turned out rather differently.	I didn't know how I could get the files back to the agency, hadn't really thought about that and I knew I couldn't keep them indefinitely, so I had a word with Jean from Admin and she said she was sorry but she'd have to tell Sunia, the team leader.	A couple of pints loosened my tongue and I guess you could say I was bragging to a friend about 'beating the system' and she told her tutor – 'snitched' is one word for it. As you can imagine, we're not talking.

Spencer and the other panel members are building a picture of Stan, essentially a moral picture of what kind of person they judge him to be. This is particularly important for Spencer because of his allegiance to *virtue ethics*, and also for Rajesh to an extent. We learn that Stan.03 has a friend who felt it was her duty to tell someone what she knew. Does this give us a clue about what she thinks about Stan.03 and ought this to colour our view?

Is Spencer's question a valid one – ought it to make a difference, the way the situation was revealed?

Selina has a question for Stan:

4 Whose 'good' were your actions promoting?
Subtext: 'Have Stan's actions added to the greater good?'

In whose interests is Stan acting? In one sense, he is acting in the father's interests, but perhaps he is acting in his own, to the extent that he is satisfying his own desires (for justice, etc.):

STAN.01	STAN.02	STAN.03
I'd like to say I was acting in the common good, in that my actions weren't just about helping the father to get a fair hearing and proper redress, but there's a broader benefit, a bit abstract, in opposing discriminatory practices.	I took this risk solely for the father and the son, so it was for their good. I felt they were getting a raw deal and this seemed to be the only way to get some justice for them.	I didn't think of it in terms of whose 'good', only that I'd have found it difficult to live with myself if I'd not done something about the situation. It's about having a sense of pride.

Developing this theme, Selina now poses the question as harm and asks Stan:

5 'Has anyone been harmed by your actions?'
Subtext: 'Have Stan's actions subtracted from the greater good?'

STAN.01	STAN.02	STAN.03
I can see that my practice teacher and the team leader at the agency might feel harmed, in the sense of being undermined. That might harm trust between the uni and the agency but I sincerely hope that isn't the case. It wasn't my intent.	Although I knew that the mother would be opposed, I don't think my actions did her any harm and there was certainly no ill intended towards her. In the long run, I hope she sees it's not caused harm, in fact, been good, for her son.	The only possible harm is to myself if this panel decides to remove me from the course. No one else has been harmed by my actions as far as I can see.

Selina wonders whether Stan's actions might be taken as an example that would in the greater scale of things prove harmful; for instance, if it sets an example whereby other students start to act on their own moral judgement and ignore agency protocols. This worries her.

Rose has been sitting with her arms folded, looking unimpressed. She challenges Stan directly:

6 What gives you the right to steal from the agency?
Subtext: 'Where does Stan believe that his duty lies?'

By accepting a placement, has Stan tacitly agreed to the agency's protocols and practices – what Singer (1973: 49) calls 'quasi-consent'? Singer uses the example of a group of people going to the pub and, in turn, buying a round of drinks. When it comes to the last round, the last person is expected to buy the round. He or she has not consented to this, but has given tacit consent by accepting the drinks in the previous rounds. Has Stan tacitly agreed to the agency's practices? Or, by not consenting explicitly, is he excused? Did the service user consent to the removal of the file? Acquiescence is not consent.

Stan might re-phrase words from Thoreau's (1866) essay on *Civil Disobedience* – 'we should be men [*sic*] first and subjects afterwards' – into 'we should be people first and professionals afterwards.' Thoreau's essay continues, 'It is not desirable to cultivate a respect for the law, so much as for the right [thing to do].'

STAN.01	STAN.02	STAN.03
I definitely don't see it as stealing as I had the intent to return them, so they were being borrowed. I'd like to see what I did as in the tradition of the Dissenters. I see disobedience as a plea for reconsideration.	Well, whose notes are they anyway? I don't know the legal position, but morally surely they are the service user's and he has a right to them, even though it should have been him who made the request. But he consented to their removal.	The only alternative to acquiescence was dissent. Under duress, I took the files as it was the only course of action left to me by that time. I didn't have any personal gain so I don't see how it could be described as theft. There was no financial gain involved.

Rose reminds Stan that there is a requirement in the agency's code of practice to protect service users' records. The student rep comes in: 'Yes, but he *was* protecting them. He didn't damage them, he returned them intact. From his point of view, he was protecting the records not just as physical objects but as what they are supposed to do, their *purpose*. At the very most, he was borrowing them and he considers they belonged to the client.'

Rose has another question:

7 'In a few years time, if and when you are a team leader and a student on placement decides to take extensive case files home, what would you do about it?'
Subtext: 'Do you understand the principle of universalizability?' (In other words, will this same principle apply then?)

If Stan is acting from a moral principle, then he must accept that if and when he becomes a team manager and one of the students on placement in his team takes a case file home because they consider that the service user has been discriminated against, Stan must accept this as a legitimate act. To do otherwise means that Stan is acting from a selfish principle, not a moral one.

Spencer feels that Stan was acting with *beneficence* because he was seeking to do good and he sees this is a critical factor in determining his culpability or not. Rajesh agrees that, at the very least, Stan was acting from a principle of *non-maleficence*, that is, seeking not to do harm.

STAN.01	STAN.02	STAN.03
It would be hypocritical of me to act against the student, given that I have done exactly the same now as a student. I'd want to remind myself of that.	In principle, yes, but I'd like to be the judge of that situation in the future – you can't just take a file, there has to be a good reason for it, and I would want to be the judge of that.	I would look on the act sympathetically, but it's hard to know what kind of person I will be then and how my different role will make me act.

Rajesh has a question for Stan:

8 Did you agonize much about this decision?
Subtext: 'Did you act from an ethic of care?'

STAN.01	STAN.02	STAN.03
Yes, I thought long and hard. I wanted to talk about it rather than coming to the decision on my own, but I didn't want to put anyone in that difficult position. In the end, it was my care for the father's situation that pushed me into the decision.	I didn't see it as a dilemma as such – more a risk, in that I was risking my place on the course. I knew it was the right thing to do, so to that extent it wasn't a dilemma. Any agonizing was whether I could afford the risk and what might happen to me.	It was the obvious thing to do. All other doors had been shut in my face by the attitude of the agency and my practice teacher. I was painted into a corner with no alternative, so I'd say no, I didn't agonize over it.

Ought it to make a difference what other avenues Stan tried, what other paths he had considered, before he decided on this course of action? Rajesh's question aims at understanding Stan's own abilities with moral reasoning, not just whether he acts from an ethics of care.

Before they leave, the student rep, a student of moral philosophy, puts her question to the panel:

9 Isn't Stan's action an example of good practice, as the UK regulatory bodies for social work – Social Work England, Scottish Social Services Council, Care and Social Services Inspectorate (Wales) and Regulation and Quality Improvement Authority (Northern Ireland) – allows confidentiality to be overridden if there is a risk to a service user? Subtext: 'He acted from an ethics of care.'

In the deliberations following the departure of Stan, his rep and the investigating leader, Selina asks the panel:

10 'Has anyone been harmed by Stan's actions?'

Rose is firm in her belief that Stan's duty was to follow the rules and that personal judgement is not central to morality. Selina believes his example might ultimately be harmful if students start to think they can act on their own will. Spencer wants to know what Stan wanted to do with the printed-out notes and, indeed, what he did do with them; on balance, he thinks the action was a good one. Rajesh feels that at least one of the 'Stans' made a good case for disobedience in this case.

The panel members are finding it difficult to come to any agreement and the emotional temperature is rising. Rajesh asks:

11 Ought our emotional responses be a factor in our determinations?

With initial resistance from the other panel members, they agree to an honest statement of how Stan's case makes them feel:

- Rose feels *anger* with what she sees as Stan's arrogance and, as he is one of her students, *embarrassment* by his actions.
- Selina feels *sympathy* for Stan's actions, but *frustration* with the way he has conducted himself.

- Spencer feels *uncertainty* about Stan and *confusion* about his actions.
- Rajesh feels *compassion* for Stan's situation and *solidarity* with his actions.

The four members of the panel have found it problematic to come to an agreement, not because of a disagreement about the facts, but because they focus on different aspects of his case. We will not necessarily change an individual's moral reasoning, but it will always help if they can each understand the basis for the disagreements.

Spencer, using a hypothetical formulation similar to Rose's Question 7, asks the panel to consider:

12 If we were the service user, the father, what would we have wanted Stan to have done?

Finally, the four members sum up their positions regarding Stan's actions:

Rose: I can say that I wouldn't want him in my agency, as I couldn't trust him to act responsibly.

Selina: On balance, I think more good than harm came out of Stan's actions. However, I'm not convinced about how much he troubled to weigh these goods.

Spencer: In all his other work, he has acted with probity and integrity and the service users have given positive feedback about his work. It's possible that he over-identified with the father in this one case, but he is a student and he is learning.

Rajesh: There is some evidence that he acted from a duty of care and he acted out of concern.

13 Does it make a difference how the story is told and re-told?

'Did you hear about the student who tried to whistleblow discriminatory practice and was nearly chucked off the course?'

'Did you hear about the student who printed off some files and stole them from his placement?'

Rightly or wrongly, in the age of the Inquiry (Stanley and Manthorpe 2004) and the viral nature of social media (see Chapter 9), the recounting of events has a significant impact. Will social media see Stan as a hero who fought for the rights of his service users and now finds himself victimized for his moral stance? Or will he be cast as a maverick, a chancer, even a bit of an idiot, who is untrustworthy and egocentric, acting on his own estimation of right and wrong without thinking of the consequences?

When moral philosophers get together, they know what kinds of difference to expect, but when social workers meet as a panel, they can be puzzled by these differences and attribute them to other factors, such as culture, coming from 'outside', cussedness, etc. So, it is important to try and tease out the subtext of questions and statements. It does not bring automatic harmony, but it will illuminate why there might not be harmony and, therefore, bring about better communication, resulting in better decisions.

The outcome

The outcome at the panel was that one member voted to remove Stan from the course and two to give him leave to stay on the course, and one abstained. Stan's progress depended upon him preparing an additional reflective assignment on the topic of confidentiality and whistleblowing.

Guidance from codes, standards and principles

The Australian code of ethics states:

> Social workers will appropriately challenge, and/or report, and/or work to improve, policies, procedures, practices and service provisions, continuing with a bulleted list to describe possible contingencies, and concludes that social workers are advised to ascertain what, if any, whistleblower protection options are provided in their state or territory.
>
> (AASW 2020)

The ninth of BASW's seventeen ethical principles reads:

> *Being prepared to whistleblow*
> Social workers should be prepared to report bad practice using all available channels including complaints procedures and if necessary use public interest disclosure legislation and whistleblowing guidelines.
>
> (BASW 2021)

Of all the national codes of ethics available in English, Norway's goes into the most detail about unacceptable conditions and how whistleblowing should be undertaken, including protection from retaliation for whistleblowers (FOKUS 2009: 15–16).

Increasingly, organizations have whistleblowing policies, probably including the agency where Stan worked. In the UK, there are criteria for whistleblowing policies at a national level (National Audit Office 2014a, 2014b). However, there can be a 'startling disconnect' between policies and practices (the phrase used by a report from Margaret Hodge's 2014 public accounts committee in relation to the generally good whistleblowing policies of the UK government and the contrasting way they are operated in practice).

Conclusion

This chapter has demonstrated how the wisest of professionals look for, and find, an abundance of paths. So, it is important to position yourself so that you give yourself choices about which paths of moral reasoning you take. When the dilemma is framed in one set of terms (for example, the *consequentialist* approach of Selina in *Stan and the files*), there is a tendency to follow unquestioningly that same path of moral reasoning. However, because the first signpost is pointed in that direction, it is not necessarily the *right* signpost to follow. The more powerful people or institutions in any situation are likely to set the signpost down the path that most favours them, rather than to offer a choice of paths; individual professionals might from time to time need to disregard (disobey) these signposts if they are to act ethically.

Think further about …

… the following situations and decide whether you think there are grounds to whistleblow.

How seriously would you view the situation about which you have become aware and would you expect to take action?

Your response might be 'it depends'. If so, what does it depend on?

1. A social worker becomes engaged to a person who until two months ago was a service user of the agency that employs the social worker.
2. A social worker over-claims mileage allowance in order to fund a group for services users.
3. A student social worker refuses to work with a same-sex couple because it contravenes their religious beliefs.
4. A social worker invites a service user to pray with them.
5. At the request of a twenty-five-year-old man who has lost use of his arms, the social worker masturbates him.
6. A social worker appears on local television with a service user to publicize the service user's plight.
7. A student social worker gives advice about where a service user can purchase cannabis.
8. A social worker becomes aware that a colleague has borrowed money from a service user.
9. A social worker qualified in the use of hypnosis uses hypnosis with a service user
10. A social worker invites a homeless service user back to their home to stay.
11. A student social worker discusses the details of a service user (without using their name), to complain about their practice teacher to other friends on Facebook.
12. A social worker is working as a dancer in a lap-dancing club in their own time. (Adapted from Doel et al. 2010)

Ethical dilemmas with twelve people

Jo Finch (Yellow star)

It was inevitable I would become a social worker, as there was no other profession where I could 'live' my politics. I grew up in a single-parent family at a time when there was stigma and shame about living in a so-called 'broken family'. I knew from an early age, my family was far from broken and I was acutely aware of the neighbours' (particularly men's) condescending attitudes towards my mum, constantly offering her unasked-for 'advice'. My brother and I felt under scrutiny and any normal childhood naughtiness was viewed as proof of our inevitable slide towards delinquency due to living in a single-parent family. Social work still battles with its conflicting roles, i.e. that of care vs control, something that cannot be resolved, but should promote constant reflection. As for those neighbours who expected my brother and I to fail … we proved you all wrong.

Further reading

Banks, S. (2024), 'Pandemic Ethics and Beyond: Creating Space for Virtues in the Social Professions', *Nursing Ethics*, 31(1): 28–38.

Bee, M. (2016), 'Social Workers Are Tied Up by Rules – Is it Time to Start Disobeying Them?', *Community Care*. https://www.communitycare.co.uk/2016/04/28/social-workers-tied-rules-time-start-disobeying/

Social Work England (2025), 'Whistleblowing Policy'. https://www.socialworkengland.org.uk/about/policies-and-procedures/whistleblowing-policy/#:~:text=You%20can%20whistleblow%20to%20Social%20Work%20England,as%20a%20reasonable%20adjustment%20for%20your%20needs)

9

Use of technology in social work practice

Introduction

This chapter considers the use of technology in social work practice and the ethical challenges presented by remote communication, social media and artificial intelligence. Technological developments bring with them new ethical dilemmas, yet many of the same challenges remain evident. In common with other chapters, a detailed case example will help to expose the dilemmas and guide you through the various ethical choices you may have to make.

Ethical dilemmas in twelve objects

Selfie

> The *Unity Group*, a Scottish group of services users state:
>
> Social work is about people and it is about involvement. We took a photograph of ourselves at one of our meetings, and not everyone was there. This made us think about the limitations of a 'snapshot' to represent who we are and what we do. We think that it is important for *Unity*, and also for social work, to recognize the missing voices and try to draw these in.

Think about …

… Would you use your placement or work laptop for personal tasks?

Is there a dilemma? If so, what is the nature of your dilemma? And what do you do?

What might make a difference to the nature of your dilemma? Consider whether this is an inappropriate use of work equipment. It can be argued that it costs the agency nothing and enables you to have a personal laptop without cost. However, compare it to the issue of using the photocopier for personal use (most agencies state that this is a firm no, as there is a cost attached), or taking a note pad home for personal use (considered theft?). Are these comparisons valid? Do they have an impact on what you consider to be ethically appropriate in terms of the work laptop?

Technology etiquette

Let us consider the etiquette that surrounds the use of technology in social work. As a social worker, the work mobile phone is never far from our hand, as we now seem to need to be instantly contactable. Many social workers take a laptop or tablet to complete forms with service users *in situ* rather than after a visit. However useful these adaptations are, they can also be a source of distraction. Turning emails off while on a Teams call enables us to focus on the service user; not answering texts or calls on a home visit respects the service user. If you are expecting a personal call about an ongoing emergency that might come while talking to a service user, ensure that they know beforehand and, if the phone rings randomly, reject the call and mute your phone while apologizing for the interruption.

An excellent coping strategy that students with a learning disability learn at university is to record lectures, seminars and tutorials so that they can listen again, to help their recall. Yet when working with service users, this may not be an ethical approach, as some people may feel that society has become too surveillance-orientated and not feel able to be open and honest if recorded. Obviously, you can only do this with permission, but is it right at all that you have a recording and they don't?

It can be helpful to reflect if there are other ways that you can ensure that technology works to enhance your practice, whilst not detracting from service users' needs.

Remote communication

Remote communication constitutes telephone calls, emails, texts, messages through social media, video calls and even letters. The use of written communication, remote communication and technology instead of face-to-face (in person) communication requires different skills (Beesley et al. 2024), but many of the ethical considerations remain the same. It can be helpful to consider:

- For whose benefit are you using remote communication?
- What are the practical benefits of remote communication?
- What are the potential pitfalls to using remote communication?

Remote communication is without doubt a time-saving method of working with service users, professionals and colleagues, as it reduces the need to commute to the office, drive to a service user's home, or get the bus to a meeting. Indeed, being able to send a regular, quick 'check-in' message or update can be very engaging within a working relationship. Furthermore, service users may feel that they connect more easily with you without a perceived intrusion into their home and feel more confident in talking without you in the room. Of course, your professional curiosity (see Chapter 7) may be piqued if someone is reluctant to admit you to their house, but an automatic assumption of risk should not be made. A 2020 study by the University of Sydney found that the benefits of technology-driven practice were:

- Isolated service user groups (geographically or through disability) are more easily engaged through digital forums;
- Creative and flexible resources can be initiated that engage service users in different ways, and
- Increased inter-professional communication.

An obvious problem in the use of remote communication is when a service user is unfamiliar with or cannot afford the required technology. Whilst we can boost skills and confidence in IT, it is important that as social workers we are aware of the impact of poverty on the way social work is accessed. Furthermore, though platforms for professional remote communication are required to be secure, it is often difficult to determine if a service user is alone or with a supportive, or unsupportive, friend/family member, as it is more difficult to take in the whole situation remotely. Reamer and Siegel (2021) suggest that we need to remind service users of the challenges of confidentiality with technology.

Messaging by text, email, or social media platforms permits a different type of relationship between social workers and service users, perhaps a more casual connection. It could make service users feel able to cancel appointments rather more readily as they don't have to tell the social worker to their face. It also means that service users can contact social workers out-of-hours and may be disappointed by the lack of immediate response that they would expect in remote communication with friends or family. Finally, written messages are open to misinterpretation as they lack nuance, especially if abbreviated language is used.

If we return to the initial question we posed, 'For whose benefit are you using remote communication?', then we are forced to weigh up all participants' perspectives and consider our response from an ethical stance: is this particular communication better undertaken in person or remotely, to ensure that the service users' needs are being met to the best of your ability? Pink et al. (2020) suggest that a hybrid combination of remote and face-to-face communication enables the benefits of both methods to be accessed and minimizes the concerns.

An interesting dilemma arises around whether to give some service users access to you via your work mobile phone, yet denying it to others. What do you consider to be the *ethical* dimension to this dilemma, and how do you try to avoid using an unthinking *convenience ethics* as your response? What criteria would you use to decide which service users are in and which are out, and would this be fair?

Social media

Social media is the use of online platforms that enable the sharing of information, ideas, opinions and/or images through virtual networks and communities. The *Selfie* ethical dilemma (one of the twelve objects above), is an important way to promote a positive service provision. Social media enables social influencers to promote themselves and products, it facilitates people to provide an account of day-to-day life, and it can unite people across the globe with a collective identity. As such, social media has become a powerful medium in contemporary society.

> ## The big picture
>
> Sadly, abuse on social media platforms appears to be prolific, with hate crimes being committed regularly and many companies prioritizing profit above ethical stance in response.
>
> Dylan Mulvaney is a social media personality who shared her gender transformation story and has millions of followers on social media sites such as Tik Tok and Instagram. She is an actor and social influencer, and campaigns for trans rights. If one weighed Plato's virtues of wisdom, courage, temperance and justice, one might argue that her fight for social justice is both ethical and admirable.
>
> However, her promoting a beer in a video created outrage in 2023: a right-wing, conservative boycott of the product for being too liberal *and* a LGBTQ+ boycott for the beer company not defending Dylan and trans rights, despite historical links supporting Pride. All of this saw the beer sales fall. Furthermore, Dylan suffered significant transphobic abuse including physical, verbal and written attacks as a result of the public outcry against her promoting a beer.
>
> Public figures have seen her as 'fair game' to vilify for their own self-promotion and furtherment. However, it should not be forgotten that social media can also challenge and respond to hate crime. Arguably, Lady Gaga posing with Dylan for 2024 International Women's Day on social media was a powerful response to the transphobic abuse of the previous year.
>
> The question is, does the nature of social media amplify these dilemmas (and, indeed, possibilities) to such an extent that they have become qualitatively different? Does the extent and immediacy with which information can be shared, and the number of people who can be linked at the click of a keypad, change the nature of the ethical dilemmas associated with social media?

An important factor is the psychology of electronic communication. In theory, there is a much greater opportunity to mediate thoughts and feelings through written words as they can be deleted and replaced, reflected on before they are dispatched, in a way that the spoken word, once articulated, cannot; yet the distance created by the typed word seems to disinhibit some people. This can lead to venting and vitriol being shared in ways unmediated by verbal and non-verbal communication (Beesley et al. 2024). As a social worker, you may experience being the target of hate crime on social media, and if this is the case, whilst Lady Gaga may not stand with you in a video, do talk to your tutor or line manager for support.

Interestingly, Reamer and Siegel (2021) reflect that the use of technology in adoption has parallels with catfishing (using a false identity to attract someone to engage with the person behind the technology), where online profiles require further scrutiny to ensure authenticity. Whilst this financial and emotional abuse for imagined babies may be more prevalent in private adoption arrangements that are less common in British social work, it still highlights the importance of scrutiny by social workers into new service provision.

On the other hand, social media offer pools of information and support for service users that are an alternative to formal, professional sources. Professionals can be sceptical about the credibility and simplicity of online information, but it is often presented in more accessible ways, by people for people in similar circumstances. Individuals who are marginalized in the physical world can move to the centres of virtual worlds, and can seek and find others in similar situations, even though these others exist at distance. They might work through dilemmas in their own lives with the assistance of this greater resource. In Chapter 5, we supported the notion of self-determination, and online self-help is one route to success in this endeavour.

Social workers' personal use of social media

The ethical dilemmas for social workers arising from social media are not dissimilar to those we have considered in previous chapters. The issues and strategies that we discussed concerning values, professionalism, power, working relationships and decision making are equally pertinent to virtual encounters and social media. You should be aware of your personal and professional value base when posting on social media, as well as your understanding of professionalism and an awareness of the power that your post may create or hold, so that you are accountable for your choices and actions. You should reflect on the appropriateness of relationships on social media and the nature of these relationships, and you should be aware of the dangers of breaching confidentiality on public access social media platforms and forums.

First, we might ask whether social workers *ought* to engage with social media. One aspect of the little-discussed ethical issues posed by social media is the fact that they are profit-making commercial companies. To open accounts with them, even if they are free, is to support their practices and the values they espouse. Should you to enquire after the tax and employment policies of the social media companies to which you subscribe, and would this affect your willingness to support them? What is their policy on taking down inappropriate posts? Ought you to consider their track record on protecting and supporting people who are in vulnerable situations?

It is a given that most social workers have personal social media accounts. However, there needs to be a separation of the personal and the professional to enable you to maintain your emotional well-being, and we would advocate never to follow or be followed by a service user on a personal social media account. This relates to a much broader notion of the social distance/proximity between social workers and the people they work with (see Chapter 6). You might consider a false name on personal social media sites and ensure your privacy settings are turned on to protect you from being followed by a service user. By virtue of the fact that you are the social worker for a service user, your mutual relationship has become different – in summary, a professional one.

You should also consider the ethical dilemma of being 'friends' on social media with a colleague. Factors that might influence your decision whether to do this are:

- Differences and similarities (in age, gender, professional background, length of time in the team, etc.).
- Power and seniority (is the colleague a peer, a supervisor, a supervisee?).
- Local culture (are other people in the team or agency 'friends'?).
- Policy (does the agency have a policy about colleagues' relationships?).
- Consequences and meaning (what do you think the colleague's invitation signifies? Is it to monitor you or befriend you?).
- Attraction.
- Your personal feelings about privacy versus your desire not to be left out.
- Trust (is this someone who will share their data and yours in a responsible manner?).

But remember, if they follow you, they can see what you are up to!

Irrespective of sharing with colleagues or not, you need to consider your social media content. The American code of ethics expects social workers to 'uphold the profession's values and to act ethically. Principles and standards must be applied by individuals of good character who discern moral questions and, in good faith, seek to make reliable ethical judgments' (NASW 2021).

An interesting ethical dilemma to consider is what makes 'good character'?

- Can you make jokes about race with friends?
- Can you follow a racist social influencer?
- Can you join an online group advocating chemical treatment for gays?

The response to each of these is clearly no. Clearly, there are some behaviours that are unequivocally wrong, such as following and liking racist propaganda or a racist joke, which further promotes their beliefs when it is so clearly against social work values. However, other suggestions are less clear. Ethical dilemmas will arise where your value-base is challenged. For example:

> Your long-time friend makes a racist joke on social media. This is not their norm and you are shocked by it. Do you:
>
> *Unfriend them on social media?*
>
> If this was a someone without personal ties to you, this is often a socially acceptable recourse: cancel culture (where people who act inappropriately lose followers or contracts) is a powerful way to make your feelings known.
>
> Should this same action be applied to friends?
>
> *Challenge them publicly online?*
>
> Your social work values are clear that social injustice must be tackled in order to change the worldview.
>
> However, you would need to consider how this might impact your relationship with them, do you want to keep the relationship or is that relationship now changing anyway?
>
> Would it impact your wider personal support network if you do or if you do not challenge them?
>
> Can you reflect on a way to do this that is tactful, does not condone racist jokes by challenging it tactfully?

You are considering here how much your professional values impact your personal actions.

Challenge them individually?

This might be online or in person.

It has the advantage of opening a dialogue with a good friend and enables you to explore why from their perspective and put forward your perspective in the hope that they can learn from this awful mistake.

However, does it leave you feeling that you have condoned the racism if you have not called out the inappropriateness of your friend's actions.

Take no action?

Might you reflect that they are your friend and have a right to act as they want to?

You might consider that there may be a good reason, or if it is a one-off, it is ok.

However, not to act is to support racism and not to challenge condones their perspective, which does not align with your social work values.

Your understanding of your own personal and professional values and ethical perspectives will support your response to these questions. Other technology-based ethical dilemmas might include:

- Can you be a social influencer who promotes a brand of vodka and work with people who misuse substances?
- Do you need to ask friends not to post pictures of you online without checking with you first, as their account does not have privacy settings switched on?
- Do you do this before posting pictures of your friends?
- Can you post stories and pictures of a drug-fuelled festival trip?
- Should you post pictures of your children on social media? Is this different in different settings, or if the children are not your own?
- Can you be openly into violent sex in a dating chat room?

You have the right to a private life and to personal choices, but they overlap your professional persona to the extent that, if concerns are raised, you may have to face a *Fitness to Practise* process and the possible consequences. Social media leaves a transparent audit trail and a permanent record, unlike previous forms of social communication, which could be denied and whose provenance was far from clear. Most people have at least one moment or incident in their life that they are happy to have forgotten. Now there is every chance that it will be captured digitally and, worse, endure through digital time. As such, it is even more imperative that an ethical approach to social media and remote communication is observed.

Social workers' professional use of social media

Social media is an excellent communication aid to engage service users. As with remote communication, it can engage isolated people on an informal basis, potentially transforming lives. Remember the quizzes of the pandemic lockdowns? Social care workers have continued to provide social interaction through online social media platforms, and even being able to sit quietly yet remotely working while a service user completes a jigsaw can address social isolation. In addition, setting up information-sharing social media sites keeps people informed of current practice and opportunities.

The University of Sydney (2020) reported that a common concern in using digital technology in social work was the technology's unclear boundaries. It is therefore important to identify your agency's social media procedure:

- Can you have a social media account in your role as a social worker?
- Is there a specific recommended platform?
- Do you set up your own professional account, or are there identified personnel for this task?
- Is your account monitored, and if so by whom?

A useful reflection can be to consider what are the principles that such a policy might be based on and are these principles ethical or practical ones, or both? Many young people communicate primarily through social media platforms, and it is a much better communication method than a rarely used email account, for example. However, with an open access social media site comes a lack of confidentiality and it is important that you do not use this communication strategy to share personal details or confidential information.

- Are there situations in which you might follow a service user on Instagram?
- If so, what are these?

- What would suggest you should not follow a service user?

If you have decided 'yes':

- What ought you to do if you view posts where you are uncertain how 'appropriate' they are?
- What factors might lead you to doubt whether the post is 'inappropriate'?

In order to facilitate communication and maintain working relationships, you would need to consider the nature of their consent:

- Does consent for you to 'follow' implicitly mean that you have consent to read all their posts?
- How do you ensure you have their informed consent, and do you record it or is their accepting you considered consent?
- Is it ethically sound for you use the content of a post as part of your work, for example, an assessment of risk or ability?
- Is that fair if you have not explicitly discussed this with the service user?
- Could it be seen as 'taken out of context'?

It can be helpful to return to the *Selfie* at the start of this chapter to remind us that a social media picture is only a snapshot of people's lives and should be respected as of that moment, and thus may require further assessment before judgement is made.

A different form of professional use of social media is following likeminded professionals. A virtual community of practice (Wenger 1998) can bring professionals together in an online forum around a specific topic of mutual interest and can offer support, advice and information irrespective of geographical location. However, an ethical dilemma is created if you hear an anecdote or comment that you judge to be unethical or unprofessional, and global cultural differences can provoke considerations of *moral relativism*. Deciding what to do when confronted online with opinions or behaviours that you consider questionable requires even more tactful exploration than usual, both because of your exposure to a distant environment, an unfamiliar one, and also because it is more difficult to achieve a nuanced approach in a virtual room. Use your social work communication skills to explore why they have that view? What beliefs underpin it? Can they see a different perspective? The weakening of lines of responsibility brought about by distance, similar to the big picture ethical challenge earlier in this chapter, perhaps explains why so many people protect themselves with insularity and do not feel compelled to challenge hate crime and abuse. Distance can reduce the feeling of duty to confront, and it should be noted that *distance* can be geographical, social, cultural, or professional.

Artificial intelligence (AI)

Artificial intelligence (AI) is an established reality in our lives, from having your favourite take-away suggestions presented to you on your laptop, to smart home technology, we are becoming much more used to the use of technology to support and potentially enhance our everyday lives. However, there is an alternative perspective on artificial intelligence in social work and social work education. At its core is the question: is it cheating?

The use of spell check is long established. Many students with a learning disability are recommended to use apps that enhance their use of grammar. This use of an AI tool to enhance work is not ethically questioned as it is custom and practice for most people: we wrote this book with spell and grammar checks switched on. Universities may ask you at the start of an assignment to state if you have used such technology, which seems a reasonable request given the professional nature of the course.

Let us apply this reasoning to writing a social work report, assessment, or case recording. The use of spell check in a Word document seems reasonable if it is part of your agency or placement provider's IT provision. However, thought should be given to applying an app such as *Grammerly* without consent from your placement provider. Is it considered a safe and secure app in which to place service users' personal and confidential information? Similar problems apply for students who use *Google Translate* (or equivalent) on their phones: are they breaking confidentiality by using an unauthorized device and app; or is the greater good being served by being able to communicate with a person in their language?

At this time of writing, the academic community is debating the ethical basis for use of AI to generate a whole assignment. What is clear is that submitting an assignment straight from AI is cheating and would be considered a breach of academic integrity. It is not your work, so it should not bear your name as author. On a practical rather than an ethical note, as AI assignment writing apps become more elaborate so, too, does AI detection technology, so it is harder to get away with it. That said, there is a debate about the value of using an AI-created assignment as an assignment plan and building your writing and references from it, provisional to you stating that you have done so, of course. However, it is important for social work students to remind themselves that they are undertaking a professional course where integrity and professional honesty is central. Claiming ownership of something that is not yours (the authorship of an assignment) is unambiguously dishonest.

Do the issues differ when writing a social work report, assessment, or case recording? AI is being trialled in English social work departments, with initial findings that using it to generate case notes and transcribe meetings saves time (Koutsounia 2024). For students with a learning disability or where English is not their first language, it was found to be beneficial, but social workers need to proofread to ensure accuracy and appropriateness of the suggested work. Yet this is an unexplored area and calls for ethical regulations remain unmet. In addition, AI does not create empathy, an important social work skill in engaging vulnerable people (Kerr 2023). When creating reports and case notes, we should always remember the importance of empathy as the people whom we are writing about will have access, be it now or in the future, to these documents. Once again, we would re-state the conclusion above: claiming ownership of something that is not yours (the authorship of a recording or professional report) is unambiguously dishonest and is not admissible.

Ethical dilemma 9: The petition

Malik is a social worker in a Multi-Agency Support Team (known as MAST). His speciality is working with families in which a child has a diagnosis of autism. An element of his work is providing support and direct advice to the child's carers, helping them respond to the child and develop strategies that are most likely to meet the child's and the family's particular needs. He gets good results, and he is much liked and appreciated by carers and colleagues.

Malik has been working with Sandra and Danny, whose child Ethan is autistic. They have noticed an improvement in Ethan's behaviour since Malik started to work with them. Sandra and Danny have a website and social media accounts promoting awareness of the support needs of children with autism. They ask Malik to promote the website with other service users, which he is happy to do. However, they also ask him to follow them on his social media accounts and send a request for them to follow Malik, which he feels requires critical thinking on his ethical position. Consider the following questions from an ethical perspective.

1 Do you feel that either following or being followed is acceptable? Is there a difference between the two?

Your agency will have a social media policy, which you should familiarize yourself with. Policies are useful shortcuts that mean you don't have to spend a lot of time explaining yourself or working out whether this circumstance justifies a particular action. Just as a parent might have a policy of no sweets before meal-time, so the agency might have a policy that its workers do not engage in social media friendships with service users. However, from our point of view in the pages of this book, agency policies are example of *convenience ethics* – they 'free' you not to have to think about these issues in any depth, and so give you time for other things. However, framing agency policies as 'taking the car' rather than the heavy duty of a walk, you can also see that there are disadvantages. Your ethical muscles get less use, and are even in danger of atrophy. And who is interrogating the policy to ensure it is ethical in the first place?

So Malik might consider that declining a request may have an impact on his working relationship. A policy is a policy (and he can always consider the ethical imperative to question it – see Chapter 8), and he considers an open and honest explanation for Sandra and Danny is needed, not just a quick 'sorry, I'm not allowed.'

Your response to this dilemma, *to Follow or not to Follow*, could depend on which part of the social work service you work in. For instance, if you work with homeless young people, it may be the only form of communication available to you, though it is always important to check with the employing or placing agency about boundaries to determine what a 'friend' constitutes on social media.

Malik decides to follow and be followed on a professional social media account and accompanies this with a discussion about frequency of communication to regulate expectations and pre-empt unprofessional actions and/or a stressful and irretrievable crossing of boundaries.

Malik has had to cut back hours with carers since one of the MAST team has left and the post is not being filled because of financial cuts. Sandra and Danny start an online petition to raise awareness of the importance of Malik's role, the impact his work has on their well-being and Ethan's progress, the impact the loss of his hours have had on them, and the general support needs of children with autism.

2 Ought Malik to start the online petition as a co-sponsor with Sandra and Danny? Ought Malik to dissuade Sandra and Danny from creating the online petition? If Sandra and Danny start the petition, ought Malik to sign it?

Social media can highlight the permeability of professional relationships and spotlight the potential for promoting social justice. What responsibility does Malik have to himself, the people he works with, his employer and to the values of his profession? Are they aligned or are there conflicts?

It can be helpful here to consider your personal values and ethics. How principled or how pragmatic is your response to the opportunities and demands of the internet? When you receive petitions, how carefully do you scrutinize each one? Do you sign them all? Do you sign none? Do you forward petitions to colleagues, friends, family? Or just some of them and how do you make that decision? Are there any circumstances in which you would forward a petition to a service user?

Different ethical stances will suggest different responses to Malik's dilemmas. A stoical response, where virtue is the discharge of duty and the ultimate good is to know one's role and to fulfil it, would indicate that Malik should do as his employer tells him: follow procedure whatever it may be.

In contrast, a Kantian perspective is that the only motive of genuine moral worth is conscientiousness, a matter of conscience. Malik considers the 'infinite worth' of all persons, so is likely to be moved to support and assist Sandra and Danny. His belief that there is a universal moral equality, that no matter how individuals differ in other ways, they are all equal in respect of their supreme moral importance, leads him to support the carers. In the twentieth century, this belief became enshrined in laws such as the Human Rights Acts.

A *consequentialist* approach is concerned about the possible outcomes of taking or not taking action and wanting to weigh up the pros and cons, perhaps via a formal risk assessment. With this perspective, Malik considers the consequences for Sandra and Danny, himself and his employer; this is a holistic approach, but is Malik giving equal value to the different parties? Ought he give an equal weight?

Ethan, Sandra and Danny's son, sees his parents using social media sites as a norm and joins one himself. He shares a video of himself 'getting cross' with a friend, which goes viral.

3 Is Ethan legally allowed to do this? Does he have the capacity to understand the potential consequences? What could the impact of both positive and negative comments be on him?

Expressing yourself on social media connects you to a larger, more unknown audience than has ever been possible. Previously, only famous people could experience such amplification of themselves; now social media has made a reality of Andy Warhol's '15 minutes of fame'. The human need for attention is exaggerated in some people, and at some developmental stages such as adolescence, and social media affords the potential for almost unlimited attention. Children are especially vulnerable because they do not yet have a fully developed sense of who they are, and they are dependent on the adult world for so many aspects of their lives. The digital age of consent in Europe is 13, but policing it is difficult.

The capacity to understand the consequences is a challenging one for parents and social workers alike. Whilst there may be a legal cut-off, every child is different and as a child nears and passes a legal age limit, parents can be understood to consider their child's individual needs and abilities. However, one can argue that if they are taking this action, then they also have a responsibility to offer support and advice to enable the young person to engage safely.

4 What protections ought to be afforded to minors in the world of social media? How ought the adult world respond to misuse of social media by children?

The parents or carers in a household should monitor and regulate what technology is being used by a child, and ethically, it could be suggested to be a problem for individual families to address. However, an equally valid argument is that society needs to react to such risks and put protective measures in placement to protect vulnerable people, in this case children, in society.

Ironically, Sandra and Danny may have lost sight of Ethan whilst advocating for him, and the social media company has failed in their due diligence to regulate age limits and content. It might also be argued that school could do more to educate young people, and peer pressure would also have influenced Ethan to think that social media is acceptable.

Social work is often at the brunt of these broad social issues with decisions needing to be made in real situations.

Guidance from codes, standards and principles

The IFSW (2018) Global Statement of Ethical Principles makes a clear statement about the ethical use of technology and social media:

> 8.2 Social workers must recognize that the use of digital technology and social media may pose threats to the practice of many ethical standards including but not limited to privacy and confidentiality, conflicts of interest, competence, and documentation and must obtain the necessary knowledge and skills to guard against unethical practice when using technology.

The British Code of Ethics (BASW 2021) states:

> Social workers should recognise that the use of digital technology and social media may impact on ethical practice, including privacy, confidentiality and conflicts of interest. Social workers need to take steps to ensure they have the appropriate knowledge of technology to protect themselves and the people they are working with.

Italy's Code of Ethics (CNOAS 2009) requires social workers to engage in training to ensure that they have the requisite skills to undertake their role, including technological progress. However, the American (NASW 2021) Code of Ethics is more specific and states:

> With growth in the use of communication technology in various aspects of social work practice, social workers need to be aware of the unique challenges that may arise in relation to the maintenance of confidentiality, informed consent, professional boundaries, professional competence, record keeping, and other ethical considerations. In general, all ethical standards in this Code of Ethics are applicable to interactions, relationships, or communications, whether they occur in person or with the use of technology. For the purposes of this Code, "technology-assisted social work services" include any social work services that involve the use of computers, mobile or landline telephones, tablets, video technology, or other electronic or digital technologies; this includes the use of various electronic or digital platforms, such as the Internet, online social media, chat rooms, text messaging, e-mail and emerging digital applications … Social workers should keep apprised of emerging technological developments that may be used in social work practice and how various ethical standards apply to them.

Continuous professional development in relation to technology, remote communication, social media and AI is very important.

Conclusion

We can use the same ethical theories to negotiate technology and social media as we used for other kinds of dilemma in this book. If used with ethical precision, the media can be a great aid, but if used without ethical forethought, it can be dangerous. It is crucial that social workers are competent and qualified to use the technology available to them and to advise service users.

Think further about …

… an online communication in your personal world that you would not wish to be shared in your professional world.

- Why would you not like this cross-over from personal to professional?
- What do you do to ensure that there isn't leakage from one world to the other?

Ethical dilemmas with twelve people

The Unity Group (Selfie)

We, Unity, are the social work service users and carers group at the University of Stirling in Scotland. The group was established in 2005 and is made up of service users, carers, staff from partner agencies, student representatives and university teaching staff. We are involved in a range of teaching sessions on the qualifying social work programmes, and also with other activities like open days and developing case studies for use in selection. We have a newsletter and a website: http://unity.wordpress.stir.ac.uk/

We are developing our involvement in teaching student nurses and we are also involved in events run by Stirling Students' Union, for instance to mark Mental Health Awareness Week and National events like conferences and research projects.

The Scottish Inter-University Service User and Carer Network: https://bettersocialwork.wordpress.com/

Further reading

The area of use of technology in social work practice is evolving rapidly and an independent search is recommended here to access the most up-to-date information and guidance.

BASW (2025), *Generative AI & Social Work Practice Guidance*, London: BASW.

Beesley, P., Watts, M. and Harlow, S. (2024), *Developing Your Communication Skills in Social Work Practice*, London: Sage. Chapter 9 is on remote communication skills.

Kerr, C. (2023), 'In Defence of Human Intelligence (and Fallibility) in Social Work', *Professional Social Work*. https://basw.co.uk/about-social-work/psw-magazine/articles/defence-human-intelligence-and-fallibility-social-work

Koutsounia, A. (2024), 'AI Could Be Time-saving for Social Workers but Needs Regulation, Says Sector Bodies. *Community Care*. www.communitycare.co.uk/2024/10/04/ai-could-be-time-saving-for-social-workers-but-needs-regulation-say-sector-bodies/

Reamer, F. and Siegel, D. (2021), 'Adoption Ethics in a Digital World: Challenges and Best Practices, *Adoption Quarterly*, 24(1): 69–88.

10

Conclusion

This final chapter may be titled 'Conclusion', but at this stage in the book the reader will be aware that *conclusive* is a notion we have reservations about. Many situations in everyday and professional life are far from conclusive, and the wisest professionals are those that continue to ask and refine the questions they use to interrogate each situation.

However, we recognize that at some point a line needs to be drawn and a decision taken – the best one available given what is known at that point. Conclusions are points when we can reflect on the process that has brought us to where we are, and to learn from these reflections so that the next stage of our journey is informed by them.

Objects

We have introduced each chapter with an object drawn from a wider collection of objects donated by various people around the globe, all with diverse perspectives and a shared commitment to social work. An object is a different, perhaps provocative, way to consider the themes that are introduced in each chapter. Focusing on an object provides an oblique perspective that can shake us out of habitual ways of thinking and doing. When we ponder objects in a physical exhibition, we can weave our own stories around the artefact in front of us before reading the side plaque that presents the story behind the object, according to the donor or maker of that object. The same is true of the objects in this book: first, weave your own story around it, and then read the donor's.

It is an experimental approach, viewing ethical dilemmas through the prism of objects, and we hope that these object-stories have worked well for you, perhaps inspiring you to consider an object from your own social work experience that can help tell the story of an ethical dilemma. If so, please visit the website socialworkin40objects.com where you can find out how to join in and donate your own object/story (Doel 2017). If you are interested in the theoretical underpinnings to the use of objects in this manner, see Doel (2019) and Espinoza et al. (2024).

The importance of questions

We have emphasized the significance of asking questions – and seeking how to ask *good* questions. Before you read on, you might take a moment to ponder what constitutes a *good* question. We would suggest that it is one that assists all parties to a better understanding of a situation. So, a pro forma of questions that have been put in order beforehand (a questionnaire) might assist the questioner to gather information, but does it enlighten the respondent? A truly empowering, and therefore ethical, questioning style is one where the questions elicit responses that enlighten everyone in the encounter.

Of course, there are times when questionnaires and other kinds of pro forma documents are necessary to speed up the process of gathering information and to ensure that all the ground is covered, but let us not confuse quantity and rapidity of information with quality and responsiveness. One of the authors remembers being asked by a street researcher to taste a new chocolate bar and to respond to a series of questions about it: not one of these questions addressed the main concern that the chocolate bar was far too sweet and, certainly, there was no question about whether the chocolate used in the manufacture was fair trade.

Unless your opinion is specifically being sought, there is usually greater value in offering questions rather than giving opinions. Even when you are asked directly, such as *what would you do if you were me?*, it is usually better to respond with questions that help people to be their own agent, such as, *rather than me tell you what to do, what would help you feel confident to make your own decision?*

Singularities

In the example dilemmas that illustrate each chapter, we used a technique of stopping the action at certain key moments. We described these as *singularities* – moments in time that correspond to forks in the road, when the nature of the questions asked and the actions taken will determine the direction of the future journey. One of the greatest challenges is to recognize these singularities at the time that they occur, as they are not always obvious. This might seem paradoxical – surely such moments of choice, such instances of dilemma are self-evident? However, we hope the case examples have successfully illustrated how this is not always the case. Too often, we unwittingly use *convenience ethics* or reach for a ready-made answer (via a protocol or procedure, for instance) to avoid having to consider the complexities of a dilemma ourselves. Like most metaphors and symbolic images, the fork in the road over-simplifies the nature of an ethical dilemma, limiting it to an either/or – left turn or right turn – when in reality the choices of direction are 360°.

If you are able to take one single element from the book directly into your regular practice, we hope it is a recognition of singularities, those moments when the opportunity is available to you to choose the best direction, and to feel growing confidence to enable yourself and others to come to an understanding of what 'best direction' means in the circumstances.

Complexity

When examining the origins of value conflicts, we presented two graphic representations of social work's reason for being and its relationship to various social systems, both of which illustrate the complexity of social work as a profession (see Chapter 3).

This complexity is further demonstrated by the range of ethical dilemmas that we have explored in this book, all of which throw light on the intricate nature of social work's moral landscape. What these specific and detailed dilemmas show clearly is the fact that social workers engage with multiple value conflicts between the persons involved (and the wider society), and the need for practitioners to navigate these situations whilst also managing their own feelings, opinions and beliefs. This requires an exceptional degree of honesty and self-awareness and a willingness to entertain different realities at the same time. Social Work England (2019: Professional Standard 3.5) describes this as 'holding different explanations in mind'.

Sometimes situations that seem to be about quite small things have complex ethical implications. We hope your journey through this book has helped you to a greater understanding of these complexities and given you frameworks to navigate these ethical waters successfully. The two story-lines from the Oaklands residential care situation (p. 5) seem widely separate in terms of their seriousness and scope – on the one hand, a major change in lifestyle, a move to cohabitation, and on the other hand, the possibility of a soft-boiled egg at breakfast. It is interesting, then, that the same ethical theories and practice frameworks are relevant in both sets of dilemmas. The size and scope of a dilemma is not necessarily related to the 'splash' it might make, and there is more that unites *everyday ethics* to *epic ethics* than we might have imagined.

Power

A consistent theme running through the book, as well as being the focus of Chapter 4, is power. In each and every dilemma, the ethical dimension needs to be viewed through the prism of power. As we have frequently stated, 'power' is not a finite commodity: if you have been part of a successful group, you will have experienced the way that it can be much more powerful than just the sum of its individuals.

The distribution of power is complex and dynamic and cannot be reduced to simple additions and subtractions, or social divisions. Of course, marginalized groups generally have less power in social situations, but we know much more about the complexity – sometimes called *intersectionality* – which is the way different identities criss-cross so that our social location (class, gender, race, age, sexuality, physical and mental ability, and other identifiers) is more fluid, more diverse, than we have often allowed or imagined. Moreover, the dimensions of power – personal, professional, knowledge, role and the like – are similarly complex and dynamic.

A recognition of the scope and limitations of your own and others' power, is an essential first step towards ethical practice. Your professional responsibility is to find ways of amplifying the power of those who are relatively powerless, of giving voice to those who are seldom heard. This is far from straightforward, as we saw in *The Petition* (p. 191), in which social worker Malik must decide whether to co-sponsor an online petition started by his service users, Sandra and Danny. Is it more ethical to follow his agency's policy whatever that policy is, or to challenge the policy if he feels it is discriminatory? How powerful (or not) is Malik's position in terms of his employer and how might he alter this, for instance, by collectivizing his power in the form of membership of a union? 'Seldom heard' might be taken to include the social work profession itself: do social workers, then, have a moral obligation to amplify the voice of their own profession?

Different ethical positions

The language used to describe the classical Western ethical theories can be off-putting to anyone who is not versed in philosophy, and we hope that the discussions and specific illustrations in this book have helped to demystify this language and to make it seem applicable to everyday life, including social work practice. We have also acknowledged the limitations of the classical theories of ethics, in particular their often unstated individualism. This focus on individual ethics is out of keeping with a social work which more often than not navigates complex *interpersonal* dilemmas, ones that have their roots in wider social policies. For these reasons, we considered the efficacy of an ethics of care and other *new ethics* to match the social nature of our profession, as well as non-Western ethical approaches such as *Surrender* and *ubuntu* (p. 60).

We hope that case examples, such as *Stan and the files* (p. 164) have demonstrated how ordinary decision making in social work is underpinned by divergent ethical approaches, even though these are very frequently implicit. The judgements of the four members of Stan's *Fitness to Practice* panel are also driven by strongly divergent, yet usually unspoken, approaches to ethics.

We have aimed to show how bringing these approaches to the surface and making them explicit can help all involved to comprehend the roots of seemingly intractable differences, in order to work with these differences from a position of mutual understanding. Of course, this will not necessarily achieve agreement, but it will always demonstrate respect and the prospect of bringing people nearer to each other's positions.

Procedures, guidance and the wise professionals

Who and what do we consult when we meet a *singularity* – a decision point where there is the possibility of different directions, often at the point of an ethical dilemma? Most social workers operate in agencies, whether small voluntary bodies or huge structures such as the British National Health Service. Wherever you are employed or placed, you will be expected to familiarize yourself with the relevant policies to guide your work. These procedures are important to ensure at least a basic level of service for the people that you serve, and also to give you some protection in terms of what is, and is not, expected of you. It is natural to turn to the procedures to guide and shape your practice.

In terms of ethics, agency protocols represent *convenience ethics* in a positive sense, in that they prevent you from having to work out everything for yourself. They can provide useful short-cuts. However, there are two problems with procedures: first, it is impossible for them to be so detailed that they cover every circumstance, so they cannot be relied upon exclusively; and second, they sometimes conflict with what an individual practitioner considers to be good practice. Agencies that are responsive to practitioners' feedback will make appropriate changes to its procedures to improve them, but unresponsive agencies are likely to find themselves in conflict with their practitioners. In these circumstances, social workers will be particularly reliant on their professional code of practice and, as we will see, also their 'wise professionals'.

Towards the conclusion of each chapter, we have quoted from the relevant sections from social work codes of practice around the globe. These codes have a parent document jointly agreed by the International Federation of Social Workers (IFSW) and the International Association of Schools of Social Work (IASSW 2018), with the understanding that social work is a profession that is particularly influenced by context and thus it is important that there are local interpretations of the general principles.

Codes of practice and other forms of written guidance can only provide general principles to assist the individual in their work. Rather like navigation charts for seagoing vessels, they map areas of risk and danger and chart the safer passages; however, they are seldom sufficiently detailed to tell you what to do in a specific situation. Developing this navigational metaphor, only you know the prevailing wind speed and direction, the tides and currents, the size of your vessel and the load that it is carrying at the particular time when you are needing navigational advice. That is why we introduced the idea of the wise professionals: these are the experienced social workers to whom you would turn for this kind of situation-specific advice and, since they are unlikely to be on board the vessel with you, you need to internalize them. This takes continuing practice and experience and is never a completed job. In essence, the wise professionals become *you* – your own inner best professional. We speak of them in the plural, because the best advice comes from a variety of perspectives, and you need to learn to give yourself advice that might point in several different directions!

Once you have navigated the difficulties and emerged the other side of the narrow straits, then it is possible to take more time to reflect and evaluate how you did, and this is where the professionals in the real world are useful. This is when an *ethical reference group* can provide a sounding board, critical friends to assist your continuing professional development and, as a member of this reference group, you are also assisting others' professional development. The 'ethical reference group' may be called something different – perhaps it is a 'case discussion group', or a 'peer supervision group' – but whatever the name, it is very important to be part of one, and to ensure that reflection on ethical dilemmas in professional practice is core to its discussion.

We highlighted two *qualities* that the wise professionals (remember, that's you) should embody: trust and care. Indeed, establishing and maintaining trust is one of the six professional standards that Social Work England (2019) consider necessary for safe and effective practice. We also proposed three 'compass points' to help you keep your bearings at all times: 'what is fair; what is generous; what is kind' (p. 62).

Procedures, professional guidance and our own wise professionals are all an important part of the ethical decision-making landscape. They are not mutually exclusive, and it is essential that they coexist. However, we ought not to pretend that this landscape is free from conflict. As we noted, organizational procedures and protocols might come into conflict with an individual social worker's notion of best practice; if the gap is sufficiently great, and the employing agency has shown no inclination to listen, the social worker will have an ethical obligation to whistleblow, supported by professional standards to 'Raise concerns about organisational wrongdoing and cultures of inappropriate and unsafe practice' (Social Work England 2019: Professional Standard 6.5). This requires considerable moral courage and is best supported by an ethical reference group of peers.

Bigger pictures

From time to time, we have drawn a distinction between *epic ethics* and *everyday ethics*. We have aimed to consider the ethics of 'small things', for instance in the *Discretion at the coffee shop* story (Chapter 2, p. 33), and link this to the bigger framework of ethical theory.

The central focus of this book has been ethical dilemmas in the realm of social work, whether everyday or epic. However, we have also sought to set these issues in a wider context. Each 'big picture' example presents a contemporary ethical dilemma in the social and public realm that reflects the professional dilemmas discussed in the corresponding chapter.

At the core of many, perhaps all, of these dilemmas is a central philosophical distinction conceptualized by Berlin (1969), a historian of ideas, and best summarized as two kinds of liberty: *freedom to* or *freedom from*. Many of the so-called 'culture wars' resolve themselves into adherents of one or other of these two camps. For example, there were fevered arguments during the Covid pandemic concerning the wearing of masks. Those who argued their right not to wear a mask were asserting a *freedom to* (choose whether to wear a mask), whereas others argued the imperative to wear a mask as a *freedom from* (the risk of airborne infection). These same philosophical positions lay at the heart of the arguments confronting the UK Parliament in 2024 about assisted dying: *freedom to* end your own life or *freedom from* possible coercion to end your own life.

An ability to engage in moral discourse, as demonstrated throughout the pages of this book, enables you to decide on the primacy of one of these liberties on a case-by-case (*casuist*) basis. In other words, we would weigh the evidence that supports the effectiveness or otherwise of mask-wearing in protecting people from cross-infection and if this evidence suggests that wearing a mask will save lives, an ethically alert person will decide to forgo the *freedom to* unmask in favour of the moral imperative of other people's *freedom from* airborne infection. This same ethically aware person might cross over into a different 'camp' on a different issue (for example, they might support a *freedom to* end your own life), precisely because they are not ideologically committed to one kind of liberty over the other.

The problem arises when ideological identification drives a person via a short-cut to arrive at a decision, perhaps based on their 'deeply held beliefs' – a commitment to libertarianism on the one hand, or state communism on the other, the prescriptions of a particular religion, or the dictums of a specific political thinker – without bothering to consider the careful steps of ethical reasoning. It is intellectually sloppy to bypass these processes, and very much easier than careful thought. One might say it is the junk food of a default position, as opposed to the handcrafted careful preparation of a balanced meal. Moreover, these default positions tend to be hardened and amplified by closed conversations within like-minded social media groups. We are not claiming that breaking into a virtuous circle of ethical reasoning is easy, but you can make a start by understanding the philosophical roots that explain commonly held positions and by modelling a process of careful questioning to achieve a better understanding. The hope is that this better understanding will achieve better (i.e., more ethical) outcomes.

The 'Bigger pictures' are a reminder that decisions which are seen as expressions of individual will are, without doubt, forged in the communities that nurture us. For example, in the archipelago at the western edge of the Eurasian landmass, the population believes that pedestrians ought to be *free to* make their own judgement about where it is safe to cross the road; in the archipelago at the eastern edge of this landmass, such activity is roundly condemned as jay-walking and is punishable with up to three months in prison. It is just a coincidence that 60 million British people are individually coming to the same conclusion, and 120 million Japanese people are individually coming to the same and opposite conclusion? Clearly not. What we like to think of as paths individually chosen are influenced by social forces that are too often misunderstood or dismissed.

Navigating the future: Thinking further about …

We concluded each chapter with a section headed *Think further about…* designed to encourage your capacity for critical reflection and building on the initial *Think about …* towards the beginning of the chapters. Now you have completed reading the book we would suggest that you return to some of these *Think further about …* sections and revisit your responses. Have they developed in any way as a consequence of your journey with us through the book? This kind of overview is sometimes referred to as *meta* – a reflection on your reflections. Has taking time to reflect on your ethical reasoning and practical decision making become a regular part of your professional life and, if so, what impact do you think this is having on your learning and practice?

You might like to revisit the ten questions that we posed in Chapter 2 (*Finding your inner moral philosopher*, p. 23). Has your response to these questions changed since you first addressed them and, if so, in what ways?

Although our time together has come to a close, it will be evident by now that the journey to ethical best practice is never completed. Just as one good question leads on to another even better one, so the art and science of navigating ethical and practice dilemmas progresses stage by stage. We hope that you are able to find or create your own ethical reference group to encourage and support your journey, and that you will develop your own ways of charting ethical social work practice to help others to navigate these fascinating waters.

Further reading

Now you have completed this stage in your journey, you might choose to return to some of the classic philosophers such as Socrates, Plato, Aristotle, Kant, Sartre, Rawls and Fletcher.

Glossary

a priori	A statement that is taken and understood as truthful in itself with no need for further proof or justification.
beneficence	Seeking to do good.
case-based ethics	*see* 'casuism'.
casuism	Treating each situation on a case-by-case basis, rather than applying principles or a strict rule book.
categorical imperative	*see* 'Kantian'.
cognitive bias	The way in which we see, process and understand things according to (often unconscious) established patterns and beliefs.
consequentialism	When giving moral weight to any action, the primary concern of consequentialism is to understand the likely consequences of the action; this is a *teleological* approach.
convenience ethics	The tendency to make an ethical decision on the basis of what least discomforts us or takes less time.
defeasible	A proposition that depends on various and varying factors that are subject to refutation, and that lead to an inconclusive *all things being equal* outcome, open to various interpretations.
deontological	Duty-based ethical theories; acting morally is doing your duty regardless of consequences and according to absolute rules that are always valid – for instance, that it is always right to tell the truth and, therefore, your duty to be honest.
dilemma, ethical and practical	Using a strict definition, an ethical dilemma is a choice between two ethically undesirable courses of action. We use an inclusive definition that incorporates everyday use of the word – that is, a choice between courses of action where the balance between what is right is complex and open to dispute. An ethical dilemma is where 'right' is used as a moral adjective and a practice dilemma is where 'right' is used a factual description (most effective),

	but frequently the same dilemma has a complex mix of ethical and practical uncertainties.
dual relationships	The boundary issues that can arise when social workers have more than one kind of relationship with a service user (professional, social, commercial, etc.). Dual relationships can also refer to situations where social workers are also service users.
duty-based ethics	see 'deontological'.
emotivism	A belief that all ethical statements are merely expressions of the speaker's emotions, their likes and dislikes, and a moral argument is to some extent meaningless.
ends and means	Part of Kant's categorical imperative to treat people as ends, not means to an end. This links with social work values concerning human dignity and the moral worth of every individual.
ethics of care	Derived from feminist theory, ethics of care place relationships at their heart and recognize that, for certain periods of their lives, humans are dependent on the care of others. Rather than seeing emotions as a challenge to rational moral reasoning, the ethics of care embrace feelings as central to ethics.
existentialism	As existentialism focuses on what *is* rather than what ought to be and is associated with moral subjectivism (i.e., morality is a matter of individual choice), philosophers query whether an existentialist ethics is possible.
free will	A belief that individuals can exercise their own choices without constraints, leading to a belief that everyone is responsible for their own actions.
intuitionism	'Goodness' is something that we know intuitively, so it cannot be defined or inferred from any facts or propositions. However, from this knowledge of what is good, it is possible to derive principles of obligation.
Kantian	In Kantian ethics, good actions are those done from a sense of duty – motivation is all-important. Duties that are unconditional (*musts*) are called *categorical imperatives*. These are universal, applying to everyone in every circumstance. There is respect for people as rational beings.

land ethics	A thing is right when it preserves the integrity, stability and beauty of the biotic community.
maleficence	Seeking to do harm.
maxim	A general principle underlying any action, similar to an axiom – for example, 'Do to others as you would have them do to you.'
meta-ethics	Meta-ethics focuses not on what is moral, but on morality itself – the status and meaning of ethical values and qualities.
moral agent	A person who is actively being and doing in ways they consider to be ethical.
moral relativism	The question as to whether ethical and moral judgements ought to differ from time to time and place to place; or whether there are moral absolutes that transcend era and location. A moral relativist asserts that there can be no universal consensus on what is right or wrong.
narrative ethics	Using stories to reveal ethical issues.
non-maleficence	Seeking not to do harm.
ontological	Ontology is the philosophy of being and the nature of existence and reality. Ontology describes the world as it is, not as it ought to be.
philosophical scepticism	Questioning the possibility of certainty of knowledge and being open to doubt and alternative perspectives. It can be used as a formal method of philosophical enquiry.
pragmatism	A belief that the best solutions are those that work in practice and are perhaps the most accommodating; a strong belief in compromise rather than sticking to principles.
principlism	A reliance on guiding principles about how to act, adapted to the particular profession in question. Principles are broader than rules.
proportionalism	A form of consequentialism that sees the rightness or wrongness of an act in terms of its consequences, so that actions ought to be measured against their results.
redemptive ethics	A strong belief in the possibility of change and the value of forgiveness; people who have committed wrongs can learn from these experiences and become better for them. Redemption plays a large

	part in much religious ethics, as in 'the road to Damascus' when the Christian-hater Saul converts and becomes the Christian saint, Paul.
relationship ethics	*see* 'ethics of care'.
relativism	*see* 'moral relativism'.
rule utilitarianism	Personal judgement is not central to morality, rather obedience to a system of social rules; following these rules exonerates a person from the consequences, since they have 'played by the book' rather than used their own judgement.
scepticism	*see* 'philosophical scepticism'.
singularity	A moment in time with potential significance.
surrender	Surrender is the First Nations', aboriginal ability to let go, central in holistic cultures where value conflicts are subsumed in the solidarity of the community and the individual's will is gifted to a collective wisdom.
teleology	Weighing good and bad in terms of what follows from an action (sometimes termed consequentialism); whether a lie is good or bad depends on the end goal and what happens as a result.
ubuntu	An African philosophy that is founded on the overall importance of collective life in contrast to the individualism of Western ethical philosophies. Literally, 'I am because we are.'
utilitarianism	Whatever brings about the greatest total happiness, or the least unhappiness.
value patterning	The particular values or ethical principles that are regularly given priority by an individual.
virtue ethics	An individual's character is what matters. It is necessary to cultivate a virtuous life in order to flourish as a genuinely rounded human being.

References

Abishevaa, K. and Assylbekovab, L. (2016), 'Risk Management and Ethical Issues in Social Work', *European Proceedings of Social and Behavioural Sciences*. http://dx.doi.org/10.15405/epsbs.2016.09.2

Action on Armed Violence (AOAV) (2024), *22% Rise in Global Civilian Fatalities From Explosive Weapons in 2023: A Year of Harm Reviewed*, London; Action on Armed Violence. https://aoav.org.uk/reports/

Acton, J. (1887), Letter to Creighton. https://oll.libertyfund.org/titles/acton-acton-creighton-correspondence

Adams, R. (2008), *Empowerment, Participation and Social Work*, 4th edn, Basingstoke: Palgrave MacMillan.

Addams, J. (1910), Twenty Years at Hull-House, New York: Macmillan,

Akhtar, F. (2012), *Mastering Social Work Values and Ethics*, London: Jessica Kingsley.

Allen, A. (1998), 'Rethinking Power', *Hyptia*, 13(1): 21–40.

Aotearoa New Zealand Association of Social Workers (ANZASW) (2019), Code of Ethics. https://www.anzasw.nz/public/150/files/Publications/Code-of-Ethics-Adopted-30-Aug-2019.pdf

Asch, S.E. (1952), *Social Psychology*, Englewood Cliffs, NJ: Prentice.

Australia Association of Social Workers (AASW) (2020), Australian Association of Social Workers Code of Ethics. https://aasw-prod.s3.ap-southeast-2.amazonaws.com/wp-content/uploads/2023/08/AASW-Code-of-Ethics-2020.pdf

Bacon, F. (1597) *Meditationes Sacrae*.

Banks, S. (1995), *Ethics and Values in Social Work*, 1st edn, London: Macmillan.

Banks, S. (2004), *Ethics, Accountability and the Social Professions*, Basingstoke: Palgrave.

Banks, S., ed. (2010), *Ethical Issues in Youth Work*, 2nd edn, Abingdon: Routledge.

Banks, S., ed. (2014), *Ethics*, Bristol: Policy Press.

Banks, S. (2016), 'Everyday Ethics in Professional Life: Social Work as Ethics Work', *Ethics and Social Welfare*, 10(1): 35–52.

Banks, S. (2020), *Ethics and Values in Social Work*, 5th edn, London: Bloomsbury.

Banks, S. (2024) 'Pandemic Ethics and Beyond: Creating Space for Virtues in the Social Professions', *Nursing Ethics*, 31(1): 28–38.

Banks, S. and Nøhr, K. [eds] (2012), *Practising Social Work Ethics around the World*, Abingdon: Routledge.

Barsky, A. E. (2019), *Ethics and Values in Social Work*, 2nd edn, New York: Oxford University Press.

Barnard, A., Horner, N. and Wild, J. (2008), *The Value Base of Social Work and Social Care*, Berkshire: McGraw Hill.

BASW (2021) *The Code of Ethics for Social Workers: Statement of Principles*. https://basw.co.uk/policy-practice/standards/code-ethics

BASW (2025), *Generative AI & Social Work Practice Guidance*, London: BASW.

BATSW (2002) 'Declaration of Ethics for Social Workers', Bombay Association of Trained Social Workers: Mumbai', in J. Joseph, and G. Fernandes (eds), *An Enquiry into Ethical Dilemmas in Social Work*, Mumbai: College of Social Work.

Bauman, Z. (1993), *Postmodern Ethics*, Oxford: Wiley.

Beauchamp, T. and Childress, J. (1979), *Principles of Biomedical Ethics*, New York: Oxford University Press.

Beckett, C., Maynard, A. and Jordan, P. (2017), *Values and Ethics in Social Work*, London: Sage.

Beesley, P. (2024), 'Supporting Students on Placement to Develop a Diligent Attitude to Social Work Student Supervision', *Journal of Practice Teaching and Learning*, 22(1–2): 7–23.

Beesley, P., Watts, M. and Harlow, S. (2023), *Developing Your Communication Skills in Social Work*, London: Sage.

Bell, L. and Hafford-Letchfield, T., eds (2015), *Ethics, Values and Social Work Practice*, Milton Keynes: Open University Press.

Beresford, P. and Croft, S. (2001), 'Service Users' Knowledges and the Social Construction of Social Work', *Journal of Social Work*, 1(3): 295–316.

Beresford, P. and Holden, C. (2000), 'We Have Choices: Globalisation and Welfare User Movements', *Disability and Society*, 15(7): 973–9.

Berlin, I. (1969), 'Two Concepts of Liberty', in I. Berlin, *Four Essays on Liberty*, 118–72, London: Oxford University Press. New edn in Berlin 2002: 166–217.

Bernard, H. and Schuttenberg, E. (1995), 'Development of the Diligence Inventory-Higher Education Form', *Journal of Research and Development in Education*, 28(2): 91–100.

Bernsen, A., Tabachnick, B. G. and Pope, S. (1994), 'National Survey of Social Workers' Sexual Attraction to Their Clients: Results, Implications, and Comparison to Psychologists', *Ethics and Behavior*, 4(4): 369–88.

Bhatti-Sinclair, K. (2022), 'De-colonising Social Work: Changing Perspectives (SWEARN)', *Social Dialogue*, 26: 5–9.

Biestek, F. (1961), *The Casework Relationship*, London: Allen and Unwin.

Boszormenyi-Nagy, I. (1987), *Foundations of Contextual Therapy. Collected Papers of Ivan Boszormenyi-Nagy, M.D.*, New York: Brunner/Mazel.

Burnham, J. (2012), 'Developments in Social GGRRAAACCEEESSS: Visible–Invisible and Voiced– Unvoiced, in I.-B. Krause (ed.), *Culture and Reflexivity in Systemic Psychotherapy: Mutual Perspectives*, London: Karnac.

Burton, V. and Revell, L. (2018), 'Professional Curiosity in Child Protection: Thinking the Unthinkable in a Neoliberal World', *British Journal of Social Work*, 48: 1508–23.

Butterfield, L. D., Borgen, W. A., Amundsen, N. E. and Maglio, A.-S. T (2005), 'Fifty Years of the Critical Incident Technique: 1954–2004 and Beyond', *Qualitative Research*, 5(4): 475–97.

CAIPE (2012), *Interprofessional Education in Pre-registration Courses*, Fareham: CAIPE.

Cantacuzino, M. (2015), *The Forgiveness Project: Stories for a Vengeful Age*, London: Jessica Kingsley.

CASW (2024), *Canadian Code of Ethics and Guiding Principles*. https://www.casw-acts.ca/en/casw-code-ethics-2024

Cavaliere, F. (2014), 'The British Code and the Italian Code of Ethics for Social Work: A Lingua-cultural Comparative Analysis', *ESP Across Cultures*, 11: 57–73.

Chard, K. (2019) ,'Working with Carers', in H. Dix, S. Hollinrake and J. Meade (eds), *Relationship-Based Social Work with Adults*, 95–108, St Albans: Critical Publishing.

Clandinin, D. J. and Huber, J. (2010), 'Narrative Inquiry', in P. L. Peterson, E. L. Baker and B. McGraw (eds), *International Encyclopaedia of Education*, 3rd edn, New York: Elsevier.

Clapton, G., Cree, V. and Smith, M. (2013), 'Moral Panics and Social Work: Towards a Sceptical View of UK Child Protection', *Critical Social Policy*, 33(2): 197–217.

Clark, C. L. (2000), *Social Work Ethics: Politics, Principles and Practice*, Basingstoke: Palgrave Macmillan.

Clark, C. (2006), 'Children's Voices: The Views of Vulnerable Children on Their Service Providers and the Relevance of Services They Receive', *British Journal of Social Work*, 36: 21–39.

CNOAS (Consiglio Nazionale Ordine Assistenti Sociali) (2009), Code of Ethics for Social Workers https://www.cnoas.info/files/000000/00000018.pdf

Cohen, S. (1972), *Folk Devils and Moral Panics: The Creation of the Mods and Rockers*, London: Routledge.

Committee of Public Accounts (2014), *Whistleblowing. Ninth Report of Session 2014–15*, London: House of Commons.

Cooper, F. (2012), *Professional Boundaries in Social Work and Social Care: A Practical Guide to Understanding, Maintaining and Managing Your Professional Boundaries*, London: Jessica Kingsley.

Crenshaw, K. (1989), 'Demarginalizing the Intersection of Race and Sex: A Black Feminist Critique of Antidiscrimination Doctrine, Feminist Theory and Antiracist Politics', *University of Chicago Legal Forum*, 1(8): 139–67.

Das, C. and Kulkarni, A. (2006a), 'Culture and Ethics' in J. Joseph and G. Fernandes (eds), *An Enquiry into Ethical Dilemmas in Social Work*, 78–91, Mumbai: College of Social Work.

Das, C. and Kulkarni, A. (2006b), 'Person vis-à-vis Profession', in J. Joseph and G. Fernandes (eds), *An Enquiry into Ethical Dilemmas in Social Work*, 92–103, Mumbai: College of Social Work.

de Beauvoir, S. (1947/1986), *The Ethics of Ambiguity*, New York: Citadel Press.

Department for Education (DfE) (2023), *Working Together to Safeguard Children 2023: A Guide to Multi-Agency Working to Help, Protect and Promote the Welfare of Children*. https://assets.publishing.service.gov.uk/media/669e7501ab418ab055592a7b/Working_together_to_safeguard_children_2023.pdf

Dickens, J. (2012), *Social Work, Law and Ethics*, London: Routledge.

Dickens, J., Cook, L., Cossar, J., Okpokiri, C., Taylor, J. and Garstang, J. (2023), 'Re-envisaging Professional Curiosity and Challenge: Messages for Child Protection Practice from Reviews of Serious Cases in England', *Children and Youth Services Review*, 152 (June).

Doel, M. and Best, L. (2008), *Experiencing Social Work: Learning from Service Users*, London: Sage.

Doel, M. (2010), *Social Work Placements: A Traveller's Guide*, London: Routledge.

Doel, M. (2023), *Social Work: The Basics*, 2nd edn, London: Routledge.

Doel, M. (2019), 'Displaying Social Work Through Objects', *British Journal of Social Work*, 49(3) (April): 824–41.

Doel, M., ed. (2017), *Social Work in 42 Objects (and More)*, Lichfield: Kirwin Maclean Associates.

Doel, M. and Shardlow, S. M. (2005), *Modern Social Work Practice: Teaching and Learning in Practice Settings*, Aldershot: Ashgate.

Doel, M., Allmark, P., Conway, P., Cowburn, M., Flynn, M., Nelson, P. and Tod, A. (2010), 'Professional Boundaries: Crossing a Line or Entering the Shadows', *British Journal of Social Work*, 40(6): 1866–89.

Doel, M., Kachkachishvili, I., Lucas, J., Namicheishvili, S. and Partskhaladze, N. (2016), 'Creating Social Work Education in the Republic of Georgia', in I. Taylor, M. Bogo and M. Lefevre (eds), *International Handbook of Social Work Education*, 96–106, London: Routledge.

Dolgoff, R., Loewenberg, F. M. and Harrington, D. (2009), *Ethical Decisions for Social Work Practice*, 8th edn, Belmont, CA: Thomson Brooks/Cole.

Dubois, B. and Miley, K. (1996), *Social Work: An Empowering Profession*, Harlow: Allyn and Bacon.

Ells, P., and Dehn, G. (2001), 'Whistleblowing: Public Concern At Work', in C. Cull and J. Roche (eds), *The Law and Social Work*, Houndmills, Basingstoke: Palgrave.

Espinoza, S., Vivanco, R., Ibacache, I. and Doel, M. (2024), 'Social Work and the Idea of Object', *Qualitative Social Work*, 23(1): 195–212.

Featherstone, B., Gupta, A., Morris, K. and Warner, J. (2018), 'Let's Stop Feeding the Risk Monster: Towards a Social Model of "Child Protection"', *Families, Relationships and Societies*, 7(1): 7–22.

Feldman, G. (2019), 'Towards a Relational Approach to Poverty in Social Work: Research and Practice Considerations', *British Journal of Social Work*, 49(7): 1705–22.

Fenton, J. (2019), *Social Work for Lazy Professionals*, London: Red Globe Press.

Ferguson, H., Disney, T., Warwick, L., Leigh, J., Singh Conner T., and Beddoe, L (2021), 'Hostile Relationships in Social Work Practice: Anxiety, Hate and Conflict in Long-term Work with Involuntary Service Users', *Journal of Social Work Practice*, 35(1): 19–37.

Fischhoff, B., Slovic, P., Lichtenstein, S., Read, S. and Combs, B. (1978), 'How Safe is Safe Enough? A Psychometric Study of Attitudes Towards Technological Risks and Benefit', *Policy Sciences*, 9: 127–52.

Flanagan, S. (2015), 'How Does Storytelling Within Higher Education Contribute to the Learning Experience of Early Years Students?', *Journal of Practice Teaching & Learning*, 13(2): 162–84.

Fletcher, J. F. (1967), *Moral Responsibility: Situation Ethics at Work*, London: SCM Press.

FOKUS (2009), *Ethical Guidelines Fokus (Code of Conduct)*, Oslo: Norwegian Union of Social Educators and Social Workers.

Fook, J. (2023), *Social Work: A Critical Approach to Practice*, London: Sage.

Foot, P. (1967), 'The Problem of Abortion and the Doctrine of the Double Effect', *The Oxford Review*, 5: 5–15.

Foucault, M. (1991), 'Governmentality', in Burchell, G., Gordon, C. and Miller, P. (eds), *The Foucault Effects: Studies in Governmentality*, 87–104, London: Harvester Wheatsheaf.

Freire, P. (1968/2018), *Pedagogy of the Oppressed*, New York: Bloomsbury Academic.

French, J. and Raven, B. (1959), 'The Bases of Social Power', in Cartwright, D. (ed.), *Studies in Social Power*, 311–20, Ann Arbor, MI: Institute for Social Research.

Gardner, P. J. and Poole, J. M. (2009), 'One Story at a Time: Narrative Therapy, Older Adults and Addictions', *Journal of Applied Gerontology*, 28(5): 600–20.

Gawronski, B. (2022), 'Moral Impressions and Presumed Moral Choices: Perceptions of How Moral Exemplars Resolve Moral Dilemmas'. *Journal of Experimental Social Psychology*, 99: 1–14.

Gergen, K. (2000), *An Invitation to Social Construction*, London: Sage.

Global Cancer Observatory (GCO) [including International Agency for Research on Cancer (IARC), World Health Organization (WHO) and Cancer Today] (2024), All Cancers. https://gco.iarc.who.int/media/globocan/factsheets/cancers/39-all-cancers-fact-sheet.pdf

Goode, E. and Ben-Yehuda, N. (2009), *Moral Panics: The Social Construction of Deviance*, 2nd edn, Malden: Wiley-Blackwell.

Gray, M. and Webb, S. (2010), *Ethics and Value Perspectives in Social Work*, Basingstoke: Palgrave Macmillan.

Green, L. and Carey, M., eds (2013), *Practical Social Work Ethics*, Aldershot: Ashgate.

Hardcastle, D. A. (2011), *Community Practice: Theories and Skills for Social Workers*, Oxford: Oxford University Press.

Hardwick, L. and Worsley, A. (2011), *Doing Social Work Research*, London: Sage.

Held, V. (2006), *The Ethics of Care*, Oxford: Ocford University Press.

Hennessey, R. (2011), *Relationship Skills in Social Work*, London: Sage.

Hill, D, Agu, L. and Mercer, D. (2018), *Exploring and Locating Social Work*. London: Bloomsbury.

HMSO (1989), Children Act 1989. https://www.legislation.gov.uk/ukpga/1989/41/contents

HMSO (2018, updated 2024), Care Act 2014. https://www.legislation.gov.uk/ukpga/2014/23/contents

Hollinrake, S. (2019), 'Theoretical Perspectives', in H. Dix, S. Hollinrake and J. Meade (eds), *Relationship-Based Social Work with Adults*, 7–25, St Albans: Critical Publishing.

Honey, P. and Mumford, A. (1992), *Manual of Learning Styles*, London: Peter Honey Publications.

Horne, N. (1999), *Values in Social Work*, 2nd edn, Aldershot: Ashgate.

Howe, D. and Hill, D. (2024), *A Brief Introduction to Social Work Theory*, London: Bloomsbury.
Hugman, R. and Smith, D. (1995), *Ethical Issues in Social Work*, London: Routledge.
Hugman, R. (2013a), *A–Z of Professional Ethics*, Basingstoke: Palgrave Macmillan.
Hugman, R. (2013b), 'Ethics', in M. Davies (ed.), *The Blackwell Companion to Social Work*, 4th edn, 379–86, Chichester: Wiley-Blackwell.
Hunt, G., ed. (1998), *Whistleblowing in the Social Services: Public Accountability and Professional Practice*, London: Arnold.
Institute for Economics and Peace (IEP) (2024), *Global Terror Index*, Syndey, Australia: Institute for Economics and Peace.
International Federation of Social Workers (IFSW) (2018), *Ethics in Social Work: Statement of Principles*, IFSW. https://www.ifsw.org/global-social-work-statement-of-ethical-principles/
Irish Association for Social Workers (IASW) (2023), Code of Ethics. file:///C:/Users/Beesle02/Downloads/65157773da1aa_82554-IASW-Code%20of%20Ethics%206pp%20DL-V3.pdf
Janis, I. (1972), *Victims of Groupthink*, Boston, MA: Houghton Mifflin.
Jarvis Thomson, J. (1976), 'Killing, Letting Die, and the Trolley Problem', *The Monist*, 59: 204–17.
Joseph, J. and Fernandes, G., eds) (2006), *An Enquiry into Ethical Dilemmas in Social Work*, Mumbai: College of Social Work.
Kahneman, D. (2012), *Thinking, Fast and Slow*, Penguin.
Kant, I. (1784/1998), *Groundwork of the Metaphysics of Morals*, M. Gregor (ed. and trans.), Cambridge: Cambridge University Press.
Karpman, S. (1968), 'Fairy Tales and Script Drama Analysis', *Transactional Analysis Bulletin*, 26(7): 39–43.
Keeney, A. J., Smart, A. M., Richards, R., Harrison, S., Carrillo, M., and Valentine, D. (2014), 'Human Rights and Social Work Codes of Ethics: An International Analysis', *Journal of Social Welfare and Human Rights*, 2(2): 1–16.
Kerr, C. (2023), 'In Defence of Human Intelligence (and Fallibility) in Social Work', *Professional Social Work*. https://basw.co.uk/about-social-work/psw-magazine/articles/defence-human-intelligence-and-fallibility-social-work
Killick, C. and Taylor, B. (2024), *Assessment, Risk and Decision Making in Social Work*, London: Sage.
Knight. T. (1921), *Risk, Uncertainty, and Profit*, Chicago, IL: Houghton Mifflin.
Koehn, D. (1994), *The Ground of Professional Ethics*, London: Routledge
Koutsounia, A. (2024), 'AI Could Be Time-Saving for Social Workers but Needs Regulation, Says Sector Bodies', *Community Care*. https://www.communitycare.

co.uk/2024/10/04/ai-could-be-time-saving-for-social-workers-but-needs-regulation-say-sector-bodies/

Krinsky, C. (2015), The Ashgate Research Companion to Moral Panics. http://www.ashgate.com/pdf/samplepages/ashgate-research-companion-to-moral-panics-intro.pdf

Kubler-Ross, E. (1969), *On Death and Dying*, New York: Scribner.

Lee, S. (1965), *Amazing Fantasy #15*. https://www.marvel.com/comics/issue/16926/amazing_fantasy_1962_15

Leigh, J., Beddoe, L. and Keddell, E. (2020), 'Disguised Compliance or Undisguised Nonsense? A Critical Discourse Analysis of Compliance and Resistance in Social Work Practice', *Families, Relationships and Societies*, 9(2): 269–85.

Long, N., Gardner, F., Hodgkin, S. and Lehmann, J. (2023), 'Developing Social Work Professional Identity and Resilience: Seven Protective Factors', *Australian Social Work*, DOI: 10.1080/0312407X.2022.2160265

Lonne, B., Harries, M., Featherstone, B. and Gray, M. (2015), *Working Ethically in Child Protection*, London: Routledge.

Lukes, S. (1974), *Power: A Radical View*, London: Macmillan.

Mann, J. (2016), 'Filling the Gap: Constructive Responses to the Erosion of Training Standards for Practice Educators', in A. Bellinger and D. Ford (eds), *Practice Placements in Social Work*, 165–80, Bristol: Policy Press.

Marsh, P. and Doel, M. (2005), *The Task-Centred Book*, London: Routledge/Community Care.

Marquis, R. and Jackson, R. (2000), 'Quality of Life and Quality of Services Relationships: Experiences of People with Disabilities', *Disability and Society*, 15(3): 411–25.

Maslow, A. H. (1943), 'A Theory of Human Motivation', *Psychological Review*, 50(4): 370–96. http://psychclassics.yorku.ca/Maslow/motivation.htm

Mason, B. (1993), 'Towards Positions of Safe Uncertainty', *Human Systems*, 4: 189–200.

Mayaka, B. and Truell, R. (2021), 'Ubuntu and Its Potential Impact on the International Social Work Profession', *International Social Work*, 64(5): 649–62.

McAuliffe, D. (2022), *Interprofessional Ethics*, Cambridge: Cambridge University Press.

McEwan, I. (2014), *The Children Act*, London: Jonathan Cape.

Meagher, G. and Parton, N. (2004), 'Modernising Social Work and the Ethics of Care', *Social Work and Society*, 2(1): 10–27.

Mental Capacity Act 2005, https://www.legislation.gov.uk/ukpga/2005/9

Mill, J. S. (1863), *Utilitarianism*, London: Parker, Son and Bourn.

Nagel, T. (1979), *Mortal Questions*, Cambridge: Cambridge University Press.

Narayan, D. (2010), 'Poverty is Powerlessness and Voicelessness'. in Gasper, D. and Lera St Clair, A. (eds), *Development Ethics*, 117–120, Abingdon: Routledge.

National Association of Social Workers (NASW) (2021), Code of Ethics. https://www.socialworkers.org/About/Ethics/Code-of-Ethics/Code-of-Ethics-English

National Audit Office (2014a), *Government Whistleblowing Policies*, London: UK Parliament.

National Audit Office (2014b), *Assessment Criteria for Whistleblowing Policies*, Supplementary Report, London: UK Parliament.

Nelkin, D. K. (2013), 'Moral Luck', in Zalta, Edward N. (ed.), *The Stanford Encyclopedia of Philosophy* (Winter 2013 edn). http://plato.stanford.edu/archives/win2013/entries/moral-luck/

Nolan Committee on Standards in Public Life (1995), *First Report of the Committee on Standards in Public Life* (aka 'Nolan Principles'), p. 14. https://www.gov.uk/government/uploads/system/uploads/attachment_data/file/263360/285002.pdf

Olusa, O. (2023), 'Racial, Social and Spatial Inequalities: Supporting Black African Students on Practice Placement Using UBUNTU Philosophy', *Journal of Practice Teaching & Learning* 20(1). https://doi.org/10.1921/jpts.v20i2.2148

O'Sullivan, T. (2010), *Decision Making in Social Work*, London: Red Globe Press.

Parker, J. (2024), *Social Work Practice. Assessment, Planning, Intervention and Review*, London: Sage.

Parrott, L. (2014), *Values and Ethics in Social Work Practice*, Exeter: Learning Matters.

Parsons, R. D. (2001), *The Ethics of Professional Practice*, New York: Pearson.

Parton, N. (2003), 'Rethinking Professional Practice: The Contributions of Social Constructionism and the Feminist "Ethics of Care"', *British Journal of Social Work*, 33: 1–16.

Payne, M. (2007), 'Performing as a "Wise Person" in Social Work Practice', *Practice* 19(2): 85–96.

Pease, B., Vreugdenhill, A. and Stanford, S. (2018), 'Towards a Critical Ethics of Care in Social Work', in B. Pease, A. Vreugdenhill and S. Stanford (eds), *Critical Ethics of Care in Social Work Transforming the Politics and Practices of Caring*, 3–15, Abingdon: Routledge.

Pink, S., Ferguson, H. and Kelly, L. (2020), *Research Briefing Three: Digital Social Work – The Emergence of Hybrid Practice During the COVID-19 Pandemic*. https://www.birmingham.ac.uk/documents/college-social-sciences/social-policy/publications/research-briefing-3-digital-social-work-accessible.pdf

Plamenatz, J. (1938), *Consent, Freedom and Political Obligation*, 2nd edn published 1968, Oxford: Oxford University Press.
Porter, E. (1999), *Feminist Perspectives on Ethics*, London: Longman.
Pullen-Sansfaçon, A. and Cowden, S. (2012), *The Ethical Foundations of Social Work*, New York: Pearson.
Rabinowitch, E. (1972), 'Living Dangerously in the Age of Science, *Bulletin of the Atomic Scientists*, 28(1): 5–8.
Rapp, C. (1988), *The Strengths Model: Case Management with People Suffering Severe and Persistent Mental Illness*, New York: Oxford Press.
Rawls, J. (1958), 'Justice as Fairness', *Philosophical Review*, 68: 164–94.
Reamer, F. (2023a), 'Ethics Risk Management in Social Work: A Primer', *Families in Society*, 104(2): 209–21.
Reamer, F. (2023b), 'Moral Disengagement in Social Work', *Social Work*, 68(3): 183–11.
Reamer, F. G. (2024), *Social Work Values and Ethics*, 5th edn, New York: Columbia University Press.
Reamer, F. and Siegel, D. (2021), 'Adoption Ethics in a Digital World: Challenges and Best Practices', *Adoption Quarterly*, 24(1): 69–88.
Rifkin, J. (2009), *The Empathic Civilization: The Race to Global Consciousness in a World in Crisis*, New York: J.P. Tarcher/Penguin.
Ruch, G., Turney, D. and Ward, A., eds (2018), *Relationship-Based Social Work*, London: Jessica Kingsley.
Saarnio, P. (2000), 'Does It Matter Who Treats You?', *European Journal of Social Work*, 3(3): 261–8.
Saleebey, D. (1992), *The Strengths Perspective in Social Work Practice*, New York: Pearson.
Samson, P. L. (2015), 'Practice Wisdom: The Art and Science of Social Work', *Journal of Social Work Practice*, 29(2): 119–31.
Sartre, J.-P. (1946), *Existentialism and Humanism*, Paris: Les Editions Nagel.
Samuel, M. (2024), '"Families First For Children" Model to be Rolled Out to all Councils, Says Chief Social Worker', *Community Care*. https://www.communitycare.co.uk/2024/12/11/families-first-for-children-model-to-be-rolled-out-to-all-councils-says-chief-social-worker/
Sicora, A., Taylor, B., Alfandari, R., Enosh, G., Helm, D., Killick, C., Lyons, O., Mullineux, J., Przeperski, J., Rölver, M. and Whittaker, A. (2021) 'Using Intuition In Social Work Decision Making', *European Journal of Social Work*, 24(5): 772–87.

Shlomo, S.B., Levy, D. and Itzhaky, H. (2012), 'Development of Professional Identity Among Social Work Students: Contributing Factors', *The Clinical Supervisor*, 31(2): 240–55.

Singer, P. (1973), *Democracy and Disobedience*, Oxford: Oxford University Press.

Smith, R. (2008), *Social Work and Power*, Basingstoke: Palgrave MacMillan.

Social Care Institute for Excellence (SCIE) (n.d.), Multidisciplinary *Teams Working for Integrated Care*. https://www.scie.org.uk/integrated-care/research-practice/activities/multidisciplinary-teams/

Social Work England (SWE) (2019), Professional Standards. https://www.socialworkengland.org.uk/standards/professional-standards/

Social Work Podcast (n.d.), 'Social Work Ethics'. https://www.socialworkpodcast.com/Barsky_ethics.mp3

Some, M. P. (1997), *Ritual: Power, Healing and Community*, Penguin Group USA.

SSR (2006), *Ethics in Social Work: an Ethical Code for Social Workers*, Stockholm: Swedish Association of Graduates in Social Sciences, Personnel and Public Administration, Economics and Social Work.

Stanley, N. and Manthorpe, J. (2004), *The Age of the Inquiry: Learning and Blaming in Health and Social Care*, London: Routledge.

Tedam, P. (2024), *Anti-Oppressive Social Work Practice*, London: Learning Matters.

Thacker, H., Anka, A. and Penhale, B. (2019), 'Could Curiosity Save Lives? An Exploration Into the Value of Employing Professional Curiosity and Partnership Work in Safeguarding Adults Under the Care Act 2014', *Journal of Adult Protection*, 21(5): 252–67.

Thompson, N. (2024), *Understanding Social Work: Preparing for Practice*, London: Bloomsbury.

Thompson, N. (2021), *People Skills*, London: Red Globe Press.

Thompson, N. (2016), *The Authentic Leader*, Basingstoke: Palgrave.

Thoreau, H. D. (1866), 'Civil Disobedience', *Resistance to Civil Government*. https://sniggle.net/TPL/index5.php?entry=rtcg

Turner, M. and Pratkanis, A. (1998), 'Twenty Five Years of Groupthink Research', *Organizational Behavior and Human Decision Processes*, 73(2): 105–15.

Ungar, S. (2001), 'Moral Panic Versus the Risk Society: The Implications of the Changing Sites of Social Anxiety', *British Journal of Sociology*, 52(2): 271–91.

UNICEF (2024), Levels and *Trends in Child Mortality*. https://data.unicef.org/resources/levels-and-trends-in-child-mortality-2024/

University of Sydney Research Centre for Children and Families (2020), Remote Social Work Research to Practice. https://www.sydney.edu.au/arts/our-research/centres-institutes-and-groups/research-centre-for-children-and-families.html

Warnock, M. (1998), *An Intelligent Person's Guide to Ethics*, London; Duckworth.

Warren, J. (2007), *Service User and Carer Participation in Social Work*, Exeter: Learning Matters.

Wachtel, T. and McCold, P. (2001), 'Restorative Justice in Everyday Life', in H. Strang and J. Braithwaite (eds), *Restorative Justice and Civil Society*, 117–25, Cambridge: Cambridge University Press.

Webb, S. (2017), 'Matters of Professional Identity and Social Work', in S. Webb (ed.), *Professional Identity and Social Work*, 1–18, London: Routledge.

Weber, M. (1922), *Economy and Society*, Berkeley: University of California Press.

Wenger, E. (1998), *Communities of Practice: Learning, Meaning, and Identity*, Cambridge: Cambridge University Press.

Wiles, F. (2017), 'What is Professional Identity and How Do Social Workers Acquire It?', in S. Webb (ed.), *Professional Identity and Social Work*, 35–50, London: Routledge.

Wilkins, D. and Meindl, M. (2024), 'Can Social Workers Estimate the Likelihood of Future Actions and Events? A Forecasting Accuracy Study', *British Journal of Social Work*, 54(3): 1150–69.

Williams, B. (1981), *Moral Luck*, Cambridge: Cambridge University Press.

Wolff, J. (2011), *Ethics and Public Policy: A Philosophical Inquiry*, London: Routrledge.

World Health Organization (WHO) (2022), *Violence Against Children*. https://www.who.int/news-room/fact-sheets/detail/violence-against-children#:~:text=Globally%2C%20it%20is%20estimated%20that,lifelong%20health%20and%20well%2Dbeing

World Population Review (WPR) (2024), *Literacy Rate by Country*. https://worldpopulationreview.com/country-rankings/literacy-rate-by-country

Wrench, K. (2024), *Skills and Knowledge for Life Story Work with Children and Adolescents*, London: Jessica Kingsley.

Yassour-Borochowitz, D. (2004), 'Reflections on the Researcher-participant Relationship and the Ethics of Dialogue, *Ethics and Behavior*, 14(2): 175–86.

Zerbe, W. J. (2008), 'Feelings About Ethical Decisions: The Emotions of Moral Residue', in W. J. Zerbe, C. E. J. Härtel and N. M. Ashkanasy (eds), *Emotions, Ethics and Decision-Making*, 109–29, Bingley: Emerald Group.

Index

Note: *Italic* page numbers denote figures.

40objetos.ulagos.cl/galeria 1

Aborigine 152
accountability 129
Addams, Jane 42
agency 46, 53, 95–96, 117, 152, 153, 158, 162, 164–165, 169–170, 192–193, 204, 206
AIDS Quilt 66
alternative paradigms 60–61
American code of ethics 186, 196
Aotearoa New Zealand (ANZASW 2019) code 121–122
Aristotle 25, 31
artificial intelligence (AI) 190–191
Asch, S. E. 162
Australian code of ethics 174
avoid 52, 53

'balance sheet' method 17, 138
Banks, S. 9, 10, 26, 87, 108, 129
Barsky, A. E. 133, 138, 140
Beauchamp, T. 110
Beckett, C. 67, 75, 110
Beesley, P. 19–20
beneficence 110, 130–131, 171
bias 118–119, 134–136
Biestek, F. 25, 26, 109
big events 16–17
The big picture 18, 50, 69, 87, 127, 155–156, 183, 206–208
Black Lives Matter 72
Boszormenyi-Nagy, M. D. 108
boundaries 111–112
British Code of Ethics for Social Workers (BASW) 12, 99, 121, 195
  ethical principles 174–175
Burnham, J. 90
Burton, V. 129

Canadian Code of Ethics and Guiding Principles 99–100
Care Act 2014, 128
case-based ethics 15
the casework relationship 25, 109
casuism(/ist) 28–29, 131, 137, 207
Cavaliere, F. 12
Children Act 1989, 128, 136
Childress, J. 110
code of ethics 11–12, 36–37, 88
  American code of ethics 186, 196
  Australian code of ethics 174
  British code of ethics 80, 99, 121, 195
  Canadian Code of Ethics and Guiding Principles 99
  Irish code of ethics 80
  Italy's Code of Ethics 195–196
coercive power 70
cognitive bias 118–119
co-habitation 5–6
collaboration 117, 121
colonization 91
commission 131
common good 141, 142, 152
communication skills 97, 112, 189
compass 22
  professional 22
compete 51, 52
complexity 201–202
compromise 51, 53
concede 51, 53, 60
confidentiality 26, 114, 195
confirmation bias 134
conflict 43–45
  long-term value 47
  manage 142–143
  short-term value 47
  for social workers 46, 48

conflict resolution 109, 142–143. *see also* value conflicts
conformity 91, 162
  bias 134
consequentialism 11, 29–30, 35, 56, 77, 156, 163, 175, 194
continuing professional development (CPD) 89
convenience ethics 34, 98–99, 137, 182, 192, 201, 204
credibility bias 134
critical incident analysis 15
critical thinking 31–32, 74, 86, 133, 141–142

Das, C. 45
decision making
  defensible 132–133, 146
  duty-based approach 130
  ethical 130–131, 133–134
  participative 131–132
  professional curiosity 129
  risk in 126–127
  in social work 125
defensible decision making 132–133, 138, 146, 148
deontological theories. *see* duty-based ethical theories
deprivation of self-determination 75–76
discretion 29
discrimination 106, 131, 165
disobedience 151–177
Doel, M. 18–19, 26, 92, 135
duty-based ethical theories 26–27
duty ethics 76, 78, 101
duty of care 142

eggs policy 7–8
emotional intelligence 80, 85, 113, 129, 130
emotional well-being 66, 185
empathy 60, 85, 92, 115, 191
empowerment 74–75
  importance of 80
epic ethics 17, 33, 206
ethical codes and guidance 11–12
ethical decision making 130–131, 133–134
ethical frameworks 30, 60, 70, 88, 95, 148
ethical literacy 110
ethical problems 9–10

ethical reference group 12–14
ethics 8, 9
  consequentialism 29–30
  convenience 98–99
  different approaches 24–31
  duty-based ethical theories 26–27
  existentialism 29
  moral relativism 31
  personal 86–87
  principlism 25–26
  professional 86, 87–89
  redemptive 30–31, 88
  relational 108, 119
  relationship 30
  situation ethics 28–29
  social work 89
  virtue 24–25, 55, 56, 137
  of whistleblowing 163
ethics of care 14, 30, 95, 129, 172
ethics of forgiveness 30–31
everyday ethics 17, 33, 202, 206
existentialism 29, 73
expert power 69–70

fairness 35, 62, 137, 153
Feldman, G. 73
Fenton, J. 86
Ferguson, H. 109
Fernandes, G. 8, 131
Finch, J. 176–177
fitness to practice 165–166, 187, 203
Flanagan, S. 16
Fletcher, J. F.
  Moral Responsibility: Situation Ethics at Work 28
Fook, J. 73, 75
Foucault, M. 73, 74
framing bias 134
Fraser, M. 102
free will 159
Freire, P. 73
French, J. 14
Friesen, B. 63

Gawronski, B. 30, 38
generosity 62
Global Statement of Ethical Principles 37
greater good 28, 30, 33, 131, 137, 156, 168, 169

Groundhog Day (film) 16
Grové, M. 81

Hardwick, L. 26
Hill, D. 74
HIV 48, 56–57
Hodge, M. 160
holistic discipline 49
Hollinrake, S. 108
honesty 71, 92, 106–107, 130, 157, 191, 202
Howe, D. 74
human dignity 11
humanism 29
human rights 11, 26–27

identity
  personal and professional 90–92
  social 72–73
India 48
Indian code 12
individual practitioners 72
information, new 6
inner moral philosopher 23–24
integrity 92–98
  in professional conduct 100
  in professional practice 99
International Association of Schools of
    Social Work (IFSW) 11, 37, 61, 79, 99,
    120, 146, 195
International Federation of Social Workers
    and the International Association
    of Schools of Social Work (IFSW/
    IASSW) 11
inter-professional education 49
inter professional working 110
inter-professional working 110
intersectionality 73
Irish Code of Ethics 80
Italian code 12
Italy's Code of Ethics 195–196

Jane Addams' coat 41–42
jigsaw puzzle 105, 122–123
Joseph, J. 8, 131
justice 110, 142

Kant, I. 26, 27, 29, 31, 158
Kantian categorical imperative 136
Kantian equality 74

Kantian ethics 26
Karpman, S. 109
Killick, C. 144
kindness 62
Knight, T. 127
knowledge, new 7
Koehn, D. 85
Koehnian ethics 86
Kulkarni, A. 45

lappieskombers (quilt) 65–66, 81
legitimate power 69
Leigh, J. 135
loyalty 162

Maslow, A. H. 30, 139
McAuliffe, D. 110
McLaughlin, A. 148
medical model of obesity 49
medication 76, 77
Me Too 72
Mill, J. S. 29, 30
Mohamed, O. 39
Moldovan, V. 63
moral cognition 135
moral compass 160, *161*
moral guardians 156–157
moral judgement 28, 135
moral luck
  causal luck 159
  circumstantial luck 158–159
  constitutive luck 159
  moral compass 160, *161*
  resultant luck 158
moral obligation 48, 49, 145–146, 152, 153
moral panics 154–155
moral question 166–167
moral relativism 31, 34, 59, 189
moral responsibility 28, 36, 152, 159
*Moral Responsibility: Situation Ethics at
    Work* (Fletcher) 28
morals 8, 9
moral worth 73, 74, 193
Muslim communities 27

Nagel, T. 158, 159, 160
narrative inquiry 15
Nicomachean Ethics 25
Nøhr, K. 9

non-maleficence 110, 131, 171
north–south axis 160

Oaklands 5
objects 199–200
object-stories 1
omission 131, 147
oppression 73, 74, 91, 106, 131
optimism bias 134
O'Sullivan, T. 145

Parker, J. 109, 131
participative 131–132
partnership 86, 105, 108, 109, 121
personal ethics 86–87
personal identity 90–92
person centred approach 32, 85, 108, 115, 131, 144
person with lived experience 32, 65, 74, 75, 85, 86, 88, 140, 144
pessimism bias 134
philosophic scepticism 13, 145
philosophy 9, 10, 13, 19, 23–24, 27, 29, 30, 31, 33–36, 73, 133, 152, 165–166, 172, 174, 203
placement 5, 19, 27, 38, 66, 95, 116–118, 164–165, 170–171, 195
Plato 25
positional power. *see* legitimate power
poverty
    alleviate 33
    digital 139
    social awareness 145
power 15, 66–67, 202–203
    coercive 70
    dimensions of 71–72
    equality 72
    expert 69–70
    legitimate 69
    referent 70
    reward 70
    social identity 72–73
    in social work 65, 80
    types of 68–69
practical dilemma 10, 68, 101, 105, 109–111, 138
pragmatism 27, 34, 162
prejudice 134
principlism 25–26, 68, 130

professional boundaries 93, 101, 111–112, 196. *see also* boundaries
professional compass 22
professional curiosity 109, 129
professional ethics 86, 87–89
professional identity 90–92
professionalism 85–86
    indicators 89
    integrity 92–98
    personal and professional identity 90–92
    professional standards 89
professional standards 89
proportionalism 95

radical low-tide 46
radical social work 19, 46, 86
Reamer, F. 131, 133, 136, 138, 184
recall bias 134
redemptive ethics 30–31, 88
referent power 70
reflection 4, 32, 88, 101, 111, 113, 129, 144, 188
relational ethics 108, 119
relationship based practice 105, 114
relationship ethics 30
relativity 125–126, 148
remote communication 181–182
repetition bias 134
resilience 92, 131, 139
Revell, L. 129
reward power 70
rights based 88, 141, 142
risk 126–127
    assessment 128
rule utilitarians 137, 153

safe uncertainty 127
Sartre, J.-P. 29, 130
scales 21–22
self-awareness 114
self-determination 75–77
self-reflection 114
Šerkšnienė, Ž. 122–123
service users 108–110
Shapiro, B. 39
Shardlow, S. M. 135
Sicora, A. 135
Siegel, D. 131, 184
similarity bias 134

Singer, P. 169
singularities 15–17, 201, 204
situation ethics 28–29
Sliding Doors (film) 16
Smith, R. 67, 75
social democracies 48
Social GGRRAAACCEEESSS 90
social identity 72–73
social injustice 186
social justice 11, 25, 39, 42, 83, 85
social media 182–183
   ethical dilemmas 185–186
   social workers' personal use of 184–188
   social workers' professional use of 188–190
social model 49
social work 3, 4
   assessments 128
   central tenets of 49
   community 157
   decision making in 125
   education and training 31–32
   ethics 89
   functions 43, *44*
   practice 83–84
   professional identity 91
   relationships 112–114
   social systems 43, *45*
   values 9, 11
Social Work England 89, 172, 202, 205
social worker 3, 4
   codes of ethics 11–12
   collaborative approach 106
   ethical responsibilities 11
   with professionals 110–111
   with service users 108–110
   in UK 11
   working relationships 106
social workers 80
   ethical dilemmas for 184–185
   moral panics 154–155
   offering solutions 48
   personal use of social media 184–188
   professional use of social media 188–190
socialworkin40objects.com 1
Socrates 25, 32
Statement of Principles 61
sticking plaster 42
Street Guide 2
Surrender 60, 203

Taylor, B. 144
technology
   American Code of Ethics 196
   British Code of Ethics 195
   ethical dilemma 191–195
   Global Statement of Ethical Principles 195
   Italy's Code of Ethics 195–196
   in social work 188
   in social work practice 179
technology etiquette 180
Tedam, P. 68
Thacker, H. 109
Thompson, N. 68, 110
Thoreau, H. D. 170
tram dilemma 33
transference 113
trust 14
trustworthy 85, 99

ubuntu 60, 91, 108, 203
uncertainty 108, 127, 129, 173
United Nations' Declaration of Human Rights 1948, 27
The Unity Group 177, 197
University of Sydney 188
Utilitarian ethics 28, 29, 34, 142, 153

value(s) 8, 9, 36
value conflicts 47
   guidance 61
   personal, professional and structural 43–44
   responses 50–51
virtue ethics 24–25, 35, 55, 56, 137, 142
Voice of Experience 13

west–east axis 160
whistleblowing 160–164
wise professionals 153, 157, 204–206
working relationships
   boundaries 111–112
   social worker 106
Worsley, A. 26